MW00610456

TExES™ BILINGUAL EDUCATION SUPPLEMENTAL (164)

Dr. Luis A. Rosado
Professor and Founding Director
Center for Bilingual and ESL Education
University of Texas at Arlington

Foreword by
Dr. José Ruiz-Escalante
Professor of Education
Prince Mohammad Bin Fahd University

Research & Education Association

Research & Education Association
258 Prospect Plains Road
Cranbury, New Jersey 08512
Email: info@rea.com

TExES™ Bilingual Education Supplemental (164) with Online Practice Tests

Published 2021

Printed in the United States of America

Library of Congress Control Number 2017946114

ISBN-13: 978-0-7386-1229-4
ISBN-10: 0-7386-1229-4

The competencies presented in this book were created and implemented by the Texas Education Agency and Pearson Education or its affiliate(s). Texas Examinations of Educator Standards and TExES are trademarks of the Texas Education Agency. All other trademarks cited in this publication are the property of their respective owners.

Cover image: ©iStockphoto.com/monkeybusinessimages

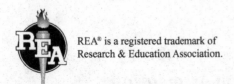

REA® is a registered trademark of
Research & Education Association.

This book is dedicated to McKinley Wardlaw Rosado, a second-generation Texas-Rican. You and your generation represent the hopes and expectations of a troubled nation searching for answers and yearning for unity.

Contents

Foreword

The preparation of dual language educators is critical to the academic success of the millions of children currently learning in two languages. In the state of Texas, English learners (ELs) now account for 18 percent of the total student enrollment. Ensuring the supply of highly qualified bilingual educators for current demand is a challenge at a time when the teaching profession has become increasingly selective. School districts no longer hire teachers with emergency certification, and before they employ an educator in Texas, he or she must be fully certified. This means passing all the certification exams required by the state. Bilingual educators, for example, must pass four exams:

- ✓ Core Subjects EC-6 (291)

- ✓ Pedagogy and Professional Responsibilities (160)

- ✓ Bilingual Target Language Proficiency Test—Spanish (190)

- ✓ Bilingual Education Supplemental (164)

Candidates earn the stamp of approval to enter the teaching force only after they have successfully obtained a passing score in their certification exams. With this goal in mind, prospective teachers like you diligently review the content covered in the exams. But even though some concepts are fresh in their minds, they may not remember information related to certain domains and competencies assessed. One thing students know for sure is that they need to review all the content covered in their preparation courses as well as the state curricula at least for PK to grade 6. Useful tools in this review process are reading manuals or study guides, especially those that concisely address information covered in the teacher preparation courses from beginning to end.

When I worked in a bilingual educator preparation program, I witnessed firsthand how, after diligently studying Dr. Rosado's study guides, students reported successful outcomes. Although I always encouraged my students to find review books that included practice questions, I never recommended any specific review materials, since I did not want to seem biased or influence my students to purchase a book. When my students informed me that they had successfully passed the exams, I was curious to hear how they prepared for this task. A great majority invariably mentioned Luis Rosado's books. So I was honored when Dr. Rosado asked me to write this foreword to this new teacher preparation book for the Bilingual Education Supplemental (164) test.

I have known Dr. Rosado for over 25 years. I know that he has dedicated his professional career to improving bilingual educator preparation programs as well as to develop quality materials to help teacher candidates with the Texas certification exams. Dr. Rosado has published study guides in several areas, including REA's bestselling book and online prep for the TExES Core Subjects EC-6, as well as a guide to the Bilingual Target Language Proficiency Test.

Dr. Rosado's years of experience in the field of bilingual education have equipped him with firsthand knowledge of the type of content information needed for the TExES certification exams. This knowledge translates into strategically designed multiple-choice practice questions that accompany this book. Within each section, the reader will find a comprehensive review of the standards, knowledge, and skills assessed.

This book includes six chapters. The first two chapters provide an overview of the Bilingual Education Supplemental exam and include test-taking strategies that teacher candidates need to review and practice to be successful on their first attempt. Chapters 3–6 cover the four competencies of the TExES 164 examination. In Chapter 3, the book offers an extensive review of the history and foundation of bilingual/ESL education. It also covers the judicial decisions and federal legislation that have impacted bilingual education at the state and national levels.

In Chapter 4, the book presents an overview of first- and second-language acquisition. This area usually presents a challenge for teacher candidates, since they might have taken just one or two courses dealing with it. The book discusses some linguistic aspects as applied to second language learners as well as the theories of first- and second-language acquisition. The book does a first-rate job in presenting the key concepts and terminology needed for the teacher examination.

In Chapter 5, the book presents a comprehensive review of the development and assessment of literacy and biliteracy. In this chapter, Dr. Rosado discusses the process of learning to read in the first language as well as how to develop biliteracy in dual language programs.

The last chapter includes information about the integration of content-area instruction with the English Language Proficiency Standards required when teaching in English. It presents an overview of the most popular Sheltered English instruction methods used in the United States to teach content to English learners (ELs). The chapter also presents sample lesson plans that integrate content areas with the English Language Proficiency Standards required when teaching content to ELs.

In summary, Dr. Rosado has designed an exceptional study guide for bilingual education teacher candidates. Future teachers should consider investing in this book as soon as they start their preparation program and use it as they go through the program. I wholeheartedly endorse REA's TExES Bilingual Education Supplemental Book + Online test prep for all bilingual teacher candidates looking to teach in Texas.

—Dr. José Agustín Ruiz-Escalante
Professor of Education
College of Sciences and Human Studies
Prince Mohammad Bin Fahd University

About the Author

Dr. Luis A. Rosado is Professor of Bilingual Education and the Director of the Center for Bilingual and ESL Education in the College of Education and Health Professions at the University of Texas at Arlington. He holds degrees from the University of Puerto Rico, Boston State College, and Texas A&I University, now Texas A&M–Kingsville.

Prior to coming to UT Arlington, Dr. Rosado held academic appointments at Pontifical Catholic University of Puerto Rico, Texas Southern University, and Texas Woman's University. Dr. Rosado has more than three decades of teaching experience at the elementary, high school, and college levels. He has taught in Puerto Rico, Massachusetts, and Texas.

In 2011, Dr. Rosado was the co-recipient of a $1.9 million grant from the U.S. Department of Education's Office of English Language Acquisition to improve preparation for teachers serving English learners. In total, Dr. Rosado has received more than $5.6 million in state and federal funding to prepare bilingual and ESL teachers as well as school administrators, and to provide services to support high school students.

Dr. Rosado has written extensively in the areas of pedagogy and professional responsibilities, parental involvement, cross-cultural communication, preparation for teacher certification exams, and Spanish for bilingual teachers.

In 2018, this *TExES Bilingual Education Supplemental (164)* test guide earned Dr. Rosado recognition as an International Latino Book Awards' award-winning author. Among his publications are a series of books to prepare pre-service teachers for certification tests, including REA's bestselling *TExES Bilingual Generalist EC-6 (192)*, and *Desarrollo del Español para Maestros en Programas de Educación Bilingüe* (Spanish Development for Teachers in Bilingual Education Programs), for which, with co-author Lidia Morris, he earned first place in the 2014 International Latino Book Awards in the category of Best Reference Book—Spanish or Bilingual. The book, which is intended, Dr. Rosado says, "to polish the Spanish proficiency of current and future bilingual teachers," is being used by several universities and a number of Texas school districts.

About REA

Founded in 1959, Research & Education Association (REA) is dedicated to publishing the finest and most effective educational materials—including study guides and test preps—for students of all ages. Today, REA's wide-ranging catalog is a leading resource for students, teachers, and other professionals. Visit *www.rea.com* to see a complete listing of all our titles.

Publisher's Acknowledgments

Publisher: Pam Weston

Editorial Director: Larry B. Kling

Technology Director: John Paul Cording

Managing Editor: Diane Goldschmidt

Copy Editor: John Kupetz

Composition Services: Caragraphics

Cover Design and File Prep: Jennifer Calhoun

Getting Started

Congratulations! By taking the TExES Bilingual Education Supplemental (164) test, you're on your way to a rewarding career as a teacher of young students in Texas. Our book, and the online tools that come with it, give you everything you need to succeed on this important exam, bringing you one step closer to being certified to teach in Texas.

This TExES Bilingual Education Supplemental test prep package includes:

- A **targeted review** of the TExES Bilingual Education Supplemental (164) test

- A **diagnostic test** to pinpoint your strengths and weaknesses and focus your study

- A **full-length practice test** to simulate the complete test-taking experience with true-to-format questions

All practice content is available both in the book and online at the REA Study Center.

HOW TO USE THIS BOOK + ONLINE PREP

About Our Review

The review chapters in this book are designed to help you sharpen your command of all four competencies assessed on the TExES Bilingual Education Supplemental test. Our content review is designed to reinforce what you have learned and show you how to relate the information you have acquired to the specific competencies on the test. Studying your class notes and textbooks together with our review will give you an excellent foundation for passing the test. We provide a comprehensive bibliography.

About the REA Study Center

We know your time is valuable and you want an efficient study experience. At the online REA Study Center (*www.rea.com/studycenter*), you will get feedback right from the start on what you know and what you don't to help make the most of your study time.

Here is what you will find at the REA Study Center:

- **Diagnostic Test**—Before you review with the book, take our online diagnostic test. Your score report will automatically pinpoint topics for which you need the most review, to help focus your study.

- **Full-Length Practice Test**—REA's online practice test gives you the most complete picture of your strengths and weaknesses. After you've studied with the book, test what you've learned by taking the practice exam. Review your score reports, then go back and study any topics you missed.

Our online exams simulate the computer-based format of the actual TExES test and come with these features:

- **Automatic scoring**—Find out how you did on your test, instantly.

- **Diagnostic score reports**—Get a specific score tied to each competency, so you can focus on the areas that challenge you the most.

- **On-screen detailed answer explanations**—See why the correct response option is right, and learn why the other answer choices are incorrect.

- **Timed testing**—Learn to manage your time as you practice, so you'll feel confident on test day.

AN OVERVIEW OF THE TEST

What is assessed on the Bilingual Education Supplemental test?

The TExES Bilingual Education Supplemental test is a criterion-referenced examination constructed to measure the knowledge and skills that an entry-level bilingual educator in Texas public schools must have. Because it's a computer-administered test, the exam is available throughout the year at numerous locations across the state and at select locations nationally. To find a test center near you, visit the official website of Texas's Educator Certification Examination Program at *www.tx.nesinc.com*.

Candidates are limited to five attempts to take any of Texas's teacher certification tests.

A Snapshot of the TExES Bilingual Education Supplemental Test

Testing Time: 4 hours and 45 minutes
Number of Questions: 80 multiple-choice questions

Competency 001: The beginning Bilingual Education teacher understands the foundations of Bilingual Education and the concepts of bilingualism and biculturalism and applies this knowledge to create an effective learning environment for students in the Bilingual Education program.

Competency 002: The beginning Bilingual Education teacher understands processes of first- and second-language acquisition and development and applies this knowledge to promote students' language proficiency in their first language (L1) and second language (L2).

Competency 003: The beginning Bilingual Education teacher has comprehensive knowledge of the development and assessment of literacy in L1 and the development and assessment of biliteracy.

Competency 004: The beginning Bilingual Education teacher has comprehensive knowledge of content area instruction in L1 and L2 and uses this knowledge to promote bilingual students' academic achievement across the curriculum.

What is the format of the TExES Bilingual Education Supplemental test?

The test includes a total of 80 multiple-choice items, a few of which may not be scorable because they're being field-tested. You won't know which is which, so they surely aren't worth worrying about. Your final scaled score will be based only on the scorable items.

Could there be unfamiliar types of multiple-choice questions?

Though all the questions on the test are multiple-choice, they may not all be the type of multiple-choice question with which you're familiar. The majority of questions on the TExES Bilingual Education Supplemental test are standard multiple-choice items. The questions are not intended merely to test your command of facts or your talent for recall but also your critical-thinking skills. For example, you may be asked to analyze information and compare it with knowledge you have, or make a judgment about it. To acquaint yourself with all the detail on the standards and competencies covered on the test, be sure to download the test framework at *www.tx.nesinc.com*.

Some multiple-choice questions are self-contained while others are clustered, relating to a common stimulus. Each question will generally have four choices: A, B, C, and D. (It's possible that an occasional question will have five options.) In addition, the test may sometimes present non-traditional formats for multiple-choice items, both to present the information and to allow you to select the best answer. The test developer, Pearson Education, reserves wide latitude to use what it terms unfamiliar question types. A rundown of these new formats follows.

What do unfamiliar question types look like?

There are several unfamiliar question types that may show up on the TExES Bilingual Education Supplemental test. First, let's look at the kind of question that asks TExES test-takers to identify more than one correct answer.

Example

1. Which of the following led to the American Revolution?

    A.   the French and Indian War

    B.   the Intolerable Acts

    C.   the French Revolution

    D.   Options A and B

Answer and Explanation

Option (D) is correct. In other words, options (A) and (B) are both correct. The French and Indian War (A), fought from 1754 to 1763, served as a powerful vehicle by which the British Empire extended its reach in North America.

The British sought to impose taxation on the colonists to finance the defense of the newly acquired territory, which aggravated growing discontent with British governance. The Intolerable Acts (B) embraced measures enacted by the British Parliament in 1774 to strike back at the colonists' defiance (e.g., the Boston Tea Party in 1773) of British rule. The move backfired, spawning the First Continental Congress later that year. Simple chronology helps you root out the French Revolution (C) as an incorrect option. The French Revolution, fought from 1787 to 1799, is an anachronistic response that could not have led to the American Revolution, which ended in 1783.

According to ETS, the Bilingual Education Supplemental test may use interactive questions that may include audio or video clips instead of, say, a static map or reading passage.

Item formats may ask you to select the correct answer(s) by any of these means:

- Click on a sentence or sentences, or on parts of a graphic representation, such as a map, chart, or figure—sometimes dubbed a "hot spot."

- Drag and drop answer options into "target" areas in a table, piece of text, or graphic.

- Use a drop-down menu.

More than anything, these innovative item types require that you read the instructions carefully to be sure you are fully responsive to the question.

The TExES Bilingual Education Supplemental test is scored based on the number of questions you answer correctly. With no penalty for guessing, you won't want to leave any item unanswered.

When should the test be taken?

The TExES Bilingual Education Supplemental is generally taken during your junior or senior year. Traditionally, teacher preparation programs determine when their candidates take the required tests for teacher certification. These programs will also clear you to take the examinations and make final recommendations for certification to the Texas State Board for Educator Certification (SBEC).

An entry-level candidate seeking bilingual education certification may take the Bilingual Education Supplemental test at such time as his or her Educator Preparation Program (EPP) determines the candidate's readiness to take the test, or upon successful completion of the EPP, whichever comes first. The EPP will determine readiness through benchmarks and structured assessments of the candidates' progress throughout the preparation program.

How do I register for the test?

To register for the TExES 164 test, you must create an account in the ETS online registration system. Registration will then be available to you online, 24/7, during the regular, late, and emergency registration periods. Visit Pearson Education's TExES website at *www.tx.nesinc.com* and follow the instructions.

The TExES Registration Bulletin provides information about test dates and locations, as well as information on registration and testing accommodations for those with special needs. The registration bulletin is available at *www.tx.nesinc.com*.

Registration bulletins are also available at the education departments of Texas colleges and universities. To address issues that cannot be solved at the teacher preparation program level, you can contact the offices of SBEC at (888) 863-5880 or (512) 469-8400.

You must pay a registration fee to take the TExES tests, and you will also incur additional late fees if registering after the scheduled date.

What's the passing score?

The TExES 164's score is reported on a 100–300 scale. A scaled score of 240 is set as the minimum passing score. To put this in context, you want to be confident you can answer between 70% and 80% of the questions correctly. To achieve the 70% level, you must get 56 questions correct; to reach the 80% level, you need to get 64 questions correct. As you work your way through our practice tests, scores in this range will suggest that you are sufficiently mastering the test content. On the actual test, some questions may be being field-tested and thus will not be scored.

If you do not get a passing score on our online diagnostic test or the practice test, review your score report and study the detailed explanations for the questions you answered incorrectly. Note which types of questions you answered wrong, and re-examine the corresponding review content. After further review, you may want to retake the online practice tests.

Bear in mind that there are various forms of this test. Because no two forms are the same, your performance on a given test form is figured on a common scale. To adjust for any even minor differences in a test form's aggregate difficulty, each test form is statistically equated versus the original test form.

When will I receive my score report?

As part of the registration process to take TExES examinations, test candidates set up an account with Pearson Education in which they are assigned a username and password. Use this account to access your score report information on Pearson's TExES website. Score reports will be posted by 5 p.m. CT on the score reporting date and will be available for 90 days.

What if I don't pass the test?

If for some reason you don't do well on the TExES Bilingual Education Supplemental test, don't panic. You can retake the test up to four times more, for a maximum of five attempts. After the fifth attempt, you still have the option of requesting special dispensation from the Texas Higher Education Coordinating Board to retake the test; however, approval is not automatic. A 30-day waiting period is required between attempts.

How should I prepare for the test?

It is never too early to start studying for the TExES. The earlier you begin, the more time you will have to sharpen your skills. Do not procrastinate. Cramming is not an effective way to study, since it does not allow you the time needed to learn the test material. It is important for you to choose the time and place for studying that works best for you. Be consistent and use your time wisely. Work out a study routine and stick to it.

When you take REA's diagnostic test and practice test, simulate the conditions of the actual test as closely as possible. Turn your television and smartphone off, and go to a quiet place free from distraction.

Read each question carefully, consider all answer choices, and pace yourself. As you complete each test, review your score reports, study the diagnostic feedback, and thoroughly review the explanations to the questions you answered incorrectly. But don't overdo it. Take one problem area at a time; review it until you are confident that you have mastered the material.

Give extra attention to the areas giving you the most difficulty, as this will help build your score. In addition, be sure to take the time to review the relevant state curricula for these grades (Texas Essential Knowledge and Skills) available at *http://www.tea.state.tx.us*.

TExES Bilingual Education Supplemental (164) Study Schedule

Time Period	Activity
Week 1	Take the online Diagnostic Test at the REA Study Center. Your detailed score report will identify the topics where you need the most review.
Week 2–3	Study the review chapters. Use your score report from the Diagnostic Test to focus your study. Useful study techniques include highlighting key terms and information and taking notes as you read the review. Learn all the competencies by making flashcards and targeting questions you missed on the diagnostic test.
Week 4	Take the Practice Test either in the book or online at the REA Study Center. Review your score report and identify topics where you need more review.

Are there any breaks during the test?

Although there is no designated break during the test, you do have some time to use for the restroom or snacking or stretching outside the testing room.

Bear in mind the following:

- You need to get permission to leave the testing room.

- The overall test clock never stops.

- Consult your test admission materials for further details, including updates from Pearson Education and the Texas Education Agency.

What else do I need to know about test day?

The day before your test, check for any updates in your Pearson Education testing account. This is where you'll learn of any changes to your reporting schedule or if there's a change in the test site. On the day of the test, you should wake up early after a good night's rest. Have a good breakfast and dress in layers that can be removed or added as the conditions in the test center require. Arrive at the test center early. This will allow you to relax and collect your thoughts before the test, and will also spare you the anguish that comes with being late. As an added incentive to make sure that you arrive early, keep in mind that no one will be admitted into the test center after the test has begun.

Before you leave for the testing site, carefully review your registration materials. Make sure you bring your admission ticket and two unexpired forms of identification. Primary forms of ID include:

- Passport

- Government-issued driver's license

- State or Province ID card

- National ID card

- Military ID card

You may need to produce a supplemental ID document if any questions arise with your primary ID or if your primary ID is otherwise valid but lacks your full name, photo, and signature. Without proper identification, you will not be admitted to the test center. Strict rules limit what you can bring into the test center to just your ID; we recommend that you consult the Texas Education Agency's "Texas Educator Certification Registration Bulletin" for a complete rundown. You may not bring watches of any kind, cellphones, smartphones, or any other electronic communication devices or weapons of any kind. Scrap paper, written notes, and books and other printed material are prohibited.

No smoking, eating, or drinking is allowed in the testing room. Consider bringing a small snack and a bottle of water to partake of beforehand to keep you sharp during the test.

Good luck on the TExES Bilingual Education Supplemental test!

Proven Test-Taking Strategies for Your TExES Exam

1. Guess Away

One of the most frequently asked questions about the TExES exams is: Can I guess? The answer: absolutely! There is no penalty for guessing on the test. That means if you refrain from guessing, you may lose points. To guess smartly, use the process of elimination (see Strategy No. 2). Your score is based strictly on the number of correct answers. So answer all questions and take your best guess when you don't know the answer.

2. Process of Elimination

Process of elimination is one of the most important test-taking strategies at your disposal. Process of elimination means looking at the choices and eliminating the ones you know are wrong, including answers that are partially wrong. Your odds of getting the right answer increase from the moment you're able to get rid of a wrong choice.

3. All in

Review all the response options. Just because you believe you've found the correct answer—or, in some cases, answers—look at each choice so you don't mistakenly jump to any conclusions. If you are asked to choose the *best* answer, be sure your first answer is really the best one.

4. Use Choices to Confirm Your Answer

The great thing about multiple-choice questions is that the answer has to be staring back at you. Have an answer in mind and use the choices to *confirm* it.

5. Read, Read, Read

It's important to read through all the multiple-choice options. Even if you believe answer choice A is correct, you can misread a question or response option if you're rushing to get through the test. While it is important not to linger on a question, it is also crucial to avoid giving a question short shrift. Slow down, calm down, read all the choices. Verify that your choice is the best one, and click on it.

6. Take Notes

Use the scratch paper provided to you to make notes to work toward the answer(s). If you use all the scratch paper you're initially given, you can get more.

7. Isolate Limiters

Pay attention to any limiters in a multiple-choice question stem. These are words such as *initial, best, most* (as in *most appropriate* or *most likely*), *not, least, except, required,* or *necessary.* Especially watch for negative words, such as "Choose the answer that is *not* true." When you select your answer, double-check yourself by asking how the response fits the limitations established by the stem. Think of the stem as a puzzle piece that perfectly fits only the response option(s) that contain the correct answer. Let it guide you.

8. It's Not a Race

Ignore other test-takers. Don't compare yourself to anyone else in the room. Focus on the items in front of you and the time you have left. If someone finishes the test 30 minutes early, it does not necessarily mean that person answered more questions correctly than you did. Stay calm and focus on *your* test. It's the only one that matters.

9. Confirm Your Click

In the digital age, many of us are used to rapid-clicking, be it in the course of emailing or gaming. Look at the screen to be sure to see that your mouse-click is acknowledged. If your answer doesn't register, you won't get credit. However, if you want to mark it for review so you can return later, that's your call. Before you click "Submit," use the test's review screen to see whether you inadvertently skipped any questions.

10. Creature of Habit? No Worries.

We are all creatures of habit. It's therefore best to follow a familiar pattern of study. Do what's comfortable for you. Set a time and place each day to study for this test. Whether it is 30 minutes at the library or an hour in a secluded corner of your local coffee shop, commit yourself as best you can to this schedule every day. Find quiet places where it is less crowded, as constant background noise can distract you. Don't study one subject for too long, either. Take an occasional breather and treat yourself to a healthy snack or some quick exercise. After your short break—5 or 10 minutes can do the trick—return to what you were studying or start a new section.

11. Knowledge is Power

Purchasing this book gave you an edge on passing the TExES Bilingual Education Supplemental test. Make the most of this edge. Review the sections on how the test is structured, what the directions look like, what types of questions will be asked, and so on. Take our practice tests to familiarize yourself with what the test looks and feels like. Most test anxiety occurs because people feel unprepared when they are taking the test, and they psych themselves out. You can whittle away at anxiety by learning the format of the test and by knowing what to expect. Fully simulating the test even once will boost your chances of getting the score you need. Meanwhile, the knowledge you've gained will also will save you the valuable time that would have been eaten up puzzling through what the directions are asking As an added benefit, previewing the test will free up your brain's resources so you can focus on racking up as many points as you can.

12. B-r-e-a-t-h-e

Anxiety is neither unusual nor necessarily unwelcome on a test. Just don't let it stifle you. Take a moment to breathe. This won't merely make you feel good. The brain uses roughly three times as much oxygen as muscles in the body do: Give it what it needs. Now consider this: What's the worst that can happen when you take a test? You may have an off day, and despite your best efforts, you may not pass. Well, the good news is that this test can be retaken. Fortunately, the TExES Bilingual Education Supplemental test is something you can study and prepare for, and in some ways to a greater extent than other tests you've taken throughout your academic career. In fact, study after study has validated the value of test preparation. Yes, there will be questions you won't know, but neither your teacher education program nor state licensing board expects you to know everything. When unfamiliar vocabulary appears, don't despair: Use context clues, process of elimination, or your response option of the day (i.e., choose either A, B, C, or D routinely when you need to resort to a guess) to make your choice, and then press ahead. If you have time left, you can always come back to the question later. If not, relax. It is only one question on a test filled with many.

Take a deep breath and then exhale. You know this information. Now you're going to show it.

Foundations of Bilingual and ESL Education

"We take it as axiomatic that every child of school age should attend school and that every child should be made literate. We take it as axiomatic, too, that the best medium for teaching is the mother tongue of the pupil."

(UNESCO, 1953)

COMPETENCY 001: FOUNDATIONS OF BILINGUAL EDUCATION

The beginning Bilingual Education teacher understands the foundations of Bilingual Education and the concepts of bilingualism and biculturalism and applies this knowledge to create an effective learning environment for students in the Bilingual Education program (TEA, 2015).

This chapter addresses Competency 001—Foundations of Bilingual Education—of the Bilingual Supplemental Exam (TExES 164). It also covers selected components of Competency 008—Foundations of Education and ESL Programs—of the ESL Supplemental Exam (TExES 154). The chapter addresses the theoretical framework and the historical development of bilingual and ESL education as well as the court cases, the federal and state legislation, and the significant events that affected the development of bilingual and ESL education in the United States. The chapter also describes the program models to address the educational needs of English learners (ELs).

Historical Development of Bilingual and ESL Education in the United States

Pre-Colonial Period

Long before the European colonization, over 200 indigenous groups that spoke multiple languages inhabited what is today the United States (USHistory.org, 2016). Most of these languages belonged to one of nine major language families native to America: Algic, Iroquoian, Muskogean, Siouan, Uto-Aztecan, Athabaskan, Salishan, Eskimo-Aleut, and Mayan (Rehling, 1996). In what is now Texas alone, 50 indigenous groups were identified, and some were native to Texas. Some of the Native Americans from Texas were the Apaches, Bidai, Coahuiltecan and Carrizo, Caddo, Comanche, Jumano, Eastern Pueblo, Karankawa, Kiowa, Kitsai, Tawakoni, Tokawa, and Wichita (Texas State Facts, 2015). Because of this linguistic diversity, indigenous groups used sign language to communicate until some of them became bilingual and multilingual. It is thus important to recognize that the European conquest did not bring bilingualism and multilingualism, as they were common among Native American groups living in America before the European colonization.

Language Loss: The European conquest and the forced assimilation to European language and values caused large numbers of Native American groups and their language to become extinct, while others became endangered. Because of conquest, tribes were sent to exile and forced to live on reservations. With the establishment of the federal Bureau of Indian Affairs, this practice became the norm. By the 1880s, most Native American tribes were relocated to reservations, most of them west of the Appalachians. Under the federal Bureau of Indian Affairs, large numbers of children were sent to live in boarding schools whose main purpose was to teach the American language and culture (Crawford, 1995). Because of this Americanization, large numbers of Native American children lost their language and culture. Despite this colonizing practice, such nations as Navajo, Cree, and Cherokee preserved their language and culture.

The term *assimilation* is used to describe the imposition of the language and culture of the dominant group.

An estimated 155 Native American languages are still spoken in the United States, and 87% of them are listed as endangered (Kraus, 1992). According to Rehling from the University of Indiana, only eight indigenous languages spoken in the United States and Canada have over 9, 000 speakers (1996). Most of these groups live on reservations in the Southwest and central regions of the United States. In Texas, three recognized groups are living on reservations—the Alabama-Coushatta (Livingston), Ysleta Del Sur Pueblo (El Paso), and Kickapoos (Eagle Pass) (Texas State Facts, 2015). Table 1.1 presents details about languages with 9,000 or more speakers currently living in the United States and/or Canada.

Table 3.1. Native American Languages in the United States and Canada

Languages	Family	United States and Canada	Number of Speakers
Navajo	Athabaskan	Arizona, New Mexico, Utah	169,369
Cree	Algic	Montana, Canada	60,000
Ojibwa	Algic	Minnesota, Nevada, Missouri, and Canada	51,000
Cherokee	Iroquoian	Oklahoma and North Carolina	22,500
Dakota	Siouan	Nevada, North Dakota, South Dakota, Minnesota, Montana and Canada	20,000
Apache	Athabaskan	New Mexico, Arizona, Oklahoma	15,000
Blackfoot	Algic	Montana and Canada	10,000
Choctaw	Muskogean	Oklahoma, Missouri, and Louisiana	9,211

The 2010 U.S. Census reported that 2.4 million people in the nation identified themselves as Native Americans or Alaskan Natives. Of those 2.4 million (70%), identified English as their native language, and 15% indicated that they were native speakers of tribal languages (Lee, June 30, 2014). The report also showed that two-thirds of speakers of tribal languages were residing in Arizona, New Mexico, and Alaska.

The 2010 U.S. Census reported the language data based on two broad classifications—Navajo speakers or speakers of other Native American languages (Ryan, 2013). The limited data gathered in the Census makes it difficult to determine the status of languages other than the Navajo. The Census also identified a Navajo population of 169,369, an increase of 20,839 speakers from the number reported in the 1990 census (Hehling, 1996). The remaining speakers of tribal languages were included in the "other" language classification, with a total of 195,407 speakers.

The Navajo Success Story: With the implementation of bilingual education programs in the United States from 1968 to the present, some tribal languages have experienced a renaissance of their language and culture. The most successful language group has been the Navajos. As part of its revitalization, the Navajo language has expanded and modernized its vocabulary to reflect technological as well as lifestyle changes. To preserve the language, the Navajos have also created radio stations to broadcast programs in English and Navajo. In addition, they have established several institutions of higher education to educate their population and to promote and preserve the language (Lee, June 30, 2014). The Navajos' attempts to preserve their language and culture is among the success stories in the history of Native American groups in the United States.

Colonial Period

The American colonization officially began with Jamestown in 1607. Most American colonists spoke English, but people from multiple language backgrounds also joined the colonization effort. With the arrival of speakers of European languages, the colonization effort brought more languages to the more than 200 tribal languages already spoken in America.

The first official census of the new nation was taken in 1790, and it showed that half of the population of the colonies was composed of English speakers. It also recorded a large number of European languages from such colonists as Scots, German, Dutch, Irish, Swedish, Welsh, and French (U.S. Census, n.d.). Because of this diversity, linguistic tolerance and multilingualism were typical of colonial America. As part of this tradition, some documents during the Revolutionary War were printed in more than one language (Crawford, 2004). This linguistic diversity played an important role in the decision to leave the identification of the official language of the nation out of the Constitution. This decision and the Tenth Amendment of the U.S. Constitution, relegated language and educational issues to the state legislatures. When the first schools were established, the state and/or local government thus made decisions about the language used for instruction.

 The Tenth Amendment of the U.S. Constitution emphasizes the principles of federalism, saying that the states have control of the powers not directly assigned to the central government in the Constitution.

17th to 19th Centuries

During the 17th to 19th centuries, multiple languages were used for instruction in U.S. schools. German schools operated in Philadelphia as early as 1694 (Crawford, 2004). In 1890, about 600,000 children were being taught in German in Pennsylvania, Maryland, Ohio, Indiana, Illinois, Missouri, Nebraska, Colorado, and Oregon. Swedish, Norwegian, and Danish were also used then as the language of instruction in Wisconsin, Illinois, Minnesota, Iowa, the Dakotas, Nebraska, and Washington. Polish and Italian were used in schools in Wisconsin, Dutch in Michigan, French in Louisiana, Czech and Spanish in Texas, and Spanish in the Southwest.

In the second half of the 19th century, many parochial and public schools in cities like Baltimore, Cleveland, Indianapolis, and St. Louis offered instruction in English and another language. The bilingual education movement was so strong in the United States that state legislatures in Ohio (1836), Louisiana (1847), and New Mexico (1848) passed laws authorizing instruction in two languages (Crawford 2004). However, military conflicts in Europe then were limiting the immigration of speakers of colonial languages. Without the linguistic support of new immigrants, the influence of French, Dutch, and German decreased, and English emerged as the national language. With fewer new immigrants, second generation immigrants stopped using their heritage languages, and bilingual education as an official policy disappeared from public view. However, expansionist policies of the United States meant that new immigrants and migrants would soon replace European immigrants. The annexation of Texas (1845), the war with Mexico (1845–1848), and the Spanish-American War of 1898 added a large number of non-English-speaking people to the nation.

The Annexation of Texas and the War with Mexico (1845–1848): Because of the 1836 Texas revolution, this former Mexican province became a free nation. For almost 10 years (1836–1846) Texas functioned as a sovereign nation. However, the Mexican government never recognized Texas independence. The economic challenges of the new nation spurred its citizens to seek U.S. support, which came in the form of an invitation to join the country. In December 1845, U.S. President John Tyler signed the legislation to annex Texas, and Texas became the 28th state. Technically, the process to become a state ended a few months later in 1846 under President James K. Polk.

When President Tyler signed the legislation to annex Texas, the war with Mexico began. The conflict ended in 1848 with the Treaty of Guadalupe Hidalgo. This treaty gave the United States official control over Texas and the territory today known as the American Southwest. With this annexation, a large number of non-English-speaking people, including those of Native American nations, found themselves living in an English-speaking country.

The Spanish-American War: After the war with Mexico, the United States engaged in its last war of the 19th century—the Spanish-American War of 1898, a conflict that ended the Spanish colonial period in America. Because of the war, Spain ceded to the United States several non-English-speaking territories—Puerto Rico, Guam, Cuba, and the Philippines. Cuba and the Philippines obtained their independence later, but Puerto Rico and Guam became territories of the U.S. Today, residents of Puerto Rico and Guam are American citizens.

With the annexation of Mexican territory, the United States became a natural immigration destination for millions of Mexicans. The annexation of Puerto Rico and Guam also resulted in the migration of Spanish and Chamorro speakers (Guam) to the United States. The influx of these groups made bilingual education a need for these new non-English speakers. However, during the late 19th and early 20th centuries, speaking a language other than English was considered a deficiency. Bilingual education thus was compensatory and not viewed as the enriching additive that bilingualism had been during the 17th and 18th centuries.

20th Century

During the first part of the 20th century, immigrants from Southeastern Europe arrived in America and brought the multiple languages spoken in the region. These immigrants did not enjoy the linguistic flexibility of earlier immigrants. They were expected to assimilate the new language and culture and abandon their own. By 1919, partly because of post–World War I xenophobia, programs to Americanize immigrants gained momentum. Fifteen states, including Texas, had enacted English-only legislation by 1919. Because of this restrictive legislation, ELs received severe punishment for using their native languages on the playground or in the classroom. With the new English-only legislation, dual language instruction virtually disappeared in the United States.

1920s through 1960s: From the 1920s through the 1960s, ELs were submerged in English without consistent support through their first language (L1). This "sink or swim" approach resulted in academic failure for many ELs. The term *submersion* was coined to describe this lack of L1 support for language-minority students. For more than five decades, bilingual and foreign language instruction was almost eliminated from public schools.

The Renaissance of Bilingual Education

The resurgence of bilingual education resulted from multiple events, including war, court cases and legislation. For example, because of the multiple language groups in the World War II effort and perhaps because of the success of the Navajo program, the public perception of foreign language instruction changed. A key event that promoted the development of foreign language instruction was the launching of a Soviet satellite into space. The *Sputnik* in 1957 showed that America was falling behind the Soviet Union. The government then allocated large grants for science as well as foreign language instruction.

Navajo Code Talkers: The Navajo language earned a distinguished place in U.S. history. During World War II, the U.S. government used Navajo radio operators—the Navajo Code Talkers—to communicate. Since Navajo was a relatively unknown language, the Japanese were never able to decipher the code. Using the Navajo language saved thousands of lives and contributed to the victory.

The expansion of foreign language instruction contributed to the development of a new field of study, English as a Second Language (ESL).

The Development of English as a Second Language

In the 1940s, as part of the Americanization program in the United States, English as a foreign language was developed as a field of study at the University of Michigan. By the 1960s, the field had evolved into what is known today as English as a Second Language, or ESL. In 1966, the association of Teachers of English to Speakers of Other Languages (TESOL) was founded to study and improve methods and strategies for teaching English. Today TESOL is an international organization with hundreds of affiliates and more than 47,000 members (TESOL, n.d.). In 2016, TESOL celebrated its 50th anniversary.

During the '70s similar organizations were established to promote bilingualism and fight for the rights of linguistic minorities. The National Association for Bilingual Education (NABE) was founded in 1972 in Austin, Texas. Texas and other states soon established NABE affiliates. These organizations fought for ELs and regulated the establishment of programs to meet the needs of language-minority students.

Policy and Legislative Context

Current bilingual education programs came via political activism as well as policy statements, legislative mandates, and court rulings. Here is a look at the policy and legislative landscape that helped shape bilingual education in the United States. A look at the relevant court cases follows in the next section in this chapter.

The United Nations Document of 1953: The United Nations in 1953 published a monograph titled *The Use of the Vernacular Language in Education.* This publication provided the theoretical foundation for the revival of dual language instruction in the United States (UNESCO, 1953). In this document, the United Nations Educational, Scientific and Cultural Organization (1953), established one of the cardinal points of bilingual education: *"We take it as axiomatic, too, that the best medium for teaching is in the mother tongue of the pupil"* (1953. P. 6). This document indirectly promoted the development of the bilingual education programs of the 1960s.

The event that paved the way for modern bilingual education programs was the triumph of the Cuban Revolution in 1959 and the resulting mass exodus of Cuban refugees to the United States. Using funds for the relocation of Cuban refugees fleeing communism, the U.S. government sponsored the creation of the first dual language program of the 1960s in Dade County, Florida. The success of this program at **Coral Way Elementary** in Florida guided other states to experiment with bilingual education programs.

Texas in 1964 implemented bilingual education programs in the United Consolidated ISD (Laredo area) and in the San Antonio ISD (Anderson & Boyer, 1970). Two more programs began in 1965, one in Edinburg, Texas, and the second in Pecos, New Mexico. In 1966, similar programs were started in California, New Mexico, Arizona, and New Jersey. Other districts that began bilingual education in Texas included Harlandale (1966), Del Rio (1966), Zapata (1966), Corpus Christi (1967), and Del Valle (1967) (Anderson & Boyer, 1970).

Title VI of the Civil Rights Act of 1964—Non-Discriminatory Clause: The passage of the Civil Rights Act of 1964 as well as the leadership of African American and Latino advocates provided the momentum needed to secure federal support for the fight against poverty and eventually for bilingual education. One component of the legislation, **Title VI**, specifically prohibited institutions that receive federal funding from discriminating on the grounds of race, color, or national origin. This legislation was used as a foundation for the multiple court cases that emerged in the '70s to seek support for the education of language-minority students.

Direct Intervention of the Federal Government: Although education is not mentioned in the U.S. Constitution, the federal government has been involved in education through legislative initiatives. In 1965, President Lyndon B. Johnson signed into law the Elementary and Secondary Education Act (ESEA) to provide financial support for public education. President Johnson, a former elementary teacher in Cotula, Texas, saw this law as an important component of civil rights legislation. Title I, a key component of the legislation, specifically helped children from low socioeconomic backgrounds. In 1968, the legislation added Title VII—The Bilingual Education Act—which provided funding for programs to address the needs of ELs. This legislation did not mandate bilingual education, but it provided funds, on a competitive basis, to develop model programs. Both Title I and Title VII remained major components of the ESEA until 2001, when the legislation was reenacted under the No Child Left Behind Act (NCLB). For more than three decades, the ESEA legislation regulated the services and programs to address the needs of language-minority students.

The Bilingual Education Act of 1968: In 1968, U.S. Senator Ralph Yarborough of Texas proposed a bill to provide services to English learners, and the legislation resulted in amending the ESEA to include Title VII—The Bilingual Education Act (Orr, 2015). The law did not mandate bilingual education or the use of the students' native language for instruction. Instead, the legislation encouraged the development of innovative programs to teach English. Title VII also provided funding:

- to prepare bilingual education teachers and teacher aides,

- for the development and dissemination of materials, and

- for the implementation of programs to involve parents in the education of their children (Ovando & Combs, 2014).

Since Title VII provided funding for the preparation of bilingual education teachers and teacher aides, the field of bilingual education was created in higher education. Since bilingual education was new, most pioneers in bilingual education came from foreign language and linguistics studies. The legislation described English learners as Limited English Proficiency (LEP), a term that was used until 2015 when the new Every Student Succeeds Act (ESSA) replaced it with a more neutral term, *English learners* (ELs).

The Memorandum of 1970: The division of the Civil Rights of the Department of Health, Education, and Welfare (HEW) in 1970 issued a memorandum that influenced the education of English learners nationwide. In this document, HEW clarified the responsibilities of the school district under Title VI of the Civil Rights Act of 1965—the non-discriminatory and equal access to education legislation. In the memorandum, HEW reinstated the responsibilities of the district to take *affirmative steps* to correct *language deficiency* that students may bring to school (HEW,

1970). Entities receiving federal funding were required to comply with this directive. The document offered help to implement the directive as well as ways to monitor compliance. Despite the simplicity of this directive, this document was used in litigation to secure better education services for language-minority students.

The Bilingual Education Act of 1974: Because of the Supreme Court ruling in *Lau v. Nichols* in 1974, the Bilingual Education Act was amended the same year to accomplish the following:

- clarify the goals and programs for bilingual education;

- promote the establishment of regional support centers (Lau Compliance Centers);

- provide funding for research and development of curricula (Orr, 2015);

- provide funding for technical help to districts starting bilingual education programs;

- establish a clearinghouse (the National Clearinghouse for Bilingual Education) to disseminate information about bilingual/ESL education; and

- increase funding for bilingual education from $7.5 million to $68.0 million.

The Equal Education Opportunity Act of the ESEA of 1974: The Equal Education Opportunity Act (EEOA), an amendment of the ESEA of 1974, resulted from two court cases, one about segregation of schools in 1973 — *Keyes v. School District No. 1 (Denver, Colorado)*, and the second about quality education for ELs in 1974 (*Lau v. Nichols*). The legislation specifically said that the state could not deny equal educational opportunity based on race, color, gender, or national origin. It also prohibited school districts from segregating students (Law & Higher Education, 2015).

Reauthorization of the ESEA of 1978: The reauthorization of the ESEA of 1978 incorporated the following changes:

- redefined and emphasized the transitional nature of bilingual education, which led to the creation of early-exit transitional bilingual education programs.

- prohibited the use of federal funding to create language developmental or maintenance bilingual education programs.

- extended the Lau ruling to all students and school districts from only those receiving federal financial support (Stewner-Manzanares, 1988).

Reauthorization of the ESEA of 1984: The ESEA of 1984 legislation broke from the compensatory model of bilingual education (early exit) to take an enrichment approach and allocated special funding to implement such programs (late exit). However, it also made ESL an alternative program to serve the needs of ELs. Some key changes of the 1984 legislation were to:

- eliminate the 1978 restrictions on the use of federal funding for maintenance programs and provide special grants to promote "developmental/maintenance bilingual education programs" (Ovando & Combs, 2014);

- allocate funding for alternative programs that did not require the use of minority languages for instruction, i.e., ESL as a program (Crawford 2004);

- provide a legal foundation for the use of English as a Second Language to serve the needs of ELs; and

- allocate special funding to improve teacher-preparation programs.

The ESEA of 1994: Under President Bill Clinton, the ESEA legislation was renamed the Improving America's School Act of 1994. This version of the legislation allowed the creation and development of dual language programs. Some key provisions of this legislation were to:

- allow the participation of English proficiency students in bilingual education programs, which opened the door to the implementation of two-way dual language programs;

- continue allowing the use of funding to support developmental/maintenance bilingual education programs; and

- provide special funding for higher education to continue the preparation of bilingual/ESL education teachers.

No Child Left Behind Act: Under President George W. Bush in 2001, the No Child Left Behind Act (NCLB) replaced the ESEA of 1965. The NCLB legislation replaced title VII—the Bilingual Education Act—with Title III—English Language Acquisition, Language Enhancement, and Academic Achievement Act. This legislation abandoned bilingual education or dual language instruction. Instead, the legislation emphasized the acquisition of English to allow students opportunities to compete with native English speakers.

Title I of the NCLB legislation redefined the concept of highly qualified teachers and required school districts to hire those teachers to serve students in Title I and III. Because of the required qualifications for teachers, state education agencies (SEAs) had to provide evidence that teachers serving low-income and language-minority students were fully qualified and proficient in the languages used for instruction.

Because of the NCLB, the preparation of highly qualified teachers became a key focus for SEAs and universities engaged in preparing teachers. Teachers in bilingual and foreign language instruction were required to show proficiency in the language of instruction. Texas engaged in the development of multiple certification exams to be sure teachers met the federal criteria. In the early childhood to grade 6 certification, the quest for highly qualified teachers resulted in the development of a demanding content-area certification exam—which has evolved into today's TExES Core Subjects EC–6 (291)—with 267 questions in five subtests: language arts and reading, mathematics, social studies, science, and fine arts, health and physical education (TEA, 2014). For bilingual education certification, the state went from a test that assessed only speaking ability (Texas Oral Proficiency Test) to a comprehensive three-and-a-half hour test, covering all language skills (listening, speaking, reading, and writing). These two tests have resulted in a reduction of teacher candidates in bilingual education in Texas.

The Every Student Succeeds Act: On Dec. 6, 2015, President Barack Obama signed into law the Every Student Succeeds Act (ESSA), replacing the NCLB legislation. This legislation changed multiple NCLB mandates. The ESSA legislation emphasized state and local control over the implementation of the education program, including assessment and reporting procedures. An analysis of key provisions of the ESSA legislation is presented in this section.

The ESSA legislation mandated the following (ESSA, 2015; USDE, n.d.):

1. Made state education agencies (SEAs) responsible for the development and implementation of college and career readiness standards.

2. Made state education agencies (SEAs) responsible for setting students' performance targets, using multiple measures.

3. Required annual assessments of all students but reduced unnecessary testing practices required under the NCLB legislation.

4. Shifted the responsibility for the development of the assessment program from the federal government to local control.

5. Required a state-developed system to identify and provide support to low-performing schools, including the achievement discrepancies among the subgroups (white, black, Latino...) represented in schools.

6. Mandated the development of programs to support schools with high dropout rates in high school.

7. Established competitive programs to reward high-performing teachers, especially those working in low-performing schools.

8. Provided funding for pre-kindergarten education.

9. Allocated funding to replicate high-performing charter school programs.

10. Required the disclosure of comprehensive per-pupil expenditures that include federal, state, and local funding.

Impact of the ESSA in Bilingual and ESL Education: Some components of the ESSA that affected the education of English learners (ELs) are listed in this section (CCSSO, 2016, February; USDE, 2016).

1. The legislation replaced the compensatory term—*Limited English Proficient* (LEP)—with a more neutral term—*English learners* (ELs).

2. It required school districts to assess within 30 days of enrollment in school the language proficiency of students who might qualify for special language programs [already required in Texas].

3. Required states to develop English language proficiency standards (ELPS) to monitor the English proficiency of ELs and to align these with the academic standards of each state's K–12 curricula [already required in Texas].

4. The state's accountability system must include long-term goals and measures to document the progress of ELs in achieving English proficiency.

5. It shifted the accountability provision from Title III (Education of ELs) to Title I (Education of Disadvantaged Students). The accountability for ELs thus will be part of the Title I accountability system. However, under Title III states are still required to establish statewide admission and exit procedures for the special language programs designed for ELs.

6. Expanded the required follow-up provisions of reclassified ELs from two years (NCLB) to four years. The state thus must follow former ELs four years after their reclassification as fluent English speakers (CCSSO, 2016, February).

7. Required states to assess the English proficiency of ELs annually in grades 3–8 and once in high school.

8. Allowed state education agencies (SEAs) to allocate funding to reward districts with programs that significantly improve the academic performance of ELs.

9. Under Title I, states must show evidence that they have adopted English language proficiency standards (ELPS) and that these standards are aligned with state academic standards [already required in Texas].

The ESSA changed multiple NCLB mandates. A comparative analysis of the differences between the NCLB and the ESSA (ASCD, n.d.) is presented in Table 3.2.

Table 3.2. Comparison of NCLB and ESSA

No Child Left Behind Act (NCLB)	Every Student Succeeds Act (ESSA)
Academic Standards	**Academic Standards**
• Requires state to set standards in reading, mathematics, and science at all grade levels. • Requires states to apply the same academic standards to all schools and children.	• Requires states to adopt academic standards in reading, mathematics, and science with three levels of achievement. • It prohibits the interference of the federal government with states' ability to set their own academic standards. This provision eliminates the possibility of forcing states to adopt the Common Core Standards use in several states.* • Permits states to develop alternate achievement standards for students in special education.
Assessment and Accountability	**Assessment and Accountability**
• Calls for states to develop annual assessments in reading and mathematics in grades 3–8 and once in high school. • Requires state testing in science annually in grade spans 3–5, 6–8, and 10–12.	• Same as NCLB, but the legislation allows states the option of using a single annual summative assessment or the summative result of multiple assessments throughout the year. • Allows districts to use or develop their own assessment instrument, with permission from the state. • The legislation prohibits the federal government from prescribing any part of the assessment.
• Requires states to administer assessments to at least 95% of students and 95% of each student subgroup.	• No changes, but the state and the school districts have the right to establish consequences for schools unable to meet the 95% assessment threshold.
• Requires districts annually to assess all students with limited English language proficiency.	• Moves the accountability for English learners into Title I (Education of Disadvantaged Students) instead of Title III and allows schools to phase in the use of English learners' test results for accountability purposes.*

* Identifies a key change to the legislation.

No Child Left Behind Act (NCLB)	Every Student Succeeds Act (ESSA)
Assessment and Accountability (cont'd)	**Assessment and Accountability (cont'd)**
• Requires that schools make adequate yearly progress (AYP) for all students and for subgroups for which data are disaggregated.	• Eliminates AYP and the 100% proficiency requirement. • Requires state-developed accountability systems that include performance goals for each subgroup. • Annually measure student performance based on state assessments. For high schools: annually measure graduation rates. • For elementary and middle schools: annually measure student growth (or another valid and reliable statewide academic indicator). • Requires identification of schools in which any subgroup is consistently underperforming. • Allows states to decide how much weight to give tests in their accountability systems and determine what consequences, if any, should attach to poor performance. Requires states to give more weight to academic factors than to other factors.
• Establishes student subgroups for accountability and data disaggregation, including students who are economically disadvantaged, English learners, students with disabilities, and students from major racial and ethnic groups.	• Same as NCLB, with three additional subgroups for data reporting only: homeless status (if statistically significant), students with parents in the military, and students in foster care.*

---

* Identifies a key change to the legislation.

No Child Left Behind Act (NCLB)	Every Student Succeeds Act (ESSA)
Reporting Requirements	Reporting Requirements
• Requires annual reporting on the academic performance of students with data disaggregated by subgroup. • Requires the disclosure of the percentage of students not tested, the state's achievement trends over the course of two years, graduation rate and information on teacher quality.	• Similar to the NCLB legislation. • Requires a description of the state accountability system, including all indicators and the weights assigned by the state. • Identification of schools in need of support and improvement. • Student performance disaggregated by subgroup, including the performance of English learners. • Teacher qualifications, including those with emergency or provisional status. • Disclosure of the state per-pupil expenditures of federal, state, and local funds.* • Identification of the number of students taking alternate assessments and the number of high school students who enroll in postsecondary education.*

English Language Proficiency Standards in Texas: The ESSA legislation requires the development of English language proficiency standards (ELPS) for ELs nationwide. With this provision, states must align the academic standards of the curriculum with the proficiency standards required from ELs. This alignment will serve as the platform to guide teachers in the implementation of linguistically accessible instruction for ELs in the United States.

Texas already complies with this mandate. The adoption of the revised ELPS as part of 19 Texas Administrative Code (TAC) Chapter 74, *Curriculum Requirements*, ensures alignment with all academic content areas (ELPS, 2016). This legislation outlines the language instruction school districts must provide to ELs in kindergarten to grade 12 so they can learn English and succeed academically. The ELPS are to be implemented as part of the instructional program in each foundation and enrichment subject of the state curriculum. Obviously, the ELPS are not required when instruction is delivered in the students' native language.

---

* Identifies a key change to the legislation.

Texas legislation requires school districts to assess the English proficiency levels of all ELs from kindergarten to grade 12, in the language domains of listening, speaking, reading, and writing and to assign one of the four language proficiency levels used in the state—beginning, intermediate, advanced, and advanced high. Based on individual language proficiency of ELs, they then must develop linguistically accommodated instruction to meet individual needs of the learners.

Relevant Court Cases at the National Level

The following section presents the court cases that laid the foundation for the litigation that influenced the development of bilingual education.

Cases That Preceded Litigation for Bilingual Education

The struggle for a meaningful education for linguistic minorities cannot be separated from the struggle for civil rights. Based on this premise, some cases that traditionally are not linked to bilingual education litigation are discussed here. These cases are included because they represent the beginning of the struggle for human rights, and the pursuit of meaningful education for language-minority students in the United States.

Meyer v. Nebraska **(1923):** This U.S. Supreme Court case challenged a 1919 English-only state law that prohibited the teaching of foreign languages in public and private schools. A teacher was found guilty of teaching a student in German. The teacher challenged the decision, which went to the Nebraska Supreme Court, where it was upheld. Using the due process clause of the 14th Amendment of the U.S. Constitution, the plaintiffs appealed the decision to the U.S. Supreme Court, which ruled in favor of the plaintiffs and overturned the Nebraska law. Using the *Meyer v. Nebraska* ruling, the 14th Amendment was used as a foundation in multiple litigations that shaped bilingual education in the United States.

Méndez v. Westminster **(1946):** This court case involved a group of Mexican American students challenging segregation laws in California. Children of the Méndez family were prevented from attending a white-only school. The plaintiffs argued that they were discriminated based on their ethnicity. The district argued that it could restrict admission to the school based on California segregation law, legally under the "separate but equal" doctrine established in the 1896 *Plessy v. Ferguson* decision.

- The U.S. District Court in Los Angeles ruled in favor of the Méndez family based on the Equal Protection Clause of the 14th Amendment. The district appealed the decision to the 9th Federal District Court of Appeals in San Francisco.

- In 1947, the U.S. 9th Federal District Court of Appeals upheld the ruling on different grounds, saying the California segregation law did not include Mexican Americans. It included such other groups as Chinese and Japanese.

- The 9th Circuit Court of Appeals did not challenge the "separate but equal doctrine" established in *Plessy v. Ferguson* but brought up several historical events that paved the road for the *Brown v. Board of Education* landmark segregation case.

- The National Association for the Advancement of Colored People (NAACP) led by Thurgood Marshall joined the appellate process as *amicus curiae* (friends of the court).

- Governor Earl Warren repealed the California segregation laws, making California the first state to ban segregated neighborhood schools (*Los Angeles Times*, 6/27/16). Warren later became Chief Justice of the U.S. Supreme Court and presided over *Brown v. Board of Education of Topeka* (1954).

***Brown v. Board of Education of Topeka* (1954):** This school segregation case was brought up on behalf of thousands of African American students attending segregated schools in the Topeka school district. Thurgood Marshall of the NAACP represented the plaintiffs. Again, Warren was now the chief justice of the Supreme Court. The U.S. Supreme Court ruled that separate educational facilities were inherently unequal and a violation of the equal protection clause of the 14th Amendment. This Supreme Court ruling declared the "separate but equal doctrine" established in *Plessy v. Ferguson* was unconstitutional, and the decision applied the desegregation mandate to the whole nation. *Brown v. Board of Education of Topeka* established the foundation for the struggle for civil rights that characterized the 1960s and '70s in America.

***Hernández v. Texas* (1954):** An all-white jury in Jackson County, Texas, found Pete Hernández guilty of murder. During the jury selection as well as the trial, his legal team unsuccessfully challenged the composition of the jury, alleging that people of Mexican descent were not represented on it. They suggested that an all-white jury clearly discriminated against the defendant. They alleged that people of Mexican ancestry represent a special classification different from whites. The legal team appealed the case to the Texas Supreme Court, arguing that an all-white jury could have not been impartial in the Hernández case.

The Texas Court of Criminal Appeals denied the motion, saying that people of Mexican descent were not a special classification under the 14th Amendment. The defendant appealed the case to the U.S. Supreme Court, which ruled unanimously in favor of Hernández. It ordered the case to be retried with a jury of peers selected without regard to ethnicity. The Court also held that the 14th Amendment protects and addresses not only white and black racial classifications but also such groups as Mexican Americans (*Hernández v. Texas,* 1954). This landmark case extended the equal protection clause of the 14th Amendment to Mexican Americans and other minority groups (Collier & Thomas, 2012).

The identification of Mexican Americans as a group different from whites was further challenged in a segregation case in *Cisneros v. Corpus Christi ISD* (1971). The plaintiffs in this case argued that the district's Mexican American students were grouped with African Americans to comply with the desegregation ruling white and black students mandated under *Brown v. Board of Education of Topeka* (1954). The Court found in favor of the plaintiffs and ordered integration of the three groups—white, black, and Mexican American (1971).

***Diana v. California State Board of Education* (1970):** Based on IQ testing scores derived from an English test, a group of nine Spanish-speaking Mexican American children from Monterey County, California, in this case were placed in a special education classroom. The plaintiffs argued that the process used to place students in special education was unfair because the children could not understand the language used in the test. The Court ruled in favor of the plaintiffs, saying that Spanish-speaking students should be retested in their native language to avoid errors in placement. It also indicated that additional testing and supporting data should be used to ensure accurate placement of students in special education programs (Yzquierdo-McLain, 1995).

***Keyes v. School District No. 1, Denver, Colorado* (1973):** Black and Hispanic parents took legal action against this school district, alleging that it placed students in racially segregated schools that were inferior to white schools. The plaintiffs argued that this segregation, intended or not, violated the equal protection clause of the 14th Amendment. The Supreme Court ruled that the district unintentionally (de facto) created and promoted a climate of racial segregation. Since most segregation cases involved Southern states, this case was significant because it addressed a non-Southern state of the country (*Keyes v. School District No. 1*, 1973).

***Serna v. Portales Municipal Schools* (1972 and 1974):** This was among the first successful court cases seeking support for bilingual education. In 1972, a federal court mandated that the school district in Portales, New Mexico, start a bilingual-bicultural curriculum, revise assessment procedures to monitor Hispanic students' academic achievement, and recruit bilingual personnel. The Portales Municipal Schools appealed, but the 10th District Court of Appeals upheld the decision in 1974, based on the *Lau v. Nichols* ruling handed down the same year (*Serna v. Portales*, 1974).

***Lau v. Nichols* (1974):** In this landmark case, Kinney Lau, representing 1,790 Chinese students, started a class action suit against the San Francisco Unified School District seeking support for Chinese students who were failing school because they could not understand English. The plaintiffs argued that the Chinese students were provided with unequal educational opportunity, a violation of the 14th Amendment and the Civil Rights Act of 1964. In 1974, the U.S. Supreme Court, based on the Civil Rights Act of 1964 and the Office for Civil Rights (OCR) Memorandum of 1970, found in favor of the plaintiffs. However, the court did not specify a remedy and left it to the district to decide how to comply with the mandate to provide "meaningful education" to students of limited English proficiency. In the consent decree that followed, the San Francisco Unified School District agreed to provide bilingual-bicultural education. Although the court did not dictate a specific remedy in its ruling, this landmark case provided the momentum and foundation for other litigations. It became the de facto tool for the implementation of bilingual education in the United States (*Lau v. Nichols*, 1974).

***ASPIRA v. New York City Board of Education* (1974):** ASPIRA, a community-based organization, sued the New York City Board of Education seeking relief for a large number of ELs in the city. While the case was being heard, the Lau ruling was handed down, and the litigation ended in a consent decree—that is, the district agreed with the demands of the plaintiffs. The court mandated a city-wide assessment to identify students who need special language services as well as the implementation of a district-wide bilingual education program to address the identified needs of ELs.

***Rios v. Reed* (1978):** This case addressed program quality. A federal court ruled that the Patchogue-Medford School District in New York had violated the rights of ELs by providing a "half-hearted" (Crawford 2004, p. 11) bilingual program that relied mostly on ESL and did not include a bicultural component. The court not only upheld the importance of teaching English to students but also recognized the need to provide meaningful education while accomplishing the language goal. This ruling clearly called for the use of L1 instruction for the content areas while developing English proficiency. The *Rios v. Reed* decision provided the foundation for many bilingual education programs developed in the 1980s and beyond.

***Castañeda v. Pickard* (1981):** The quality of the bilingual programs was addressed again when the school district of Raymondville, Texas, was charged with violating the Equal Educational Opportunities Act (EEOA) of 1974. In its decision, the Fifth Court of Appeals mandated three steps to develop quality bilingual education programs. The Court ruled that program implementation must be based on sound research, with adequate resources and opportunities for students to have access to the full curriculum. These guidelines were used as the model to enforce the Lau Remedies to be discussed in this chapter.

***U.S. v. the State of Texas* (1981):** U.S. District Judge William Wayne Justice ordered Texas to offer a bilingual education program for Mexican American students in kindergarten through grade 12. The judge indicated that the state had segregated children to inferior schools and had "vilified" the language and culture of the Mexican American children. Although the ruling was reversed a year later, the case led the Texas governor to appoint a bilingual education task force to draft a plan for bilingual education. The work of the task force was instrumental in the drafting of Senate Bill 477, the current Bilingual Education Law in Texas.

Plyler v. Doe **(1982):** This federal case challenged a law that permitted Texas to withhold state funds for districts educating children of undocumented parents. The U.S. Court of Appeals for the Fifth Circuit ruled that children of undocumented parents are protected by the equal protection clause of the 14th Amendment. The ruling prohibited public schools from denying children of undocumented workers admission to school. It also prohibited schools from asking about the legal status of the parents and from requiring a Social Security number to enroll.

The ruling was used to declare unconstitutional a proposition designed to control illegal immigration to California. In 1994, California voters approved Proposition 187. It required school personnel to report to law enforcement agencies and the federal Immigration and Naturalization Service children or parents unable to prove their legal immigration status. In a decision based on *Plyler v. Doe*, the reporting requirement of Proposition 187 was declared unconstitutional. The judge ruled that immigration is a federal responsibility and the states cannot establish their own systems (*Plyler v. Doe*, 1982).

Roles of the Federal Government and the Office for Civil Rights

The judiciary and federal government have been used in litigation seeking support for language-minority students. Because of litigation, the Office of Civil Rights started programs to ensure compliance with court decisions. This section discusses some of the documents and actions.

1. **The 14th Amendment**—No state shall make or enforce any law which shall abridge the privileges or immunities of citizens of the United States; nor shall any state deprive any person of life, liberty, or property, without due process of law; nor deny to any person within its jurisdiction the equal protection of the laws.

2. **Title VI of the Civil Rights Act of 1964**—Title VI prohibits discrimination on the basis of race, color, or national origin in any program receiving federal funding.

3. **Office for Civil Rights Memorandum of 1970**—The OCR, part of the U.S. Department of Health, Education, and Welfare, issued this memorandum to school officials nationwide. It required districts to offer appropriate instruction to address the educational needs of language-minority students. The document also prohibited the use of data relying strictly on language as the key reason for assigning students to special education programs. Based on the historical value of the memorandum, the OCR incorporated its content into the compliance procedure for Title VI of the Civil Rights Act of 1964 (Castro Feinberg, 1990).

4. **Equal Educational Opportunities Act of 1974**—The EEOA prohibits any state that receives federal funds from denying equal educational opportunity to people based

on race, color, sex, or national origin. Unlike Title VI of the Civil Rights Act of 1964, the EEOA applied to all schools, not just those receiving federal funding. This civil rights statute provided additional support for the *Lau* ruling and put more pressure on districts to offer meaningful education to ELs.

5. **Lau Remedies (1975)**—Using the OCR memorandum, the Equal Educational Opportunities Act, and the *Lau* ruling, the OCR instituted the **Lau Remedies** in 1975. The 1974 ruling in *Lau v. Nichols* got little attention until a year later, when the U.S. secretary of education introduced a document to guide districts in the implementation of the *Lau* ruling. Called the Lau Remedies, this document described how to identify and evaluate students in bilingual education programs. It further established that school districts must not assign students to classes for the "educable mentally retarded" by applying criteria that measure language development in English.

The document also mandated bilingual education for elementary schools and ESL instruction for older students. It also described the guidelines for exiting students from the program as well as the professional standards required for teachers to participate in the program. The Lau Remedies evolved into the de facto compliance standards of the OCR. However, the Ronald Reagan administration in 1980 described the Lau Remedies as unreasonable and eliminated them.

English-Only and English-Plus Movements: In 1981, U.S. Senator S.I. Hayakawa of California started a campaign to declare English the official language of the United States and eliminate bilingual education. The **English-only movement** gained momentum through the 1980s and remains viable. Currently, 30 states have passed legislation banning dual language instruction (U.S. English, n.d.). These include states with a large Hispanic population like Massachusetts, Illinois, Florida, and Arizona.

In 1985, the **English-plus movement** was founded by the League of United Latin American Citizens (LULAC) and the Spanish American League Against Discrimination (SALAD) as a reaction against the English-only movement. This movement led to an increase in funding for bilingual education in 1994 and an increased interest in the growth of developmental or late-exit programs.

Texas Bilingual Education Legislation: Historical Background

In 1969, New Mexico and Texas became the first two states to pass legislation repealing English-only laws, opening the path to bilingual education legislation. In 1971, Massachusetts became the first state to mandate bilingual education. It was the most comprehensive legislation mandating bilingual education for multiple minority languages in K-12 schools. In 2002 Massachusetts voters approved English-only legislation and the elimination of the state bilingual education law.

The history of bilingual education in Texas has been characterized by multiple legal challenges and court cases. Here is a timeline of key events that shaped bilingual education in Texas:

- **1918**—Following the lead of other states as well as the xenophobia and isolation tendencies that resulted from World War I, Texas instituted the English-only rule in education. ELs then were submerged in English-only instruction. Although some children learned English, others could not cope and dropped out of school.

- **1920**—Schools in South Texas offered home-based reading and writing instruction in Spanish—the "Escuelitas" program. This program was active until the 1960s (Rodríguez, 2016).

- **1964**—Under the leadership of Superintendent Harold Brantley, the Laredo School District became the first district in Texas to offer bilingual education. Districts including San Antonio, McAllen, and El Paso followed Laredo's lead and started bilingual-education programs for Mexican American children.

- **1969**—Under the leadership of Rep. Carlos Truán, and Sen. Joe Bernal, the Texas Legislature officially ended the English-only legislation of 1918 by enacting HB 103. The bill launched the development of bilingual education in the state by allowing—but not requiring—bilingual education through grade 6.

- **1972**—The Texas Association for Bilingual Education was founded in San Antonio.

- **1973**—Nineteen school districts in Texas received Title VII (ESEA, 1965) funding to start bilingual education programs (Rodríguez, 2016).

- **1973**—SB 121 amended the Texas Education Code to allow the establishment of the first Bilingual Education and Training Act. It mandated bilingual education from grade 1 to grade 6.

- **1981**—SB 477 expanded bilingual education or special language programs for children in kindergarten through grade 12. Bilingual education was mandated through the elementary grades, bilingual or ESL for middle schools, and ESL for high schools. Dual-language instruction became an optional program that could be used in place of the traditional bilingual education. It also allowed dual-language instruction from pre-kindergarten through high school (Chapter 89 as amended in 2012).

For a historical analysis of bilingual education in Texas and to see the pioneers of this movement, see the Texas Association for Bilingual Education (TABE) video titled "The History of Bilingual Education" (Rodríguez, 2012).

Current Texas Bilingual Education and Special Language Programs

The commissioner of education in collaboration with the State Board of Education (SBE) issued rules guiding the implementation of the state's education law. They were titled the Commissioner's Rules Concerning State Plan for Educating Limited English Proficient Students (19 Texas Administrative Code, Chapter 89, Subchapter BB, 1996). The rules provide a detailed interpretation of bilingual education and special language legislation, as authorized by the Texas Education Code (TEC §§29.051–29.064, subchapter B). School districts follow this document for the implementation and administration of bilingual and special language programs. An analysis of the legislation follows.

Goals of Bilingual and ESL Education: The key goal of the legislation is to guide ELs to become competent in comprehension, speaking, reading, and composition of the English language through the development of literacy and academic skills in the primary language and English. Additionally, this legislation attempts to enable:

A. ELs to master English language skills as well as mathematics, science and social studies as integral parts of the academic goals for all students.

B. ELs to become competent in the comprehension, speaking, reading, and composition of the English language through the integrated use of second-language methods.

Components of the Bilingual Program: The bilingual education program encompasses three major components—the affective, linguistic, and cognitive.

A. Affective Component: Introduces basic concepts of the school environment in both the native language (L1) and English (L2), instills confidence and self-assurance, and develops a positive identity with the student's cultural heritage as well as U.S. culture.

B. Linguistic Component: Instruction in L1 and L2 is used to develop and master English skills in comprehension, speaking, reading, and composition.

C. Cognitive Component: Instruction in L1 and L2 is used to develop and master ELs' Essential Knowledge & Skills (TEKS) and higher-order thinking skills in mathematics, science, health, and social studies as well as other content areas.

Programs under the Texas Legislation: Some key provisions for development of the language program are:

1. Bilingual education from kindergarten through the elementary grades (kindergarten grade 6). Districts have the option of using dual language immersion as a substitute for education in prekindergarten through the elementary grades.

2. Districts are authorized to establish a bilingual education program at grade levels in which the bilingual education program is not required. This statement allows the implementation of dual-language programs in K–12 schools.

3. School districts are authorized to use bilingual education, instruction in ESL, or other transitional language programs approved by the state in post-elementary grades through grade 8.

4. The use of ESL instruction can be used in grades 9–12.

5. The legislation also allows voluntary Pre-K bilingual programs.

Home Language Survey: Under the legislation new students to the district are required to complete a home language survey containing two basic questions:

1. What language is spoken in your home most of the time?

2. What language does your child speak most of the time?

If the answer to either of these questions is a language other than English, the child must be tested for language dominance or proficiency.

Screening for Admission to the Program: Districts shall administer the following to students who have a language other than English as identified by the Home Language Survey:

1. In PK through Grade 1, an oral language proficiency test within four weeks of their enrollment) and

2. In Grades 2–12, a TEA-approved oral language proficiency test and the English reading and English language arts sections from a TEA-approved, norm-referenced measure (40th percentile), or another TEA-approved test.

Students with Special Needs: For students in bilingual or special education programs, the Admission Review and Dismissal Committee (ARD) in conjunction with the Language Proficiency Assessment Committee (LPAC) will determine if the student qualifies for admission to the special education program. Once admitted, the LPAC and the ARD committees will design the individualized education program (IEP), which will identify appropriate assessment instruments and level of performance required.

Exit and Reclassification of English Learners: LEP legislation requires school districts to follow a specific process to be sure ELs can be exited from the program with a level of language skills needed to succeed in the mainstream classroom. Reclassifying students from ELs to fluent English speakers requires:

1. Satisfactory performance on a TEA-approved test that measures the extent to which the student has developed oral and written language proficiency and specific language skills in English;

2. Satisfactory performance on the reading assessment instrument, or a TEA-approved English Language Arts assessment instrument administered in English, or a score at or above the 40th percentile on both the English reading and the English language arts sections of a TEA-approved, norm-referenced assessment instrument;

3. Passing grades on all subjects, and

4. A reclassification decision of LPAC and ARD (if applicable).

In making the decision to reclassify students, the LPAC must consider the overall academic performance of the child, teachers' evaluations, and parental input. Once in the program, students cannot be exited in grades K to 1. The earliest grade for reclassification thus is second grade.

Two-Year Monitoring Services: After reclassification as a fluent English speaker, a student is monitored for two years to ensure success in the English-only classroom. The LPAC evaluates the student's academic performance in class as well as the results of the TEA basic academic skills examinations and additional instruments used in school to measure progress. If a reclassified student experiences academic problems, the LPAC can return the child to the bilingual or ESL program or make the necessary changes to be sure the student succeeds.

 The ESSA of 2016 legislation expanded the monitoring period to four years.

Language Proficiency Assessment Committee: The Language Proficiency Assessment Committee (LPAC) is a board composed of at least one administrator as well as teachers and a parent representative. This committee regulates admission, treatment, dismissal, and follow-up services to students in the bilingual or special-language program. When students are exited from the program, the LPAC follows their progress for two years and makes decisions based on data.

Functions of the LPAC

1. Identifies the language proficiency and the level of academic achievement of each English learner;

2. Designates, subject to parental approval, the initial instructional placement of each student in the required program;

3. Facilitates the participation of students in other special programs for which they are eligible and which are provided by the district with either state or federal funds; and

4. Reclassifies students as English-proficient in accordance with the established criteria.

5. Monitors reclassified students over a period of at least two years.

Documentation Required for Bilingual/ ESL Students

The student's permanent record should contain documentation of all actions impacting students. Some of the documents are:

1. the identification of the student as English learner;

2. the designation of the student's level of language proficiency;

3. the recommendation of program placement;

4. parental approval of entry or placement into the program;

5 the dates of admission, and placement in the program;

6. the dates of exemptions from taking the criterion-referenced test, the criteria used for this determination, and additional instructional interventions provided to students to ensure academic and linguistic progress;

7. the date of exit from the program and parent notification; and

8. the results of (two-year) monitoring for academic success.

Bilingual and ESL Program Models

Several bilingual education programs are available to meet the language needs of ELs in Texas. These programs can be divided into two broad categories—early exit and late exit. Early-exit programs provide language support for two to three years. The transitional bilingual education (TBE) program is an example of this type of approach. Generally, the goal of the TBE program is to exit the child to the mainstream classroom as quickly as possible. The late-exit model provides from four to six years of treatment. This program is also called **language enrichment** and **language maintenance**, and the goal of these programs is to become bilingual and biliterate. A summary of these programs follows.

Early-Exit Transitional Bilingual Education Programs: The early-exit transitional bilingual education (TBE) program is the choice for most school districts in the United States. In Texas,

Senate Bill 2, Chapter 29B calls for transitional bilingual education. The main goal of the program is to mainstream students as quickly as possible. This program promotes literacy in L1 and native language instruction in kindergarten through grade 2 with at least 45 minutes of ESL instruction. Traditionally, the transition to English begins in third grade, and by grade 4, students are mainstreamed or placed in a class using the sheltered English approach discussed later in this chapter.

In a self-contained elementary model, a bilingual teacher provides instruction in L1 and L2. In the upper-elementary grades, one instructor might teach in L1 while an ESL specialist promotes language development. This program is perceived as remedial, too complex for teachers to follow all the guidelines, and not long enough for ELs to develop English proficiency.

Late-Exit Dual Language Programs

Under the late-exit model, programs offer four or more years of treatment. Although originally designed for students in kindergarten through grade 12, most programs are implemented through fifth or sixth grade. Two types of late-exit programs are described in this section: developmental bilingual education (DBE) and dual language immersion programs.

Developmental Bilingual Education: The developmental bilingual education (DBE) program emerged in the 1970s as an alternative to the TBE model (Crawford, 2004). The program is also known as maintenance bilingual education or bilingual-bicultural education and more recently has been labeled one-way bilingual education. In this program, language-minority children with a common language (i.e., Spanish) are placed in a program that encourages them to maintain their native language and add English. Opponents of bilingual-bicultural education have attacked the program for not placing enough emphasis on English development. Because of this opposition, the program was declared ineligible for federal funding in 1978 (Crawford, 2004). However, the program was reauthorized in the Bilingual Education Act of 1984 under the name Developmental Bilingual Education (DBE). The DBE program looks similar to the early-exit TBE program but has fundamental differences.

Two-Way Dual Language Immersion: The two-way bilingual education program is a form of developmental bilingual education because it promotes the maintenance of both languages. The program serves language-majority (native English speakers) and language-minority students (ELs) in an instructional setting in which both groups learn from each other. In addition to the language benefit of peer instruction, the program contributes to a better cultural understanding among the students (Christian, 1994). This program views students as gifted, unlike the compensatory perspective of the early-exit model. The positive nature of the program and its inclusion of language-majority students make funding and support more palatable to the public. Table 3.3 presents a comparison of the TBE and DBE programs.

Table 3.3. Comparison of the TBE and DBE Programs

Components	Transitional Bilingual Education	Developmental Bilingual Education
Duration of the Program	2–3 years	4–5 years
View of L1 and L2	The native language is considered a handicap that needs to be corrected. The program provides initial language and content support in both languages. In the later stages of the program, L1 is reduced or eliminated to allow instruction mostly in English.	Language is perceived as an asset. Enrichment and additive in orientation. The native language is considered an asset that should be preserved. Students begin with different levels of proficiency in L1 and L2 and finish with similar levels of proficiency in both languages.
Literacy Goal	The goal is to develop literacy in English. The early-exit nature of L1 support in TBE does not allow enough time for the child to become proficient in L1. As a result, students do not benefit from possible language skills transferred from L1 to L2	Development of literacy in L1 and L2 (biliteracy). The late-exit nature of the program allows more time to develop the proficiency in L1 and L2. With a stronger literacy background, students can transfer literacy skills and content from L1 to L2.

Program Implementation

Both models—early- and late-exit—are implemented in several ways throughout the United States. These versions are structured based on content areas or days of instruction, or by percentage, by language.

1. Instruction Divided by Content

In one model, some content areas are delivered in L1 and others in L2. For example, social studies and mathematics can be delivered in L1, and art and music can be presented in L2. Switching the language of instruction exposes students to the content areas in both languages. Teachers are organized in one of two ways:

A. **Two Teachers (Mixed) or Team Teaching.** This approach uses two teachers, with one teacher delivering instruction in the minority language and the second teaching in the majority language. At some point in the day or week, students switch teachers. One benefit is that students identify the teacher with a given language, which discourages code switching.

B. **Single Teacher.** In this approach, one teacher alternates the use of the languages across disciplines. The teacher must be fully bilingual and must guide students to separate the uses of the two languages. Because students know that the teacher is bilingual, they often switch from one language to the other. The teacher thus must guide students to communicate in the language of instruction.

2. Instruction Divided by Time Percentage

In the early or late exit programs, a specific percentage of the instructional time is assigned to each of the two languages. Two models are commonly used:

A. **Balanced Program, or the 50/50 Model.** Students receive equal instructional time in L1 and L2. This percentage is maintained throughout the program. This is the second-most popular U.S. model, implemented by 33% of the programs.

B. **Minority/Majority Language Program, or the 90/10 or 80/20 Model.** The largest percentage of instruction is done in the minority language, which means that language-majority (English-speaking) students are immersed in their second language. This program is used in Canada, with English speakers learning French as a second language. The amount of instruction in the majority language increases to a point at which balanced instruction is achieved (50/50) by third or fourth grade. This is the most popular U.S. model, implemented by 42% of the programs.

3. Instruction Organized by Days

The two most common formats for the dual language program are the half-day and the one-day alternating organizations.

A. **Half-Day Alternating Bilingual Program.** In this format, morning lessons are delivered in one language, and the second language is used in the afternoon. To cover all content areas in both languages, the program alternates the languages used in the two parts of the day.

B. **One-Day Alternating Bilingual Program.** Under this format, one full day is delivered in L1, and the following day the content is delivered in L2.

Alternating approaches to bilingual content area avoid the repetition of lessons in each language within the class period. However, for students with very limited proficiency in one of the languages, the alternating model may not be appropriate because the student may miss too much content when teaching is in the second language.

Canadian Total Immersion Programs: The Canadian French-English total immersion program began in Montreal, Quebec, in the early 1960s for native English-speaking students who wanted to learn the minority language, French. The program begins with 100% immersion in the second language during the first two to three years. English language support is provided in the community and in the home. Literacy instruction is developed first in French and then in English. The percentage of instruction in French then decreases by 10% each year, finishing junior high with a balanced French/English instruction (50/50).

Historical Development of the ESL Field

ESL is a system of instruction designed to teach language to children whose native language is not English. The term *ESL* evolved from foreign language instruction as part of the Americanization efforts of the late 19th and early 20th centuries (Crawford, 2004). In 1941, English as a foreign language became a field of study under the leadership of researchers at the University of Michigan (Ovando & Combs, 2014). As part of their research, University of Michigan educators prepared instructors to teach English abroad. In the 1960s, the field shifted its emphasis and began preparing instructors to teach English to immigrants. This new emphasis created the field of English as a Second Language (ESL). Following the creation of the field, the association called TESOL — Teachers of English to Speakers of Other Languages — was founded in 1966. Currently, the terms *ESL* or *ESOL* (English for speakers of other languages) are used to describe instruction used in public schools to meet the needs of English learners.

English as a second language programs are part of the curriculum in most school districts in the United States. The field is perceived as compensatory and transitional. The program has experienced multiple changes in the last two decades, becoming a permanent feature in most school districts in the nation. Currently, ESL programs are used in multiple formats and types of programs.

Types of ESL Programs

1. ESL as a Component of Bilingual Education

ESL is a component of Bilingual Education in which students get native language instruction in the content areas and English language development through ESL. In early-exit TBE models, ESL is the bridge that moves students from native language instruction to instruction in English. In such late-exit programs as one-way developmental and two-way dual language programs, ESL develops the English proficiency needed to be taught in a dual language format.

  A. **Self-contained Classroom Early Childhood.** Students in a self-contained (one instructor teaching all subjects) bilingual education program get content instruction in L1 and at least 45 minutes of ESL instruction to promote English language development.

B. **Self-contained Classroom in Upper Elementary.** In upper elementary (4–6), districts might use a variation of the typical self-contained model. One instructor teaches the content area in L1, and a second teacher pulls out the child to provide ESL instruction. A description of this and other models using English-only instruction follows.

2. ESL as a Stand-alone Program

ESL is also used as a "program" when bilingual education is not feasible because of the large number of foreign languages spoken in the district. In this case, the program is designed to support instruction while students develop the English proficiency to function in the all-English classroom. In Texas when a district is unable to find bilingual teachers, it asks for special permission from the state to use ESL instead of bilingual education. This permission must be renewed every year. To get the renewal, districts must document efforts used to find bilingual teachers.

A. **ESL Pullout.** One approach used in public schools to teach English to ELs is the ESL pullout system. Students spend most of the day in mainstream classes and are "pulled out" of their classes for one or two periods per day to get English instruction. This approach is perhaps the most expensive and least effective ESL method currently used (Crawford, 2004; Thomas & Collier, 2002). Schools with a large number of ESL students may have a full-time ESL teacher, but some districts use an ESL teacher who travels to several schools to work with small groups of students scattered throughout the district. This program has been criticized for its cost and its shortcomings (Crawford, 2004; Ovando & Combs, 2014).

B. **Structured English Immersion.** Structured English Immersion (SEI) was conceptualized in the 1980s under the U.S. Department of Education, the leadership of conservative members of Congress, and the English-only movement (Crawford, 2004). The origin of SEI can be traced to the Baker and de Kanter Report (1981), a Department of Education-commissioned study to investigate the effectiveness of TBE programs in the United States. These researchers concluded that the literature did not provide consistent evidence of the effectiveness of TBE programs.

Despite the multiple flaws of the study (Crawford, 2004; Ovando & Combs, 2014), it convinced legislators to search for a different way to address the language needs of ELs. After analyzing the success of the French bilingual immersion programs in Canada, the researchers proposed a similar program to replace TBE. The model is today known as the Structured English Immersion program. Contrary to the additive nature of the Canadian bilingual immersion programs, the SEI is a subtractive program designed to teach English only. In the self-contained ESL classroom, the teacher delivers instruction in English to ELs. To ensure comprehension, teachers use techniques to simplify and contextualize instruction. Through "sheltered instruction," children learn content and language concurrently.

C. **Sheltered English or ESL Content.** Developed in the 1980s, this model shifts from programs that emphasize only English language development to more content-based ESL instruction (Crawford, 2004). The sheltered English approach tries to make academic instruction in English comprehensible to ELs while promoting English language development. Teachers use hands-on activities, concrete objects, simplified speech, and the use of concrete objects to teach concept development in the content areas. Before this model, ESL teachers taught language development at the expense of content-area instruction. Students thus fell behind academically.

Sheltered English or ESL content is used most often at the secondary level and works best for students with intermediate-to-advanced proficiency in English. It focuses on the delivery of content in contextualized situations with the addition of language objectives. Two of the better-known commercial programs that emphasize content and language development are the Cognitive Academic Language Learning Approach (CALLA) model developed by Chamot and O'Malley (1994) and the Sheltered Instruction Observation Protocol (SIOP) Model, developed by Chavarria, Vogt, and Short (2000). The CALLA model was developed for secondary students, and the SIOP addressed both the elementary and secondary levels. These programs are often used in the traditional classroom and in newcomer centers to promote language development.

Newcomer Centers: Newcomer centers address the needs of recent immigrants or students who are new to the English language. In a newcomer center, ESL is used to support ELs in their linguistic and cultural adjustment to life and schooling in the United States. The program provides linguistic and psychological support to unschooled and other nontraditional English learners. This program was designed mainly for students in middle and high school, but today it is also used at the elementary level.

The instructional language approach and methods used in newcomer centers vary by district and state. Some centers provide intensive English language development, and others adopt a sheltered English approach in which students can keep up academically while developing proficiency in English. Traditionally, students remain in the center a year or less before they are sent to mainstream classrooms.

Research on Program Effectiveness

Ramírez Study: The 1992 Ramírez study was a federally sponsored study comparing the effectiveness of three program models: early-exit (TBE), late-exit (developmental TBE), and structured English immersion. This longitudinal study began in 1984 and included more than 2,000 children attending schools in California, Florida, New Jersey, New York, and Texas. A preliminary report issued in 1986 showed that students in the late-exit bilingual education programs were outperforming students in the immersion programs. Keith Baker, program director for the study and a sheltered English instruction (SEI) proponent, quickly dismissed the report and insisted that conclusions should not be drawn from incomplete data. After the initial report, data from the study were kept secret until the final report was released in 1992.

According to Ramírez (1992), the complexity of the study design did not permit a direct analysis of the three models. Instead, the direct comparison was done only between the SEI and early-exit models. This comparison revealed no significant differences in student performance in mathematics, reading, and English language acquisition as measured by the Comprehensive Test of Basic Skills (CTBS).

Ramírez (1992) found the growth curves for ELs in late-exit instructional programs continued to grow in English language arts and reading and mathematics, catching up to the mainstream group. Early-exit and mainstream programs had gains in the lower grades, but growth declined as they progressed to higher grades.

Thomas and Collier Study: Thomas and Collier (2002) conducted a longitudinal study (1996–2001) on school effectiveness for language-minority students including more than 700,000 students from five large urban and rural school districts from the Northeast, Northwest, South-Central, and Southeast regions of the United States. The research divided the programs into three large categories, English or ESL-based program, early exit, and late exit. An analysis of program characteristics follows.

The Department of Education developed the Normal Curve Equivalent (NCE) to replace the traditional Percentile Rank to measure educational achievement. This measure is more appropriate because it preserves the valuable equal-interval properties, and these measures can be averaged. Today, NCEs are the standard instrument in educational research to measure academic achievement in public schools.

Language Policy in the World

Some policymakers in the United States see language diversity as a threat to national security. However, several countries in the world have multiple linguistic groups co-existing within their borders and still keep the integrity of the nation. Bilingual or multilingual countries outnumber the monolingual nations (Tucker, 1999). However, fewer than 25% of countries officially recognize more than one language (Tucker, 1999). For example, in the United Kingdom multiple languages are spoken, but the majority of the citizens (95%) are monolingual (BBC Online, n.d.). However, India uses Hindi and English as lingua francas (common languages) to communicate with speakers of over 200 additional languages, 33 of which have more than 1 million speakers (Grosjean, 1982). In India, the average citizen speaks more than one language. In China, Mandarin is the unifying language of the government, but Cantonese and many other languages are used within the country. In Hong Kong, English and Chinese Mandarin are the official languages, but in practice the population speaks mostly Cantonese, and English is the language for business.

At the end of apartheid in South Africa in 1994, the country recognized its linguistic diversity. Today, the government recognizes 11 official tongues, including nine indigenous languages, English and Afrikaans (Conner, 2004). In Paraguay, Spanish is the official language, but Guarani is the national language of the indigenous population. Ninety percent of the people in Paraguay speak Guarani as their first language, and half of the population is bilingual.

 Apartheid describes the strict racial segregation and the oppressing practices imposed on non-white citizens in South Africa. Nelson Mandela was instrumental in the elimination of this regime.

In Sweden, non-native children get instruction in L1 while developing proficiency in Swedish. By the fifth grade, instruction in all subject areas is done in two languages. Canada is probably one of the best examples of an official bilingual nation. Its experiments with French-English immersion programs have been used as a model in the United States. Canada holds both French and English in high regard, and large numbers of Canadians are bilingual. Other countries with official dual or multilingual language policy follow (Anderson & Boyer, 1970; Grosjean, 1982):

1. **Belgium**—Flemish, French, and German

2. **Belarus**—Belarusian and Russian

3. **Finland**—Finnish and Swedish

4. **Ireland**—English and Gaelic

5. **Israel**—English and Hebrew

6. **Singapore**—Chinese, Malay, Tamil, and English

7. **Switzerland**—German, French, Romansh, and Italian

8. **India**—Hindi and English

The American Council on the Teaching of Foreign Languages estimates that in the United States about 3% of high school students can be considered bilingual, and only 5% become bilingual after college (Ovando & Combs, 2014). Bilingualism and multilingualism seem to be the rule in the world, but they are still considered the exception in the United States.

Key Takeaways for Competency 001

1. The use of the students' cultural background and language for instruction can enhance achievement because students feel that their language and culture are valued in school.

2. Teachers must teach the required curriculum with the same rigor required for native English speakers, but they can modify the delivery, so that instruction becomes accessible to English learners.

3. Teachers are required to integrate the English Language Proficiency Standard with content-area instruction, and use linguistic accommodation to make content cognitive accessible to ELs.

4. Quick and forced assimilation of ELs to the U.S. culture and language should not be among the priorities in school.

5. Education standards should not be changed to address the needs of the learners. Instead, instruction should be modified and enhanced to guide students to master the required education standards.

6. The *Lau v. Nichols* (1974) litigation was the landmark case used for further litigation and legislation used to provide equal access and meaningful education to ELs.

7. Learning a second language requires a degree of acculturation to the U.S. culture, because language is part of the culture and most of the ideas presented through language require an understanding of the culture.

8. Idiomatic expressions are challenging for ELs because the meaning is implied, and they allude to cultural referents not readily known to ELs.

9. The *Plyer v. Doe* (1980) court case granted free public education to undocumented students in the United States.

10. The concept of equity versus equality was presented in the *Lau* ruling. Providing the same books, instruction, and facilities is not enough (Equality). Instead, the *Lau* ruling calls for equity—provide instruction based on the needs of the learners.

11. *Castañeda v. Pichard* dealt with the issue of program quality. The result was that a number of guidelines were issued to guide the development of quality bilingual programs.

12. Additive programs in bilingual education develop a strong foundation in L1, which can enhance the acquisition of the second language (L2). The stronger the linguistic and academic foundation is acquired in L1, the easier the transition to the language and culture of the second language.

13. Teachers can celebrate diversity by posting and discussing materials from cultural and linguistic groups. However, they should go beyond the superficial or overt components of culture such as foods and celebrations.

14. Teachers should celebrate language diversity and guide students to value the benefits of bilingualism and diversity.

15. In transitional bilingual education programs, the students' first language is used so that students do not fall behind academically, while ESL is used for English language development.

16. The total language immersion programs in Canada were conceptualized for middle-class native English speakers interested in learning French as a second language. However, the structured English immersion programs in the United States are designed mostly for poor immigrants learning English as a second language.

17. Strategies to promote biliteracy and biculturalism should incorporate materials from the students' native culture as well as readings in L1. Materials should include English language versions of stories, folktales, and other narratives from the students' home cultures to validate and affirm their cultures.

18. Maintenance bilingual education programs, like one-way and two-way dual language programs, provide the most extensive instruction in L1.

19. Since the 1960s, bilingual education has gradually shifted from the early-exit model to the late-exit model. The number of dual language and late-exit programs in general continue increasing in the Texas and in the nation.

20. Students who spend four to five years in quality programs will develop cognitive-academic skills in L1 and have a better chance of succeeding academically in L2.

21. If a student has mastered the on-grade Spanish (L1) state basic skills, but he/she is not ready to study content areas in English, the LPAC should allow the student to stay in the bilingual program.

22. A bilingual education program should emphasize students' self-esteem and present the learning of English as an additive rather than a replacement for the student's native language.

23. To improve their opportunity of achieving academic parity with native English speakers, ELs should get content area and language arts instruction in L1 and L2 for at least six years (Ovando & Combs, 2014).

24. The first federal bilingual education act was signed in 1968 as part of the ESEA of 1965. Since then, the legislation has undergone multiple changes. Some key changes are:

    A. The 1974 reauthorization provided funding to establish the Lau compliance centers and to create the National Clearinghouse for Bilingual Education.

    B. The 1978 federal legislation prohibited the use of federal funding for maintenance bilingual programs and allocated funding to develop transitional bilingual programs.

    C. The 1984 federal legislation moved away from the compensatory nature of bilingual education when it allowed the use of federal funding for maintenance bilingual education. It also allowed the use of ESL programs as an alternative to bilingual education.

D. The 1994 version allowed the participation of language-majority students (Native English speakers) in bilingual education. With this provision, the federal legislation opened the doors for the creation of two-way dual language programs.

References

Anderson, T. & Boyer, M. (1970). Bilingual schooling in the United States. Southwest Educational Development Laboratory, Austin, Texas. Available at: *http://bit.ly/2dhE9mm*

ASCD (n.d.) Elementary and Secondary Education Act: Comparison of the No Child Left Behind Act to the Every Student Succeeds Act. Retrieved from *http://bit.ly/1TjBSRk*

BBC News (n.d.) Online available at *http://bbc.in/1CNr6Os*

CCSSO—Council of Chief State School Officers (February 2016). Major provisions of Every Students Succeeds Act (ESSA) related to the education of English learners. Retrieved from *http://bit. ly/2bVQvhg*

Collier & Thomas (2012). Dual language for a transformed world. Dual Language Education of New Mexico: Albuquerque, NM.

Conner, T. (2004). Global perspective on human language: The South African Context. Leland Stanford Junior University. Retrieved from *http://stanford.io/2cLuDXt*

Crawford, J. (2004). Educating English learners: Language diversity in the classroom. 5th ed. Los Angeles: Bilingual Education Services, Inc.

Crawford, J. (1995). Endangered Native American languages: What is to be done, and why. The Bilingual Research Journal, winter, 19 (1). Pp. 17–38. Retrieved from *http://bit.ly/2cVSjdM*

DHEW Memorandum (1970). Department of Health, Education, and Welfare, Division of Civil Rights. Available from *http://bit.ly/2ctJPcf*

ELPS—English Language Proficiency Standards (2016). Chapter 74. Curriculum Requirements, Subchapter A: Required Curriculum. Available from *http://bit.ly/2cxlQqe*

Every Student Succeeds Act (ESSA), S.1177, 114th Cong. (2015). Retrieved from *http://bit.ly/1M5L3Rd*

Grosjean, F. (1982). Life with two languages: An introduction to bilingualism. Cambridge, MA: Harvard University Press.

Hanna, J. (2005). The Elementary and Secondary Education Act. The Magazine of the Harvard Law and Higher Education (2015). The Equal Education Opportunity Act. Retrieved from *http://bit. ly/2cBSdqr*

Hehling, J. (1996). University of Indiana. Retrieved from *http://bit.ly/1s52gH4*

Hernández v. Texas (1954). Oyez. IIT Chicago-Kent College of Law at Illinois Tech. Retrieved from *http://bit.ly/2d7FEDn*

Keyes v. School District No. 1, Denver, Colorado (1973). Oyez IIT Chicago-Kent College of Law at Illinois Tech. Retrieved from *http://bit.ly/2d7McBO*

Krauss, M. (1992). The world's languages in crisis. Language, 68(1), pp. 4–9. Available from *http://bit.ly/2dCfBX9*

Lau v. Nichols (1974) Oyez. Chicago-Kent College of Law at Illinois Tech, n.d. September 28, 2016. Retrieved from *http://bit.ly/2d6TuIs*

Law and Higher Education (2015). The Equal Education Opportunity Act. Retrieved from *http://bit.ly/2cBSdqr*

Lee, T. H. (6/30/14). Seven most popular Native American languages in the world. Indian Country Today Media Network.com. Retrieved from *http://bit.ly/1mSF1Ne*

Los Angeles Times (6/27/16). The California schools named after the parents who led desegregation are now almost 100% Latino. Does it matter? Retrieved from *http://lat.ms/291xxGT*

No Child Left Behind Act of 2001, Public Law 107–110. (2002). Retrieved from *http://bit.ly/1PWe35z*

Orr, A. J. (2015). The Bilingual Education Act of 1968. Immigration to the United States website. Available from *http://bit.ly/2cISgye*

Ovando & Combs (2014). Bilingual and ESL classrooms: Teaching in multicultural contexts (5th Ed.) New York: McGraw-Hill Education.

Plyler v. Doe. (1982). Oyez. Chicago-Kent College of Law at Illinois Tech. Retrieved from *http://bit.ly/2dkfUUF*

Rehling, J. (1996) Native Americans language. University of Indiana. Retrieved from http://bit.ly/1s52gH4

Rodríguez, R. (2016). *Handbook of Texas online.* "Bilingual Education," accessed September 29, 2016 *http://bit.ly/2dv8Fej*

Rodríguez, R. (2012). The history of bilingual education in Texas — Video. Texas Association for Bilingual Education (TABE). Available from *http://bit.ly/2doGfxb*

Ryan, C. (2013, August). Languages use in the United States: 2011. U.S. Census Bureau. Retrieved from *http://bit.ly/1U6Mxl5*

Serna v. Portales Municipal Schools (1974), Open Juris, Retrieved from *http://bit.ly/2cCjJVS*

Stewner-Manzanares, G. (1988, fall). The Bilingual Education Act: Twenty years later. National Clearinghouse for Bilingual Education (NCBE), Focus #6. Retrieve from *http://bit.ly/2c49jMB*

TEA (2015). Texas Examinations of Educators Standards (TExES) Program: Preparation Manual for the Bilingual Education Supplemental (TExES 164). Available at http://bit.ly/1t0MVlU

TEA (2014). Texas Examinations of Educators Standards (TExES) Program: Preparation Manual for the Core Subjects EC–6 (TExES 291). Available at *http://bit.ly/1t0MVlU*

TESOL (n.d.). Teachers of English to Speakers of Other Languages. Retrieved from *http://bit.ly/2cVxCgh*

Texas State Facts (2015). American Indian Cultures. Retrieved from *http://bit.ly/2dxlvsd*

Tucker, R. 1999. A global perspective on bilingualism and bilingual education. CAL Digests.

Thomas, W. P., & Collier, V. P. (2002). A national study of school effectiveness for language-minority students' long-term academic achievement. Retrieved from *http://bit.ly/2cDw3Rq*

U.S. Census (n.d.) First Census of the United States 1790. Available from *http://bit.ly/1IdFkIo*

USDE (n.d.) Every Student Succeeds Act Highlight. Retrieved from *http://bit.ly/2cFpQ8n*

USDE (2016). Non-regulatory guidance: English learners and Title III of the Elementary and Secondary Education Act (ESEA), as amended by the Every Student Succeeds Act (ESSA). Retrieved from *http://bit.ly/2cXmz59*

UNESCO (1953). The use of vernacular languages in education. United Nations Monographs on Fundamental Education VII. Paris. Retrieved from *http://bit.ly/2dqjIjo*

U.S. English Foundation, Inc. (n.d.). Retrieved from *http://www.us-english.org/view/13*

USHistory.org (2016). Native American society on the eve of British colonization. Retrieved from *http://bit.ly/1gCeuNa*

Yzquierdo-McLean, Z. (1995). History of bilingual assessment and its impact on best practices used today. New York State Association for Bilingual Education Journal, 10, pp. 6–12. Available from *http://bit.ly/29Z58zk*

First- and Second-Language Acquisition

This chapter addresses each of the subcomponents of Competency 002 of the Bilingual Supplemental Exam (TExES 164). It also covers selected topics of Competencies 001, 002, and 009 of the TExES ESL Supplemental Exam (TExES 154). In addition, it covers the process of first- and second-language acquisition, factors that affect the acquisition of English, and major components of language.

BILINGUAL COMPETENCY 002

The beginning Bilingual Education teacher understands processes of first- and second-language acquisition and development and applies this knowledge to promote students' language proficiency in their first language (L1) and second language (L2).

Language: A Global Perspective

In the United States, when people think about language, they probably think about traditional Indo-European languages spoken in Europe and the Americas—North, Central, and South. However, many languages are spoken in remote places, where we have limited knowledge and access to their speakers. An estimated 7,097 known languages exist in the world (Lewis, Simmons, and Fenning, 2016). The number changes annually because a third of these languages are endangered (Lewis, Simmons, and Fenning, 2016). The same source indicated that 23 of these languages are spoken by half of the world's population, and two-thirds of the world languages are spoken in African and Asian countries. The country with the largest number of languages is Papua New Guinea with 840 unique tongues. This linguistic diversity is all the more remarkable because the country's population is under 8 million. Other countries with hundreds of languages spoken within their boundaries are Indonesia with 709, Nigeria with 527, and India with 453 (Lewis, Simmons, and Fenning, 2016). To function in these multilingual societies, the average person must communicate in multiple languages. On the other hand, Europe has only 4% of the world languages, and the Americas have 15%. Aside from Chinese Mandarin, the best known languages in the world are from the Indo-European family and include Hindi, English, and Spanish (Anderson, 2012).

English and Spanish: Both English and Spanish are of Indo-European origin. English is Germanic, while Spanish is a Romance language. According to the Nation Online Project, English, with 339 million speakers, is the third most widely used language in the world, surpassed only by Chinese with 1,052 million and Spanish with 427 million (1998–2016). English is also among the languages spoken in the largest number of countries: 106. Conversely, the top two languages in the world—Chinese and Spanish—are spoken in fewer than 36 countries of the world. Spanish is the second largest language in the world with 417 million speakers. Table 4.1 presents an analysis of how English and Spanish compare with the largest languages in the world (Lewis, Simon, and Fennig, 2016). The United States is not only the country with the largest number of native English speakers but also the country with the second largest number of Spanish speakers. The United States has 41 million native Spanish-speakers and 11.6 million Spanish–English bilingual speakers. Counting these two groups, the Spanish population in the United States is second only to Mexico (CNN, July 1, 2015).

Table 4.1 Most Widely Used Languages in the World

Language	Countries Spoken	Number of Speakers in Millions
Chinese	35	1,302* (note)
Spanish	31	427
English	106	339
Arabic	58	267
Hindi	4	260

Chinese is comprised of 13 language varieties, some of which are not mutually intelligible. Chinese Mandarin has the largest number of speakers with 897 million (Lewis, Simon, and Fennig, 2016). *Chinalanguage.com* (2011) suggests these linguistic variations are identified as dialects from the social and political view, not from the linguistic standpoint.

Standard Language: The identification of the standard version of a language is a subjective and non-linguistic decision. Standard language is the variety spoken and accepted by the government and those in power. For example, from the linguistic view American English is a variety of British English. That is, both are mutually intelligible and have a common grammar. Most differences between these two varieties are from the lexical and pronunciation stands. Based on these differences, American English can be considered a dialectical variation from British English. However, from the political and economic view, American English is the standard language in the United States. American Standard English has at least 24 distinctive regional and social dialects.

Dialects: Dialect describes the development of linguistic variations that differ from the standard language endorsed by the central government. Dialects might differ from the standard variety in grammar, pronunciation, and vocabulary. The key distinction of a dialect is that it must be mutually intelligible with the standard variety. If speakers of the standard variety cannot understand speakers of this new version of the language, it is not a dialect but instead a new language or the beginning of one. For example, Romance languages evolved from Latin. At the beginning, they probably sounded like the mother tongue, but throughout the years these varieties underwent such structural and linguistic changes that they became new languages. They still share common elements, but they are not mutually intelligible.

These linguistic variations can be described as regional or social dialects. For example, most people are familiar with the New England or the Southern dialects. However, these two generic dialects have multiple regional dialects. A social or cultural dialect is a variety of the language linked to a social or occupational group. For example, urban dwellers might speak the African American Vernacular English (AAVE), while Latinos living in the same area might share features of AAVE but add the use of Anglicism typical of bilingual speakers. These social dialects might differ at the grammatical, phonological or lexical level, but they still can communicate with speakers of Standard English.

African American Vernacular English (AAVE): AAVE combines features of Standard American English and African languages. It might have started as a pidgin (a provisional language) and for a time functioned as a creole (new language). However, through contacts with speakers of Standard American English and through a process called decreolization, AAVE eventually became a dialect of Standard American English. Most features of AAVE, also known as Ebonics and Black English, can be found among the speech of Southern white speakers. However, these features are more frequent among speakers from African American communities. Some key features of AAVE are listed below (Fromkin, Rodman, and Hyams, 2014; Peñalosa, 1980):

Double Negatives—two forms of negation are used

EXAMPLE

I *don't* want to know *nothing* about you.

Copula Deletion—this omission occurs in Standard American English phrases that use contractions (phonological issue). Contractions can be confusing for English learners. AAVE speakers solve this problem by deleting the contracted verb form, resulting in a nonstandard form.

EXAMPLE

He__ crazy (sic), for *He's crazy*. They __ happy (sic), for *they're happy*.

Use of the Habitual Tense—"The habitual indicates continuation of an action or a state over time, rather than a temporary condition or action which takes place only once" (Peñalosa, 1980, 152). The tense exists in some African languages, but it does not exist in Standard American English. It is not a simplification of the verb *to be* but the creation of a new tense.

EXAMPLE

"He be home early from school." This example implies that the child gets home early every day—the habitual.

Deletion of Postvocalic *Rs*—as in some British dialects, and the Bostonian dialect, the *r* following a vowel is omitted.

EXAMPLES

park and *for* become [pak] and [fo].

Simplification of Final Consonant Clusters

EXAMPLES

Firs for *first*; car for *card*.

From the linguistic standpoint all dialects have equal value. From the social view, the standard language is always preferred for school as well as the business sector. Teachers should accept and recognize the linguistic variety that children bring to school but teach and promote the use of the standard language. Teachers should model the standard language in the formal school environment so that children establish the difference between the two language varieties and become bi-dialectal.

Components of Language

Language is a system that allows communication among speakers of a linguistic community. It is composed of several sub-systems: phonology, morphology, syntax, lexicon, discourse, and pragmatics. Effective ESL teachers must understand how these components are acquired in L1 and L2 and how they affect language and cognitive development.

Phonology: Phonology studies the sound system of languages. The basic unit of sound is the phoneme. English has 44 phonemes (sounds) represented by 26 graphemes (letters). An English phoneme can be represented by more than one grapheme, and the grapheme-phoneme correspondence is often inconsistent. For example, the word *through* has seven graphemes representing only three phonemes. This inconsistency can create problems for English language learners (ELs), especially Spanish-speaking ELs, since Spanish has a relatively consistent grapheme-phoneme correspondence. Spanish has 27 graphemes to represent 27 sounds, but this does not mean a perfect one-to-one correspondence. Spanish has one silent letter, *h*, and letters that represent more than one sound. Some letters of the Spanish alphabet represent challenges, even for Spanish native speakers. Compared with English, Spanish is much more consistent. This consistency can lead to negative transfer when Spanish-speaking ELs try to pronounce each letter in English words like *island,* where the *s* is silent, or *thought*, a word with consonant digraphs. For an overview of the difference between Spanish and English, see Morris & Rosado, 2013.

Consonant Digraphs: Consonant digraphs and blends can be difficult for ELs from all language groups. The first challenge is to identify when it is a digraph and when it is a blend. English has multiple consonant digraphs whereby two letters represent one sound. These digraphs include words with any of these consonant clusters: *gh, ng, ph, sh, wh, wr, ch, th, ll* . . . Table 4.2 presents examples of consonant digraphs.

Consonant Clusters and Blends: *Consonant cluster* is a generic term to describe a group of consonants together in a word. For example, the word *spring* has an initial and final consonant cluster [spring]. In this word the sounds of the initial consonant cluster are identified as a consonant blend. The letters in the cluster are not pronounced as individual sounds. Instead, the sounds of the cluster are blended in such a way that individual sounds might not be fully recognized. However, the final cluster, *ng*, is a consonant digraph because both letters represent one sound—[sprɪŋ]. In the transcription of the word *spring*, the *ng* was transcribed with one sound /ɲ/, which complies with the definition of a digraph, two letters representing one sound.

Vowel Digraphs and Diphthongs: English also has multiple vowel combinations to create vowel digraphs or diphthongs. These combinations can create both digraphs and diphthongs: *ai, au, aw, ay, ea, ee, ei, eu, ew, ey, ie, oi, oo, ou, ow, oy*. For ELs it is a challenge to determine when the combined vowels create a digraph (two vowels representing one sound) or a diphthong (two vowels in a syllable creating a gliding sound). Most linguists recognize only three diphthongs in English—cow (au), boy (oi) and price (ai). However, in literacy textbooks, they consider diphthong most long sounds like in the words *bay* /ei/ and *old* /ou/. In the linguistic literature, these examples are identified as diphthongized sounds.

A vowel digraph is created when a word contains two adjacent vowels representing only one sound. For example, notice how the two vowels in the following words represent only one sound: *took* [tʊk], *pool* [pul], *blue* [blu]. However, if the sound of the first vowel glides to the sound of the second vowel, the two vowels create a diphthong. For example, words like m**ou**th, n**ow**, **cow**—contain the diphthong /aw/ or /au/.

Contrary to English, Spanish also has only three consonant digraphs—*ch, rr, ll*—and multiple diphthongs, and no vowel digraphs. This makes Spanish much more consistent than English.

The lack of grapheme–phoneme correspondence in the English language creates problems for all ELs. Table 4.2 presents examples of vowel digraphs and diphthongs.

Table 4.2. Consonant and Vowel Digraphs

Consonant Digraphs	Vowel Digraphs	With Diphthongs
Phone	**Soo**n	**Mou**se /aw/ /au/
Shower	**Foo**t	**Choi**ce /oi/ /oy/
Chalk	**Cou**ld	**Buy** /ai/
Write	**Boo**k	**Pou**nd /aw//au/

Morphology

Morphology studies the structure of words or word formation. Words are made of units of meaning called **morphemes**. For example, the word *called* is made of two morphemes: the basic or root word *call* and the letters *ed*, representing the regular past tense. Morphemes are classified into large categories—bound and free, and derivational and inflectional.

Free and Bound Morphemes: Free morphemes are words that convey a clear meaning in isolation or when they are used with other morphemes. In the previous example, with *called*, the first part of the word, *call*, is a free morpheme because it can stand alone and convey the intended meaning. However, the past tense morpheme *ed* of the word, does not convey meaning by itself. It must be attached to another morpheme to convey the intended meaning.

Derivational Morphemes: Derivation morphemes describe morphemes that can (but may not) change the grammatical classification of a word. Most of these morphemes are loans from foreign languages, mostly Greek and Latin, and can be used as affixes—prefixes and suffixes. For example, the word *subconsciously* contains the root word *consci* (conscience) and three derivational morphemes. The first (*sub-*) is the prefix morpheme, the second (*-ous*) is an adjectival suffix morpheme, and the third (*-ly*) is a suffix that creates an adverb. Transforming the word *subconscious* to *subconsciously,* changes the grammatical classification from an adjective to an adverb.

Inflectional Morphemes: Inflectional morphemes do not change the syntactic or grammatical classification of the words. These morphemes are always attached at the end of derivational morphemes. English has eight inflectional morphemes:

1. present participle (*-ing*)—She is runn**ing**.

2. third person singular (*-s*)—She often walk**s** too.

3. possessive (-'s)—Mary**'s** dog also runs.

4. plural (-s, -es)—She brought home two box**es** of food for her pet**s**.

5. regular past tense (-ed)—Mary walk**ed** to the store.

6. past participle (-en)—She has tak**en** her pets to the store.

7. the comparative (-er)—Her pets are bett**er** and bright**er** than some people.

8. the superlative (-est)—Her dog is the **best** and the bright**est** of the neighborhood.

All inflectional morphemes are native of English, and they are always placed at the end of the word. For example, the word *greater* is composed of the adjective *great* and the comparative *er*. Adding the inflectional ending to change the word *great* to *greater* did not affect the syntactic classification of the words. Both are adjectives.

Syntax

Syntax describes the organization of words in a sentence to communicate information. English has specific syntactic rules to account for the grammaticality of the sentence, the structure of phrases, and sentences. The order of words and phrases determines whether the sentence is grammatical. It also determines whether it is a complete sentence or a phrase. In the creation of sentences, speakers use syntax and the different components of grammar to avoid structural ambiguity and to determine the logical relations within sentences (Fromkin, Rodman, and Hyams, 2014). For example, Chomsky (1957) presented two sentences that might be ambiguous for listeners, but not necessarily when seen in writing. Through an analysis of syntax, he clarified or disambiguated the two messages. The first sentence has two words *brief case* is made of an adjective (*brief*) and a noun (*case*). While in the second, it is a noun (*briefcase*). Based on that grammatical clarification, the sentences become easier to understand.

1. The lawyer lost a brief case. [The lawyer lost a court case.]

2. The lawyer lost a briefcase. [The lawyer lost a portfolio or an attaché case.]

Lexicon or Vocabulary

The lexicon is the vocabulary of a language. It is also the most changeable and versatile component of a language. This language component can change meaning based on context of usage. For example, the word *hot* can refer to temperature, fashion, sex appeal, or luck, and its meaning depends on the context of usage. It is difficult to separate the concepts of lexicon and semantics because they must work together to create the intended meaning.

Traditionally, people develop two sets of lexicon—the productive and the receptive vocabulary. The productive lexicon is the set of words that people use to speak and write. The receptive lexicon is the one people use to understand written and oral communication, but that might not be readily available as part of their oral or written repertoire. The receptive lexicon is much larger and more sophisticated than the productive lexicon. The number of words that people understand from books is larger than the number of vocabulary words they use in oral or written communication.

Semantics

Semantics describes how languages create meaning using words and expressions. Semantics uses literal and implied meanings to achieve this goal. That is, semantics relies on the denotative and connotative language.

Denotation refers to the literal meaning of words and ideas. The literal meaning of the American expression, "I am a meat and potatoes man," is simple. I enjoy eating meat and potatoes. However, pragmatics of communication will guide people to go beyond literal meaning and understand the intended meaning of the statement: I am a simple person with basic needs and wants.

Connotation refers to the implied meaning of words and ideas. Idiomatic expressions and figurative language often use implied meaning as a communication tool. Speakers thus must know the implied cultural framework to understand the communication. English uses metaphors, similes, hyperbole, and allusions to communicate information. For example, English has multiple idioms to indicate how easy things are: "easy as pie" or "a piece of cake." However, the intended meaning might elude a person who is unfamiliar with cakes or pies. Hyperbole and allusions also can confuse people. A sentence like "I am so hungry that I can eat a horse" (hyperbole) or a reference like the "Trojan horse" (allusion) can confuse many children, especially children new to the language and culture.

English learners might also have problems getting the intended meaning of idiomatic statements like "passing the buck." They might know the two meanings of the word *buck*—male deer or a dollar—but fail to understand the implication of passing the responsibility to someone else. Idiomatic expressions like "you are as nutty as a fruitcake," "you drive me nuts," or "you drive me bananas" can challenge students who might not connect fruits with the intended meaning of these idiomatic expressions.

Discourse

Discourse refers to the ability of speakers to combine sounds to create words and the use of these words to create sentences and larger units in a cohesive manner to achieve oral or written communication. The cohesive devices used in L1 might be different from the ones required in L2. The speaker's culture affects the spoken and written discourse. For example, English follows a linear written and spoken discourse, while languages like Italian and Spanish follow a more associative or circular development. These differences can create problems for English learners when they try to apply the discourse of their native language while speaking or writing in English.

Pragmatics

The term *pragmatics* describes how the context of the communication affects the interpretation of communication. It describes the hidden rules of communication shared by native speakers of the language, and these rules are often not evident for ELs. Pragmatics is part of the culture shared by the native speakers of the language. Native speakers learn pragmatics as part of their socialization. Children often experience difficulties learning basic rules to communicate with adults. Since they are unfamiliar with the rules to join conversations, they often interrupt adults or say things that are inappropriate for the interaction. It takes several years for native English speakers to understand and apply the social rules of the language. Pragmatics is one of the most difficult components of the language for ELs. Most of these hidden norms are not explicitly taught. They are acquired subconsciously, as part of the interaction with native speakers. Even students in the advanced stage of second language acquisition experience problems developing the communicative competence required to master the pragmatics of the language. Because of the complexity of pragmatics, older learners might be better than younger learners in acquiring the abstract components of language, including pragmatics (Shovel, 1999). The development of communicative competence will determine how well students adapt to the new language and culture. Some of the activities that children need to master to achieve mastery of the language are listed here (American Speech Language-Hearing Association, n.d.):

- Taking turns in communication

- Responding to common greetings in a culturally appropriate way

- Using languages for different purposes, i.e., making requests versus demanding outcomes

- Changing from social to formal language, depending on the context

- Using culturally appropriate nonverbal communication to convey and understand messages

- Following rules used in communication, i.e., listening for information, rephrasing, asking for clarification, initiating, developing and closing communications

The Process of First-Language Acquisition

The acquisition of the first language is natural and universal. Children around the world acquire the language with minimal or no direct instruction. However, children must be immersed in their linguistic environment, with natural exposure to native speakers. As part of that immersion, the language is used for meaningful communication in a highly contextualized environment. Acquisition happens within a socially supportive environment, where sympathetic listeners (caregivers) interact with children to achieve communication. In communication activities, children expect language to make sense, and they engage in testing rules continuously.

First-language acquisition is a natural, meaningful, and purposeful communication process by which children acquire the grammar of the language subconsciously. This idea implies that children eventually will learn to apply the rules of the language without the ability to conceptualize or verbalize them. When they start school, they get exposed to formal language support.

Overview of L1 Process: The acquisition of the first language appears to be the result of a combination of innate abilities and environmental influences. The key provision to acquire a language is that children must need to communicate and must be immersed in natural settings and a language-rich environment. Imitation appears to be a learning strategy for young children, and they use it often through age 2, but this strategy works less as language learning becomes more complex (Stewig & Jett-Simpson, 1995). At the one-word stage, children use imitation as a strategy for language development. During the initial stages of language development, children appear to pay attention to the end of words and sentences. For example, when a parent asks, "Do you want me to pick you up?" the child might raise his or her arms, and say, "Up, up." This linguistic behavior is probably the result of the limited short-term memory typical of children at this stage of development. However, imitation cannot explain such idiosyncratic statements as "I *wented* (sic) home yesterday" or "You are my *bestest* (sic) friend." Adults do not produce these statements, and the child is thus testing language rules. The creation of these sentences shows that language creativity and manipulation are also part of language mastery. The child conceptualizes the function of the irregular past tense (*went*) and the superlative (*est*), but he or she does not use them appropriately. These examples suggest that children are rule makers and often use strategies to help in learning how the language operates.

Language is first acquired in meaningful social settings. The social interaction will determine the kind and quality of language that the child will develop. In mainstream American cultures, parents often allow their children opportunities to become full-fledged participants in conversation with adults. Children who get these opportunities often come to school with stronger language skills than do children who are excluded from adult conversation (Rosado, 2005).

Theories of L1 Acquisition

The three main theories of first-language acquisition are behaviorist, innatist, and interactionist (Peregoy & Boyle, 2017).

Behaviorists' Views

Behaviorists believe children are born with a clean slate, or *tabula rasa*, and language is added by imitating parents and caregivers. Children add information to the *tabula rasa* through stimulus, response, and reinforcement. Children hear a word, link the word to a concept, imitate the pronunciation of the word, and get rewarded for their efforts. This theory explains the initial stages of L1 acquisition but fails to explain the linguistic creativity typical of children beyond the first stage of development. When a parent of a 3-year-old boy says "You stink," and the child replies by saying "I stink," the response shows that the child is not merely repeating or mimicking the speech of the adult. The child is processing and hypothesizing language rules by adding the appropriate personal pronoun.

Innatists' Views

Innatist or nativist theory opposes the behaviorist theory. Innatists believe that children are born with innate capabilities for language learning. They believe children enter the world with what Noam Chomsky calls a language acquisition device (LAD). The LAD is equipped with a grammar template or universal grammar that enables children to construct the grammar of their native language through hypothesis testing (Chomsky, 1957). Chomsky says children develop the rules of their language with minimal support from their parents. The role of adults in this theory is restricted to building the lexicon of the language and modeling or teaching rules to develop socio-linguistic competence or the pragmatics of the language.

Interactionists' Views

Interactionists emphasize the importance of both nature and nurture as vital components to achieve language mastery. They conceptualize the existence of the LAD but believe that the role of parents and caregivers in the innatist theory is too narrow. Interactionists believe that caregivers play a vital role in adjusting language to facilitate language acquisition. Parents and caregivers become sympathetic listeners and provide needed language support through conversational scaffolding. Parents scaffold conversation through repetition, and they model the words that the child produces. As part of scaffolding, parents check for understanding by prompting questions at the end of the child's statements and by assuring the child feels confident in his or her ability to communicate. The interactionist theory is currently the prevailing theory used to explain L1 acquisition.

Theories of L2 Acquisition

Healthy young children acquire a first language in natural settings with minimum conscious effort. Following this universal achievement, researchers in L2 acquisition studied L1 acquisition to identify ways in which this process can be replicated to teach a second language. Their views are presented based on the three dominant theories of L1 acquisition: behaviorist, innatist, and interactionist.

Behaviorists' Views

Behaviorists see second-language learning as habit formation through stimulus, response, and reinforcement. Following these principles, behaviorists developed the Audio Lingual Method. The method uses imitation, repetition, and reinforcement to teach a second language. Behaviorists promote the use of memorization of dialogues and pattern drills as a foundation to teach the grammar. Errors are corrected immediately to avoid the formation of bad linguistic habits, and reinforcement is used to maintain the correct structures. This method influenced the teaching of second and foreign languages during the 1950s and 1960s, but its influence virtually ended in the late 1970s.

Innatists' Views

Following Chomsky's view of language, innatists developed the creative construction theory. Proponents of this theory suggest that L2 learners follow similar strategies and make the same errors as native speakers in achieving language mastery. Following these principles, Krashen (1983) developed one of the most comprehensive theories of L2 acquisition. This theory comprises five hypotheses. This section presents an analysis of these hypotheses as well as their educational implications.

Krashen's Theory of Second-Language Acquisition

1. Acquisition versus Learning

Acquisition and learning represent two different processes. Acquisition takes place through meaningful and natural language interaction with speakers of the language, with no conscious efforts to comply with grammar conventions. It is driven by meaning and is characterized by language discovery in a low-anxiety environment. In opposition, learning describes the formal and highly restrictive activities typically found in teacher-centered classroom instruction. It directly teaches students the rules of grammar, as opposed to using language to communicate.

Educational Implications—Strategies that resemble L1 acquisition can promote L2 acquisition. Teachers must expose children to the language inductively and without emphasizing the grammar. Through fun and interactive activities that lead to self-discovery, children will internalize the grammar.

2. Comprehensible Input

The key provision of this hypothesis is that children must understand the content of the communication in the target language to internalize the language structures used in the communication. However, for real acquisition to take place, the input must be slightly above the current linguistic competence of the learner.

Educational Implications—Teachers need to use meaningful activities in contextualized situations to ensure that ELs understand the content of the communication. ESL methods used in the classroom should try to recreate how children acquire a first language. Two of these methods are the Total Physical Response (TPR) and Natural Method (NM). The TPR and NM use commands and concrete objects as well as highly contextualized situations to make language comprehensible.

3. The Monitor Hypothesis

Learners exposed to formal language instruction develop an internal mechanism enabling them to assess language and make corrections. To use this language editor, children must have explicit knowledge of the rules and be given the time to apply them.

Educational Implications—The monitor hypothesis has limited implications for the development of the speaking ability in L2. However, teachers can guide students to internalize the rules so that the rules become automatic and can easily be applied subconsciously and automatically. Conscious knowledge of the rules can help polish the language and monitor writing.

4. Affective Filter Hypothesis

Students perform better when they feel motivated and relaxed. When they are relaxed, the affective filter is lowered, allowing linguistic input in the LAD. This hypothesis is a key principle of humanistic psychology, developed in the late 1970s.

Educational Implications—Teachers should create a low-anxiety environment in which students feel secure. Students should not be forced to communicate **orally** before they are ready. Studies show that children new to the language and culture can go through culture shock. Students experiencing language and culture shock go through a silent phase of second-language acquisition. The teacher thus should not force them to speak. Instead, the teacher must provide ELs with comprehensible input to develop the vocabulary and language structures needed to begin oral communication. As a third grade bilingual teacher, this author observed this behavior in the classroom. After a few weeks of linguistic and cultural support, students ventured into the language.

5. Natural Order Hypothesis

ESL students acquire English structures in a predictable sequence with small variations depending on the influence of L1. This sequence is guided by the communicative value of the structures and the frequency of required usage. For example, forms of the verb *to be* are used more frequently in communication, and they convey more information than the third-person singular. They are thus acquired earlier.

Educational Implications—Teachers should avoid following a grammatical sequence when teaching English. Instead, they should develop rich linguistic activities to encourage students to use structures. The communicative acts and the needs of the learners will determine the acquisition sequence of the language structures.

Interactionists' Views of L2 Acquisition

Krashen's concept of comprehensible input is an important part of the interactionist view of L2 acquisition. Interactionists emphasize how native speakers deliver comprehensible input and how they negotiate meaning with ELs. The interaction with speakers of the target language and the resulting negotiation of meaning are strategies for the acquisition of the second language. The hypothesis testing and the resulting trial and error typically used in conversation will provide learners with the practice to develop communication skills in a natural and relevant environment.

Educational Implications—Teachers should use nonverbal communication as well as drawing and exaggerated speech patterns (foreign talk) to deliver comprehensible input. They should also develop strategies for ELs to interact with native speakers and negotiate meaning in real-life situations. Table 4.3 compares first- and second-language acquisition.

Table 4.3. Stages in the Acquisition of L1 and L2

First Language	Second Language
Babbling Stage, 0–10 Months	**Preproduction or Silent Stage**
1. Sends and receives messages 2. Uses reflexive crying to communicate 3. Produces vowel- and consonant-like sounds 4. Identifies the voice of the parents and family members 5. Understands intonation patterns to show anger, and declarative statements or questions, etc.	1. Communicates with gestures and actions 2. Lacks receptive vocabulary and shows problems comprehending messages 3. Remains silent while trying to decipher the new language (silent phase) 4. Exhibits signs of frustration and anxiety during the initial stages of L1 acquisition/learning 5. Relies heavily on nonverbal communication, which can lead to miscommunication
Holophrastic Stage 11–18 Months (1-Word Stage)	**Early Speech Production**
1. Understands word concepts 2. Conceptualizes complete ideas through one-word sentences 3. Uses adults as tools	1. Increases comprehension 2. Communicates using *yes* or *no* and one-word statements 3. Expands receptive vocabulary 4. Understands language in contextualized situations
Telegraphic Stage, 18 Months and Up	**Speech Emergence**
1. Conceptualizes whole sentences 2. Uses the minimum number of words to get the point across 3. Uses content words with high semantic values (e.g., nouns, verbs, adjectives, etc.) 4. Conceptualizes and imitates the reading and writing processes	1. Communicates in phrases using words with high semantic context: nouns, verbs, and adjectives 2. Continues gaining receptive vocabulary 3. Communicates more effectively in contextualized situations, face-to-face interactions 4. Understands more than what he or she is able to communicate
School Age	**Intermediate and Advanced Stages**
1. Improves language skills through explicit instruction (deductively) 2. Begins formal instruction 3. Learns the social functions of the language 4. Develops a personal communication style or idiolect 5. Gets exposed to different registers (dialects)	1. Communicates using simple sentences 2. Overgeneralizes language rules because of the complexity of the second language (intra-lingual interference) 3. Relies on the rules of the native language to deal with L2, resulting in inter-lingual errors 4. Becomes more acculturated and feels more comfortable in school 5. Develops the academic language and might be ready for mainstreaming

Elements that Influence Second-Language Acquisition

Strong cognitive and academic development in the first language helps in acquiring a second language. Academic skills, content knowledge, literacy development, and metacognitive strategies transfer to L2. Cummins (1979; 1984) called this interdependence the Common Underlying Proficiency (CUP). Cummins' (1979; 1984) analogy of dual icebergs in juxtaposition represents the concepts of CUP. In Figure 4.1, the tip of the two icebergs represents the easily perceived features unique to L1 and L2, and the underwater section (underlying language) represents the hidden components of language common to both L1 and L2. The superficial components include pronunciation, grammar and communication in general. The common hidden components include semantics, content area knowledge, cumulative knowledge and experiences, and abstractions acquired through both languages. The CUP analogy has been used to support the benefits of late exit bilingual education and dual language programs.

Figure 4.1. Dual Iceberg Analogy (Adapted from Cummins, 1984)

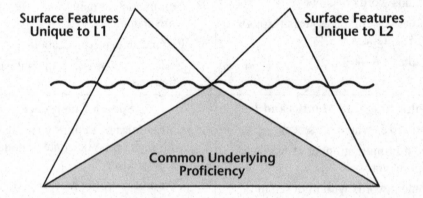

Surface Features Unique to L1 • Surface Features Unique to L2 • Common Underlying Proficiency

Age of Initial Exposure: The age of exposure plays a role in acquiring a second language. Traditionally, people think that young second-language learners have advantages over older children and adults in the acquisition of languages. Early exposure to the second language has advantages primarily at the phonological level. Young second language learners develop a native-like pronunciation, while those exposed to the language after puberty do not. Older second-language learners develop a language ego, which affects the spontaneity and the risk-taking attitude that facilitates oral development and the acquisition of a second language. However, second-language acquisition is complex and cannot be described only in terms of oral communication.

Acquiring a second language is related to cognitive development as well as all the socio-cultural components of language acquisition. Learners with on-grade level academic development and a strong foundation in the first language can transfer those skills to the second language. Thus, students who are strong in the first language can learn the second language better than those with limited development in the first language. Research suggests that when the second language replaces first-language support and instruction in the early grades, these students may never develop full second-language proficiency (Bialystok, 1991; Collier, 1988). Older second-language learners thus might be superior to younger learners in acquiring literacy, vocabulary, and pragmatics as well as the application of prior content knowledge (Shovel, 1999).

In summary, young children exposed to the second language have advantage in developing oral communication, but older learners who have developed a strong foundation in L1 have advantage in acquiring the more complex and abstract components of the language. The Critical-Period Hypothesis and the Threshold Hypothesis provide research support for the development of a second language.

Critical-Period Hypothesis: (Penfield & Roberts, 1959; Lenneberg, 1967.) Researchers have conceptualized a possible critical period for the acquisition of languages. They place this critical period from age 2 years to puberty. During this period, the lateralization of the brain occurs, and language functions are assigned to specific parts of the brain. The lateralization of the brain mainly affects the development of native-like pronunciation. A child exposed to a new language during the critical period thus can develop a near-native accent, while a child contacting a second language after puberty might develop a foreign accent.

Children are also more willing to take risks than adults and thus might develop the language faster. Adults have developed a "language ego," which may affect their willingness to seek contacts with native speakers to practice the language.

The Threshold Hypothesis: Cummins (1991) believes language learners must arrive at a given academic and literacy level in L1 (a threshold) before they can benefit from language transfer from L1 to L2. This age-appropriate threshold is reached after four or five years of effective and on-grade level instruction in L1. This theory explains why ELs taught only in L2 may experience academic difficulties in school, while ELs who receive services through late-exit programs may have cognitive advantages over monolingual students (Baker & Jones, 1998).

Extroversion: Extroversion describes people who have well-developed social skills. Extroverted people seek contacts and negotiate meaning with native speakers of the language. Extroversion can be linked to the interpersonal intelligence described by Gardner (1983, 1999). This type of personality contributes to the acquisition of the language and culture.

Tolerance for Ambiguity: Tolerance for ambiguity is the ability to avoid frustration in instructional situations characterized by lack of organization and guidance. To cope with these situations, most people create their own structures to complete tasks. Students who can cope with ambiguity are good language learners and do better academically.

Positive Self-Esteem: Self-esteem is defined as the value that people assign to themselves. Research shows that positive self-esteem correlates to language learning and academic success. Students with positive self-esteem are risk-takers, which also correlates with language learning.

Impulsiveness versus Reflection: The impulsive student tries to address an issue or answer a question without having a clear view of what the issue or question entails, but the reflective student analyzes the issue or question before trying to address or answer it. Impulsive students might develop a second language faster than reflective students, but students who take time to analyze the language will develop a more polished form.

High Anxiety: Environments characterized by high stress can impair learning and L2 acquisition. However, some levels of anxiety (e.g., facilitating anxiety) can guide students to take responsibility for learning and become effective language learners. The Affective Filter Hypothesis, one of Krashen's L2 acquisition hypotheses, suggests that students with low anxiety perform better than those with to high anxiety.

Type of Motivation—Instrumental or Integrative: Highly motivated students succeed in school. Students with integrative motivation want to learn the language because it lets them socialize and interact with native speakers. Second-language learners with instrumental motivation want to acquire the language to accomplish a specific task. For example, they may want to travel to a country or to pass a language test. People with integrative motivation will seek contacts with native speakers and can acquire the language faster. Both motivations contribute to L2 acquisition.

Previous Schooling or the Absence of Schooling: Students with strong academic backgrounds in L1 can transfer academic and language skills to the new language. However, students who have experienced interrupted schooling or have never attended school represent a unique challenge to educators. Most of these students need help to fill their linguistic and academic gaps before they can be placed in regular classrooms. Traditionally, they are served in newcomer centers or through ESL pull-out programs.

Socioeconomic Background: Traditionally, students from low socioeconomic backgrounds do not get the necessary verbal, literacy, and social stimuli to succeed in school. Most of these students are served through specialized programs funded via Title I of the federal education law, now the Every Student Succeeds Act (ESSA).

Home and Community Environment: Children living in ethnic enclaves, where L1 is used extensively, might not get adequate support in the second language. Because these children have little need for the second language in their environment, they are not highly motivated to learn it. Because they might not have direct exposure to native English speakers, their language and cultural adjustment might be affected. Because of this lack of interaction between ELs and native speakers, misconceptions and stereotypical views can develop between the groups.

Expected Time of Residence in the Country: Students who plan to remain in the country for a long time will try to learn the language. Groups like the Cubans, who did not have the option of returning to the island, tried to learn the language and adjust to U.S. culture. However, transitory or migrant students might not be motivated to learn the language because they know they will return home. Mexicans and Puerto Ricans fall under this category. Many undocumented immigrants work to save money to return to Mexico. Puerto Ricans follow a similar path. Puerto Ricans are American citizens who travel to the mainland in search of better economic conditions, but they have the option to return home. Their ability to return home as well as the availability of ethnic enclaves that meet their linguistic needs affects their motivation to learn the language and adjust to U.S. culture.

Language Status: The prestige of the languages affects the willingness to acquire and maintain the languages. English and Spanish are prestigious world languages. However, because most Spanish-speaking U.S. immigrants are poor and sometimes uneducated, Spanish is perceived as less prestigious than English. Based on this perception, young English learners often replace Spanish with English as their native language, which results in language loss. Other second-language learners might stop the development in their native language but keep the social version as a cultural marking as well as to communicate with monolingual relatives.

Academic Development and Proficiency in L1: Students with a strong background in their first language fare better in transferring skills from their native language to the second language. To do that, however, students must arrive at a plateau in L1. Cummins (1991) addressed the importance of arriving at a linguistic plateau in his Threshold Hypothesis. Students who arrive at the threshold in L1 can better identify similarities and differences between languages. They also are better equipped to identify similar words in L1 and L2—cognates.

Cognates: Cognates are words pronounced and spelled similarly in two languages. Cognates were identified because of the association of modern languages with such classical languages as Arabic, Greek, and Latin. Because of the influence of these three cultural and linguistic groups, English has multiple cognates in mathematics, natural sciences, music, art, theater, and social studies. Teachers must make children aware of the similarities in these vocabularies and guide learners to transfer cognates from L1 to L2 and vice versa. Examples of Spanish cognates are: *abandon* (abandonar), *accent* (acento), *accept* (aceptar), *band* (banda), *bank* (banco), *family* (familia), and *animal* (animal). Spanish speakers use many cognates. For a list of cognates from different languages, see Kress (2008).

False Cognates: A false cognate is a word that resembles a word in a second language but has a different meaning. For example, the English words *embarrass* and *support* resemble the Spanish words *embarazar* (to get pregnant) and *soportar* (to tolerate). This similarity can create communication problems. Teachers can guide students to identify cognates and false cognates and use this knowledge to expand their academic vocabulary.

Processes and Concepts in Second-Language Acquisition

Interlanguage and Fossilization: An interlanguage describes a transitional construction that students develop in mastering a second language. Interlanguage is usually caused by language interference or by the complexity of the structure of the second language. Interlanguages are developmental and should disappear when students achieve complete mastery of L2. When the nonstandard structures of the interlanguage persist, they are said to be fossilized. For example, ELs of Spanish background might use features of Spanish as a foundation for pronouncing English, creating nonstandard constructions like *espeak* and *estring*. Traditionally, fossilized versions of the language are passed to other generations until it becomes the norm for speakers of the language.

Pidgin and Creole: A pidgin is a transition type of language that results from the interaction of speakers of two or more different languages in their attempt to communicate. Traditionally, one language is used as a foundation for the development of pidgin. Eventually, one group masters the second language, and the pidgin disappears. Sometimes the pidgin remains as the means of communication between the two languages, and it is passed as the first language to a new generation. When the pidgin is learned as the first language of a group, technically it ceases to be a pidgin and becomes a creole. Creoles are natural languages with the same value and consistency. For example, in Haiti speakers of African languages and French created a simplified version of the French to communicate among themselves. This pidgin language evolved into a creole and became the native language of the majority of the people of the island. Today, Haitian Creole and French are the official languages of the country.

BICS and CALP: Cummins (1984) used the term Basic Interpersonal Communication Skills (BICS) and the Cognitive Academic Language Proficiency (CALP) to describe two proficiencies that English learners develop in mastering language. The BICS is the social language that children develop at home and on the playground. This language is used in highly contextualized situations and in face-to-face communications. It takes two to three years for a child to acquire this language. ELs need this language to interact socially and to communicate needs and wants. The CALP describes the formal academic language taught in school. ELs need CALP to understand information from textbooks to succeed in the content areas. It takes four to five years to master this version of the language.

Lingua Franca: Lingua franca refers to a common language used for communication in multilingual communities. For example, English and Hindi are often used in India as lingua franca to facilitate communication among speakers of the multiple languages used in that country. Yiddish for many years was the lingua franca of European Jews. With Israel's founding in 1949, Jewish people brought English and Yiddish as their languages. Currently, Hebrew and Arabic are the official languages, and Yiddish has become the language of orthodox Jews. English is still spoken but does not have an official status.

Language Interference: The interference of L1 over the structures of L2 can cause students to make errors. For example, because Spanish does not have the voiced alveolar sound /z/, Latino students might substitute the sound with its equivalent in Spanish, /s/. This substitution can result in nonstandard homonyms when speakers replace the /z/ for /s/, creating confusion with words like *zoo*, which can be pronounced as *Sue*.

Language Transfer: Positive transfer occurs when the structures of L1 help in acquiring the structures of L2. For example, most concepts related to Spanish writing transfer to English. Children do not have to learn to read again. They instead must learn the vocabulary and the syntactic and semantic features of the language to obtain meaning. Reading directionality in English (left-to-right, top-to-bottom) is identical to Spanish. It thus will transfer and make reading easier.

Code Switching: Code switching describes alternating the use of two languages within a sentence (intra-sentential) or across sentences (inter-sentential). The following list of four sentences provides examples. In sentences 1 and 4, the speaker used two languages within a sentence, making them a form of intra-sentential code switching (within the sentence). Sentences 2 and 3 are written with sentence 2 in English and sentence 3 written in Spanish, making them examples of inter-sentential code switching (across languages).

1. *Me encanta ir a las movies* on Christmas Day.

2. On Christmas Eve, my parents take me to church and then to dinner.

3. *Después de la cena es que empieza la verdadera fiesta.*

4. *Me encanta el* Christmas Day.

Code switching is natural in bilingual communities, but teachers must be sure that students can separate L1 and L2 and use each appropriately and consistently.

Translanguaging: Translanguaging was first conceptualized by Cen Williams (cited in Gwyn, Jones, and Baker, 2012). The term describes the ability to move information and skills from one language to the other, using the integrated repertoire of knowledge and skills accumulated through two or more languages (cited in Gwyn, Jones, and Baker, 2012). Translanguaging works when bilingual students deploy their full linguistic knowledge to address their language and cognitive needs (García, Johnson, & Seltzer, 2017). Bilingual people use translanguaging to make themselves understood, to analyze and compare the two languages, and to combine features of the two languages. Translanguaging goes beyond code switching because children are not merely switching linguistic codes. They are using the entire repertoire of cumulative knowledge acquired through the two languages. This cumulative knowledge is similar to Cummins' concept of the Common

Underlying Proficiency (1984) in which students use their cumulative knowledge to communicate in L1 or L2 or a combination of both.

From the instructional point of view, translanguaging should not be used to justify the combination or amalgamation of the two linguistic codes. Instead, teachers should recognize it as a natural process used by bilingual people in the process of mastering the two linguistic codes. From an instructional standpoint, translanguaging can also guide students to understand the socio-emotional implications of growing up and functioning with two languages (García, Johnson, and Seltzer, 2017). The results should be the same: the development of successful bilingual students who function in both languages, jointly or separately, and with identical ease and comfort.

Key Takeaways for Competency 002

1. Language development occurs more readily in situations in which language is nurtured and modeled in contexts to make it meaningful.

2. The key components of language are phonology, morphology, syntax, lexicon, semantics, and pragmatics.

3. The three main theories of L1 and L2 Acquisition are behaviorist, innatist, and interactionist.

4. Languages have levels of interdependence that can be used to learn a second language. Cognitive and academic language proficiency in L1 thus helps the academic acquisition of L2.

5. The Critical Period Hypothesis suggests a critical period exists (age 2 to puberty) for acquiring native-like pronunciation.

6. Personality factors can affect the rate and quality of second language acquisition (e.g., self-esteem, high anxiety, and tolerance for ambiguity).

7. When children struggle with understanding written or oral instruction, teachers can adapt instruction to make content accessible to children. Some strategies to improve comprehension include the use of simplified vocabulary, demonstrations, visuals, and graphic organizers.

8. Translanguaging differs from code switching. It lets bilingual students use their cumulative knowledge of skills acquired through L1 or L2 to meet language and academic challenges.

References

Anderson, S. R. (2012). How many languages are there in the world? Linguistic Society of America, Retrieved from *http://bit.ly/1fu2kri*.

American Speech-Language-Hearing Association (n.d.). Available from *http://bit.ly/1wRYRd8*.

Baker, C., and S. Jones. 1998. Encyclopedia of bilingualism and bilingual education. Philadelphia, PA: Multilingual Matters.

Bialystok, E. (1991). Language processing in bilingual children. Cambridge, UK: Cambridge University Press.

Chinalanguage.com (2011). Retrieved from *http://www.chinalanguage.com*.

Chomsky, N. (1957). Syntactic structures. The Hague, Paris: Mouton.

CNN (July 1, 2015). United States has more Spanish speakers than Spain does. Retrieved from *http://cnn.it/1I6VG5z*.

Collier, V. P. (1988). The effect of age on acquisition of second language for school. Washington, DC: National Clearinghouse for Bilingual Education.

Cummins, J. (1979). Linguistic interdependence and the educational development of bilingual children. Review of Educational Research, 49, 222–251. Available from *http://bit.ly/2fjWEI5*.

Cummins, J. (1984) *Bilingual Education and Special Education: Issues in Assessment and Pedagogy* San Diego: College Hill.

Cummins, J. (2000). Language, power and pedagogy: Bilingual children in the crossfire Tonawanda, NY: Multilingual Matters.

Fromkin, V., Rodman, R, & Hyams, N. (2014). *An introduction to language* (10th Ed.). New York: Cengage.

Gardner, H. (1983). Frames of mind: The theory of multiple intelligences. New York: Basic Books.

Gardner, H. (1999). Intelligence reframed. Multiple intelligences for the 21st century. New York: Basic Books.

Gwyn L, Jones, B., & Baker, C. (2012) Translanguaging: origins and development from school to street and beyond, Educational Research and Evaluation: An International Journal on Theory and Practice, 18 (7), 641-654. Online at *http://bit.ly/2fp9lgT*.

Krashen, S. D. and Terrell, T. D. (1983). The natural approach: Language acquisition in the classroom. Hayward, CA: Alemany Press.

Kress, J. E. (2008). The ESL/EFF teacher's book of lists (2nd ed.). San Francisco, CA: Jossey-Bass.

Lenneberg, E. H. (1967). Biological foundations of language. New York: Wiley.

Lewis, M., Simmons, G. F., Fennig, C. D. (2016). Ethnologue: Languages of the world (19th Ed.). Dallas, Texas: SIL International. Online version: *http://www.ethnologue.com.*

Morris, L & Rosado, L (2013) Desarrollo del Español para Maestros en Programas de Educación Bilingüe. Arlington, Texas: LM Company (Modified and Enhanced).

García, O., Johnson, S. & Seltzer, K. (2017). The translanguaging classroom. Leveraging student bilingualism for learning. Philadelphia: Caslon.

Peñalosa, F. 1980. Chicano sociolinguistics. Rowley, MA: Newbury House Publishers, Inc.

Penfield, W., Roberts, L. (1959). Speech and brain mechanisms. Princeton: Princeton University Press.

Peregoy, S., and O. Boyle. (2017). Reading, writing, and learning in ESL: A resource book for K–12 teachers (7th ed.). New York: Pearson.

Rosado, L. 2005. Cross-cultural communication: A Latino perspective. Academic Exchange Extra. January.

Shovel, T. (1999). "The younger the better" myth and bilingual education. In R. D. González & I. Melis (Eds.), Language and ideologies: Critical perspective on the English-only movement (pp. 114–136). Urbana, IL: National Council of Teachers of English.

Stewig, J. W., and Jett-Simpson, M. 1995. Language arts in the early childhood classroom, Belmont, CA: Wadsworth.

Development and Assessment of Literacy and Biliteracy

This chapter addresses Competency 003 of the Bilingual Education Supplemental Exam (TExES 164). It also covers Competency 005 of the ESL Supplemental Exam (TExES 154). The chapter covers the development and assessment of literacy and biliteracy and the implementation of the state language arts curriculum in grades EC-12.

BILINGUAL COMPETENCY 003

The beginning Bilingual Education teacher has comprehensive knowledge of the development and assessment of literacy in L1 and the development and assessment of biliteracy.

Literacy Development

U.S. literacy programs in the United States have been developed via two main schools of thought. The first conceptualizes reading and literacy as a sequenced set of subskills with specific prerequisites for the introduction of subsequent literacy skills and further development—reading readiness. The second views literacy as simultaneous, natural, integrated, and complementary processes—emergent literacy.

Reading Readiness: Reading readiness was the dominant reading theory in the latter part of the 20th century. In this perspective, formal reading instruction was delayed until children developed their speaking ability and could perform specific reading subskills linked to auditory and visual discrimination. Students develop these skills by age 6, which in theory delayed formal reading instruction until first grade. The implementation of reading readiness components follows the **bottom-up** analysis of language. This approach to reading follows an inductive approach, beginning with letters, words, sentences, paragraphs, and whole texts. This inductive and skill-based process is based on behaviorist psychology. This behaviorist approach is best represented by the phonics reading program. Educators who practice a bottom-up approach emphasize the teaching of discrete skills sequentially and systematically. A product of this approach is the concept of reading readiness, which gained momentum in the 1960s and became a prerequisite for formal reading instruction, as in basal readers.

Basal Readers: The term Basal or Scientifically Based Reading program describes a grade-leveled series of textbooks designed to teach reading. It follows the bottom-up approach for language analysis and development. The program emphasizes the teaching of decoding or word attack skills as a foundation for reading. It contains spelling programs and uses flash cards and sentence strips as foundation for language development. It relies on instant recognition of sight words or high-frequency words that cannot be easily decoded following the traditional word attack strategies.

Most school districts have moved to a top-down approach from traditional basal readers, embracing whole language practices. They consider basal readers too rigid and say they fail to provide adequate modifications to address the needs of such non-traditional students as the gifted and talented, those with cognitive disabilities, and English learners. They also maintain that the content of the stories mainly represents middle-class values and thus is out of the schemata (previous knowledge) of students from low socioeconomic backgrounds as well as the schemata of linguistic minorities.

Emergent Literacy: In the late sixties, researchers noticed that some children could read before first grade with minimal or no formal reading instruction. To accommodate this learner, a new view or perspective of literacy was conceptualized: the emergent literacy perspective. In this perspective, literacy development is viewed as parallel to oral development and emerging when children observe adults engaging in such meaningful literacy activities as reading newspapers, writing notes, and looking at environmental print and other printed materials that children see all around them. Observing these literacy activities, children engage and imitate the literacy process. Because this development occurs mainly at home, family literacy programs became an important part of literacy education. These programs support the whole family to create a home environment conducive to literary development. This support at home combines with formal classroom instruction to guide students to become literate and often biliterate. The emergent literacy perspective is compatible with the top-down approach for reading instruction.

The **top-down** approach to reading relies on the schemata that readers bring to the text in trying to derive meaning from print. This deductive approach proceeds from the whole to the parts—paragraphs, sentences, and words. This approach recognizes that each word is not a prerequisite for comprehending the passage. Teachers do not interfere with students' reading aloud and encourage students to use the context or meaning of the passage to identify unrecognized words. The best representation of the top-down model is the **whole language approach**. From its start in the 1960s, the whole language approach was the program of choice in public schools during the 1980s and 1990s. Phonics instruction came back at the start of the new millennium, and teachers now use a **balanced reading** approach that combines phonics and whole language.

Although literacy can occur informally at home with simultaneous development of skills, students go through specific stages, especially in reading and writing development. This section describes these stages of development.

Stages of Reading

Lapp et al. (2001) describe children's literacy development in three key stages: emerging readers, early readers, and newly fluent readers.

Emerging Readers: Children at the emerging stage of reading show curiosity for print and understand that it contains meaningful messages. They mimic the reading behaviors of adults and subconsciously acquire such print conventions as directionality and print awareness. Children at this stage also develop phonemic awareness, the connection between letters and sounds. Children use illustrations and other graphic representations to get meaning and predict the story. They also can retell a story that has been read to them. They also can recognize the name of a store by its logo, not necessarily because they are decoding the letters in the store's name. The skills developed during this stage become the centerpiece of the metalinguistic awareness that children need for further development in reading and writing.

Early Readers: Early readers connect words with their written representations (e.g., using phonics to decode) and recognize a number of sight words. They also develop awareness of such features of printed text as punctuation, bond print, and text format. Early readers can retell stories with specific details about the plot and characters. They use illustrations, syntax, and punctuation as well as their experiences to make sense of print. They recognize the meanings of words in different contexts and distinguish between narrative and non-narrative texts. Children at this stage enjoy listening to narratives and choosing their favorite stories.

Newly Fluent Readers: Newly fluent readers internalize the cuing or decoding system of the language. They use inferences and deduction as well as their experiences to infer meaning and generalize from text. They can discuss the point of view of the author and identify similarities and differences between two stories. As the cuing systems (decoding skills) of the language become automatic, students at this stage become more fluent and independent readers.

Instructional Implications: Children at the early stages of reading can be immersed in functional reading and writing experiences to show their value in daily life. These activities can be tailored to show and model reading and writing. Teachers can use routine activities to provide a rich print environment. For example, teachers can post classroom rules, read them to the children and rehearse the meaning of each rule. They can also post signs identifying parts of the classroom, the available equipment, and the guidelines for activities in the learning centers. Teachers can enrich dramatic play centers with functional print, including lists, phone books, and props to encourage experimentation with reading and writing during play activities. Finally, teachers must guide children to succeed in their attempts to develop literacy. Teachers thus should accept and celebrate the children's gradual progress toward literacy.

Role of Environmental Print in Early Reading: Environmental print describes forms of written communication available to children in their community. The most common print materials include road and store signs, magazines available in public areas, shopping guides, and billboard announcements. Parents can use these high-profile written samples to motivate children to read and guide them to discover the information available in their environment.

Home Environment and Early Literacy: Parents can model literacy through daily activities like reading newspapers and magazines, writing grocery lists, clipping coupons, putting notes on the refrigerator, labeling household items, and posting rules. Parents can also read books to their children and guide them to identify parts of books. They can also read stories with simple and predictable plots and ask children to predict the story based on pictorial clues. They can guide children to identify parts of the story and which part they found most interesting. Parents can also use computer programs and interactive books to promote literacy in fun ways. Parents can use the captions on television to guide children to link speaking with its written representation. Taking advantage of the natural interest children have for smartphones, parents can guide them to read instructions to manage the device. Some phones can record and transcribe oral messages, and such features can promote the development of literacy in an enjoyable way.

Classroom Activities to Promote Early Literacy Skills

The school exposes children to explicit instruction in reading, including reading conventions, the alphabetic principle, sound–symbol correspondence (graphophonemic awareness), and common sight words (Peregoy & Boyle, 2017). These components are presented through such whole texts as poems, songs, and short stories. When students make sense of simple texts, teaching phonics and sight words can supplement the instruction. Classroom routines can also enhance literacy development among early readers. Here are a few examples of activities that can help develop initial literacy:

1. Use pocket charts with labels for the days, months, and year. Ask students to update the day and the date every morning. The same activity can be done in the second language so that students can see differences between English and the second languages. In Spanish, model the appropriate use of capital letters and accent marks.

2. Write the daily schedule and guide students to follow the activities during the day.

3. Post classroom rules and procedures and read them often so that students can see the connection between written and oral communication.

4. Use a word wall containing vocabulary that students can already read and continue adding new words to expand their oral and written vocabulary.

5. Write the names of students and place each on the appropriate desks. Emphasize names with accent marks or any special Spanish markings.

6. Use an attendance pocket chart with the date and sections labeled "Present" and "Class Roster." Print cards with the names of students and organize them alphabetically under the "Class Roster." In the morning, guide students to move their names from the "Class Roster" to the "Present" section. At the end of the day, guide students to move their name back to the "Class Roster" in alphabetic order.

7. Post students' writing samples inside and outside the classroom. This activity is used to represent publishing.

8. Use language experience charts or the language experience approach to show the connection between spoken and written language.

Activities and Concepts for the Early Reader

Early readers need multiple opportunities to be exposed to reading in an enjoyable and relaxed environment. This section lists key activities and concepts that can expose children to reading.

1. **Big books** contain short repetitive stories that can be used to teach sight words and the sound–symbol correspondence. The size of the letters permits children to follow the story while the teacher reads and points to the words. Enlarged text or online books that can be projected on a screen can help students. The big books or projected texts on screen can model the reading process. By using a pointer, students can see the connection between the written text and the pronunciation of the words. These activities are ideal to promote interest in reading for students at the emergent stage. In the dual language classroom, big books in Spanish can enhance reading instruction and lead children to biliteracy. **Sight words** are high-frequency words introduced to children visually for easy recognition. Traditionally, teachers use flash cards and games to teach sight words found in stories. Practice of word recognition and meaning can be done with students organized in whole group or in small or peer groups. A strong foundation of English sight words can support students in the emergent and early stages of reading, and it can promote reading fluency. Sight words in Spanish are not as important as in English. In Spanish, the teacher relies more on decoding skills using the syllable as the basic unit to teach reading.

2. **Phonics** instruction can guide students to recognize words based on how they are pronounced. Students apply rules to "sound out" words, and based on the way the words sound, students can recognize and assign meaning to them. Phonics instruction should always be introduced within a meaningful context. First, the teacher should read the story and let the children to enjoy it. The teacher then can introduce the skills for word recognition. Phonics instruction is a bottom-up reading model because it proceeds from the parts to the whole. Phonics instruction and components of the whole language approach (top to bottom) are currently used as a component of a balanced reading approach. These reading approaches were described earlier in this section. Typically, phonics instruction is introduced in a specific sequence (Peregoy & Boyle, 2017):

1. Consistent single consonants—*m, p, t*

2. Short and long vowels—*ca t* (short) and *boy* (long)

3. Word families, or onset and rime—*-ake*, as in *lake, bake, take*

4. Digraphs (two consonants combined to produce one sound)—*ch-, th-*

5. Blends (two or more consonants combined to produce a blended sound)—*pl-, cl-, scr-*

6. Rules for syllabication.

From Learning to Read to Reading to Learn

In pre-kindergarten to second grade, children learn to read—that is, to decode language and get meaning from it. In third grade and beyond, students must develop a new literacy skill—reading to learn. Reading to learn is a required skill for further development into literacy and scholastic success. To succeed in school, children must identify different texts and how they organize information. The two key types of writing are narrative and expository.

Narrative writing describes events or tells a story using context and often repetition to communicate ideas. It uses a predictable format containing three major components—beginning, middle, and end. In the beginning, the characters, the setting, and the problem are introduced. In the middle, the topic is further developed, creating a climax. In the end, the problem is usually solved. Children usually can identify this format and use it to make predictions and get information. ELs who are exposed to this format in L1 can transfer this information to L2. Mastering the reading components of narrative text is the foundation to engage in a briefer and more sophisticated and technical writing—expository.

Expository writing explains processes or concepts. It uses more technical vocabulary and is less redundant and less contextualized than narratives. This kind of technical writing is more succinct, linear, and hierarchical. The information in expository writing is structured topically, chronologically, or numerically. In the topic format, the information is organized into chapters, each covering a topic and divided into subtopics. For example, a chapter on the Amerindians of Texas might be organized by types of Indian groups and by the location, economic activities, and cultural features of each group, or the information might be organized chronologically. The information can also be supplemented with visuals, charts, graphs, tables, and other graphic representations arranged numerically. Understanding the format of expository writing is vital to get precise information effectively.

Development of Writing

Children at the early stages of writing use several strategies to convey meaning. They rely on drawings or concrete objects to gain and convey meaning. They often scribble to mimic the action of writing. Scribbling signifies growth because it is a transition from drawing to creating meaningful writing. This stage can also be used with invented spelling (pseudo letters). This stage represents a more advanced stage of scribbling because the child is conceptualizing how speech can be represented with letters. Some children can recognize these pseudo-letters, which suggests that they are developing graphophonemic awareness.

Children develop phonetic spelling to produce nonstandard spelling that they can read. Phonetic spelling represents an advanced degree of the emergent literacy stage and the beginning of the development of the **alphabetic principle**—the idea that sounds are represented by letters and letter sequences (Peregoy & Boyle, 2017). As part of the alphabetic principle, children notice the sound–symbol correspondences of the language. Graphophonemic awareness leads the child to notice that certain letters represent sounds, and these sounds represent words, which leads to the mastery of **phonemic awareness**. The development of phonemic awareness prepares children for formal phonics instruction, and it constitutes the foundation for becoming fluent readers and writers. Children follow a path similar to how they learn reading, with specific writing stages—emerging writers, early writers, and newly fluent writers (Lapp et al., 2001).

Emerging Writers: Children at the emerging stage of writing understand that writing symbolizes speech. They combine drawings, scribbles, and conventional letters to begin writing. First, children use the initial letter of a conventional word to represent the entire word. This invented spelling represents a degree of phonemic awareness because children are connecting the sound of the word with its equivalent graphic representation.

Early Writers: Children at the early stages of writing are developing phonemic awareness and use that knowledge to progress through the stages of spelling development. Children's phonetic spelling becomes more conventional as they use rules for capitalization and punctuation. Despite the use of phonetic spelling, their writing is comprehensible.

Newly Fluent Writers: Newly fluent writers consistently use conventional grammar, spelling, and punctuation. They use prewriting strategies to achieve a writing function (e.g., writing for a specific purpose or responding to a prompt). They can produce unique writing samples that contain a beginning, middle, and end. With guidance, they can revise and edit their written work.

Strategies and Concepts in Writing: Children at these stages of writing can benefit from real-life and functional writing activities. Activities for functional writing include labeling objects, note taking, writing about a drawing, and writing a list. With the concepts and strategies that follow, these activities can promote writing skills among all students.

Word families are words that have common spelling patterns in English. The main purpose of teaching English word families is to help students recognize frequently occurring letter patterns in the language, such as *-ack* in words like *pack*, *back* and *lack*. Word families are introduced through onsets and rimes. **Onset** refers to the initial consonant or consonant clusters of a syllable. **Rime**, or **phonogram**, refers to the combination of vowels and consonants that follow the onset. The *p* in *pump* is called the onset, and the *ump* is the rime. Traditionally, onset and rimes are introduced with monosyllabic words. Examples of common word families include:

- **ack**—Attack, black, lack, rack, track, tack, and back

- **age**—Cage, age, rage, sage, stage, wage

- **ake**—Brake, bake, fake, make, rake, take, wake

- **at**—Bat, cat, chat, fat, flat, hat, mat, rat, sat, what

- **ail**—Jail, pail, nail, rail, sail, snail, tail, mail, fail

- **ay**—bay, decay, gay, gray, lay, may, okay

The concept of word families can be extended to include words that derive from a common root word and have similar or related meaning. For example, in English we have words like *boy, boys, boyish, boyhood* that share a common root and have a semantic connection. That is, these words are related based on meaning, not related based on spelling pattern. Traditionally, these types of word families are not used for initial reading and writing instruction.

In Spanish, onset and rimes are not used to teach reading because Spanish has a relatively consistent spelling pattern. However, word families linked with meaning are used to expand the vocabulary of children. Some examples of Spanish root words and the words derived from them are included:

1. **Caballo:** caballero, caballerizas, caballito, caballote, cabalgar

2. **Flor:** florero, florecita, florista, floristería, florido, florecer, floral, enflorar

3. **Niño:** niñito, niñez, niñita, niñera, niñear, niñería, aniñado

4. **Amor:** enamorado, enamorada, enamorar, amoroso, enamoramiento

5. **Libro:** librería, librero, librito, librote

Journal Writing

Teachers can use three kinds of journal writing to guide students toward writing for meaningful purposes:

- **Personal Journals**—Students analyze their experiences and write for self-expression. Teachers should be involved only when invited.

- **Dialogue Journals**—Students communicate with teachers, adults, or other students about topics of interest. Teachers respond to the content of the writing by modeling standard language usage without overemphasizing corrections.

- **Reflective Journals**—Students reflect on situations or content. This journal can be used for self-assessment.

- A **learning log** is a functional journal in which students summarize what they have learned and analyze difficulties experienced while learning. Teachers can use the information in learning logs to provide additional support or to reteach concepts.

Language Experience Approach: The language experience approach (LEA) is used for early reading development among native English speakers and language minority students. The approach assumes that students' experiences should be used as a bridge to new ideas and concepts. This approach is also known as experience charts or shared writing and was developed as an alternative to basal readers to teach initial reading to language minority students. LEA proponents maintain that the vocabulary, topics, and ideas of the stories in basal readers did not match the schemata and the vocabulary of language minority students and thus created comprehension problems. To provide reading opportunities that better matched students' schemata, the LEA has students share an experience, such as a science experiment or a playground activity. After the initial activity, students are guided to talk about it and to dictate a story to the teacher. When the story is written, the teacher reads the story while pointing to the words as they are read. Following this initial reading, students join the teacher in a choral reading. Students later are asked to correct the story or add to it. When these first revisions are done, students copy the story and take it home. The next day, the story is read again and is used for follow-up activities. For example, teachers can use a cloze activity, deleting key words from the story to check for comprehension. The story can also be used to teach grammar conventions and promote vocabulary development.

Language Logic: The language logic in Standard American English progresses in a linear fashion without allowing for digression. English speakers are expected to progress from point A to point B with minimal deviations from the topic. Russian, Spanish, and most Romance languages have a linear structure, but the grammar allows for much digression in formal and informal interactions. Native American and Semitic languages allow for even more flexibility and digression. When ELs or speakers of English dialects impose the logic of their native language on Standard American English, communication problems can occur. ESL teachers need to guide ELs in using the linear logic of English. Through prewriting activities, teachers can help students organize their thoughts following the linear progression. Process writing can guide children to organize ideas and write using the linear progression required in English.

Process writing should guide students to write following specific steps:

1. **Prewriting** activities generate and organize ideas. When children identify the task, they are guided to develop an outline or a web to ensure that the ideas are interconnected and follow a logical pattern. In this stage, the teacher can help ELs organize their ideas following a linear progression.

2. **Drafting** puts the ideas in writing, keeping in mind audience and purpose.

3. **Conferencing** with the teacher or peers provides feedback to the writer.

4. **Revising** is done based on the input from conferencing and emphasizes the overall content of the piece as well as the clarity of ideas.

5. **Editing** corrects errors in spelling, grammar, punctuation, and mechanics.

6. **Publishing** represents the last step, and the document is presented in final form to be shared with an audience.

Cross-language Connections: With appropriate instruction, simultaneous and sequential bilinguals can identify and use cross-language connections to develop literacy in both languages. English and Spanish have multiple elements that transfer from one language to the other. However, establishing this cross-language connection is not natural for children, and it must be taught. English/Spanish bilingual students may be unable to identify cognates, even if guided to identify them in text (August, Carlo, Dressler, and Snow, 2005). Cognates as well as multiple features of literacy in English and Spanish can be taught to empower bilingual students to use the knowledge from both languages to master content and become biliterate.

Similarities between English and Spanish: English and Spanish have had a historical connection with the Greek, Roman, and Arab civilizations. Based on the linguistic and cultural impact of these civilizations, a large number of concepts and words from these groups have enriched the lexicon of English and Spanish. The Romans and the Greeks contributed in science, mathematics, architecture, the fine arts, and politics. The Romans developed the alphabet system used in most European languages. The Arabs contributed in astronomy, architecture, medicine, and mathematics. They developed the number system currently used in the Western World.

English and Spanish are part of the Indo-European language family. English is from the Germanic branch, and Spanish is one of the seven major Romance languages that evolved from Latin—Spanish, French, Italian, Portuguese, Romanian, Provençal, and Catalan.

Through conquest and assimilation, the Greeks, Romans, and Arabs passed their linguistic and cultural legacy to Europeans. The Europeans, especially the English and the Spaniards, in turn transmitted this knowledge across the world. With the legacy of these civilizations came a system of cognates, with similar root words and affixes (prefixes, infixes, and suffixes) common across multiple European languages. Common cognates between English and Spanish have been the most significant tool for the development of biliteracy for Spanish/English bilingual children.

This historical association between Spanish and English has resulted in the development of common grammar rules and concepts. For example, the grammar of both languages shares multiple similarities. Common elements across the two languages include:

1. The grammar—Parts of the sentence—prepositions, nouns, verbs, adjectives, adverbs.

2. Punctuation marks—Comma, final period, semicolon, colon, and quotation marks.

3. Capitalization—Except for the days of the week, the months, adjectives of nationality

4. Comprehension skills—Finding the main idea, supporting details, topic sentence, and gist of the story.

5. Story grammar—Setting, characters, plot, climax, resolution, mood, and theme.

6. Composition—Topic sentence, transition words, sequencing, words to promote fluency (*moreover, however, finally* . . .).

7. Process writing—Prewriting, first draft, editing, publishing.

8. Types of essay—Persuasive, expository, argumentative, descriptive, narrative, opinion.

9. The concept of phonemic awareness—Connection between the letters and the sounds that they represent.

10. The alphabetic principles—Understanding that the letters of the alphabet represent the sounds of the language.

11. Directionality in reading is the same, following a top to bottom, left to right progression.

12. Word recognition strategies—Context clues, structural, syntactical.

13. Phonological similarities—A large number of consonants are identical or similar in both languages.

Contrary to popular beliefs, English and Spanish also have similar basic syntax. Table 5.1 presents an overview of the common syntactic features of the two languages.

Table 5.1. Common Basic Sentence Structures

Basic Sentence Structure	Example in English	Example in Spanish
1. Subject-Intransitive Verb	Jerry cried.	Jerry lloró.
2. Subject-Transitive Verb-Direct Object	She hugged the cat.	Ellas abrazó al gato
3. Subject-Transitive Verb-Indirect object-Direct object	Mary gave me the cat.	Mary me dio el gato.
4. Subject-Intransitive Verb-Predicate Adjective	Melania is polyglot.	Melania es políglota.
5. Subject-Intransitive Verb-Predicative Nominative	Trump is the president.	Trump es el presidente

Elements that May Not Transfer

Elements that may not transfer from Spanish and English and thus can cause language interference include:

1. The grapheme-phoneme correspondence of Spanish is more consistent than in English. English has 26 letters to represent 44 sounds, while Spanish has 27 letters to represent 27 sounds.

2. English uses multiple consonant clusters in initial position, which does not happen in Spanish. Some examples: are *st* (stop), *str* (string), *sp* (spot), *spl* (splash), *spr* (spring), *sn* (snow), *sm* (small). In Spanish, these clusters only happen in medial position, and they are preceded by the vowel **e**. Some examples are: e**st**oy, **esp**ero, de**sn**udo, **esm**alte.

3. English has multiple consonant diagraphs, and Spanish has only three—*ch* (choza), *ll* (llanta), and *rr* (carro). See Table 5.3 for examples of English digraphs.

4. The Spanish vowel system is simpler than the English system. English has five letters to represent 12–15 vowel sounds, while Spanish has five letters to represent five sounds.

5. Spanish does not have the concept of long and short vowels. All Spanish vowels have a similar duration. This difference creates pronunciation problems for ELs of Spanish background.

6. English has multiple vowel diagraphs while Spanish does not. Spanish pronounces all vowel sounds. For example, English has words like—*cool, book*, and *feet*—where the two vowels represent one sound. In Spanish two vowels are pronounced, and together they will create a diphthong—c**iu**dad, c**au**sa—or a hiatus—**a**éreo (a-é-re-o).

7. Spanish has a large number of diphthongs, while English has large number of vowel diagraphs and only a few diphthongs—*I* (ai), *oi* (boy) and *au* (cow).

8. English has multiple contractions commonly used in conversations and in writing. Speakers have the option of using the long or the contracted version. Spanish has only two contractions, and these are not optional—a el (al) de el (del)—like in English.

9. English has a complex system of prepositions to show location. For example, the prepositions **in, on, at** do not have a direct equivalent in Spanish, which uses the preposition **en** in place of all three English prepositions. Mastering the use of these three English prepositions challenges Spanish-speaking ELs.

10. English has unique sounds not present in Spanish. Sounds like the "th" in *think*, and /z/ create major problems for Spanish-speaking ELs. They will use similar Spanish sounds to produce these unique sounds. These substitutions often can affect pronunciation and create communication problems.

11. The difference between the sounds of the labia-dental /v/ and bilabial /b/ has disappeared from Spanish phonology. Spanish speakers thus will not establish the difference between words like: *vowel—bowel, vest—best, vase—base, very—bury,* and *vote—boat.*

12. The phonemes of the *ll* (elle) and the *rr* (erre) represent unique sounds in Spanish. The letters appear in English words like in the words *call* and *arrange,* but they represent different sounds.

13. The grapheme ñ is not present in English. English has a similar sound where the *n* is pronounced like the ñ, in words like o*n*ion and ca*n*yon.

14. Since most Spanish words are easy to decode, Spanish does not rely on sight words as much as English does.

15. The system of onset and rimes, commonly used in English to teach spelling, has minimal value to teach spelling in Spanish. Instead, Spanish relies on the syllabication as the main system to decode and recognize words.

16. Spanish uses orthographic accent marks and dieresis (lingüística) to guide the pronunciation of words that deviate from the traditional pronunciation rules. It also uses these markings to clarify the intended meaning. For example, the word **te** can have two meanings, the drink (té) with accent, and *te* (no accent) to represent a personal pronoun.

17. Spanish has only one silent letter—*h*—*hola* versus *ola* (same pronunciation). English has several silent letters, creating pronunciation problems for all English learners. Table 5.2 presents examples of English words with silent letters.

Table 5.2. Silent Letters in English

Silent Letters	Examples
H	Echo, cholera, ache, monarch, school
L	Calm, palm, salmon, half, walk, chalk, calf, could, would
B	Lamb, tomb, bomb, womb, climb
C	Scene, scissors, disciple, fascinating, conscious
P	Pseudo, pneumonia, receipt, psychology, pneumatic
T	Castle, whistle, Nestle, hustle, listen
N	Autumn, column, condemn, solemn, hymn

18. The inconsistency of the pronunciation of the English consonant digraphs *ch* and *sh* create pronunciation problems for ELs of Spanish background. The grapheme *ch* can be pronounced as /sh/, or in certain words the letters *ss, t, s,* and *c* are pronounced as /sh/. Examples of the discrepancy between letters and sounds are listed in Table 5.3.

Table 5.3. Grapheme-Phoneme Discrepancies in English

Letter	Pronounced as	Examples
CH	/SH/	chef, chevron, machine, Chevrolet, chauffeur
SS, T, S, C	/SH/	mission, caution, sugar, delicious
CH	/K/	chrome, chemistry, chaos

The following table presents an overview of the most significant differences between English and Spanish.

Table 5.4. Key Differences between English and Spanish

Key Components	English	Spanish
Initial consonant clusters/blend	Multiple examples: *speak, spring, street, splash slate, plate, smoke, snow, scream*	None. These clusters happen only in the medial position, preceded by the vowel "e"—e*spero*, e*sprimir*, e*scuela*
Letters of the Alphabet/ Number of Phonemes	26 letters/44 sounds	27 letters/27 sounds
Letters to Represent Vowel Sounds	5 letters/12–15 sounds	5 letters/5 sounds

Table 5.4. (continued)

Key Components	English	Spanish
Diphthongs and Hiatuses	Three identified with multiple diphthongized sounds: *Boy* (oi), *cow* (au), and *buy* (ai)	Large number of diphthongs and hiatuses: Diphthongs: ag*ua*, c*iu*dad, c*uida*do, *au*to; Hiatuses: a*é*reo, p*eo*r, pel*ea*r . . .
Consonant Digraphs	Multiple examples: k*n*ow, sc*h*ool, c*h*urch, *sh*irt	Spanish has five consonant digraphs. Three are linked to the alphabet: • CH (che)—*Choza, muchacho* • LL (elle)—*calle, llorar* • RR (erre)—*carro, perro* Two occur under special conditions: • QU (The *qu* is pronounced as /K/. The "u," occurring in the medial position, is silent in words with *que* and *qui*.—*quiero, queso*.) • GU (The "u" is silent in some words when "e" or "i" follows: *gue* and *gui*—as in *guerra, guitarra*. In words in which the "u" should be pronounced, we add a dieresis to indicate it—for example *pingüino, vergüenza*.

The English Language Arts Curriculum for EC-6

The Texas elementary English language arts and reading program is designed around five major components: reading, writing, research, listening and speaking, and oral and written conventions. In **reading,** learners are exposed to numerous literacy and informational texts (TEA, 2007–2015). In kindergarten, learners become familiar with print awareness as well as phonemic and phonological awareness. In **writing** students must perform several written tasks each with a clear thesis, supporting details and coherent organization. They also must develop written responses based on a given prompt. In the research component, students must identify sources of information for their writing. They must identify relevant research and analyze and synthesize it. In **listening and speaking**, students must understand and respond to others' ideas as well as apply the norms for entering a conversation, contributing to it, and closing it. In **oral and written conventions**, students must use the grammatical features of English to converse and then to transfer their oral skills to the written skills.

The development of phonological and phonemic awareness constitutes the students' main challenge in the early grades. Identifying the connection between written and spoken words is required to "crack" the written code. A dozen key challenges students face in early grades experience are in the following list:

1. Learn the names of the letters of the alphabet as well as their pronunciation.

2. Identify the connection between graphemes and phonemes in words, phrases, and sentences.

3. Establish the connection among letters, words, sentences, and larger written segments.

4. Identify word boundaries and the concept of the complete sentence.

5. Identify the different parts of a book.

6. Connect spoken words and their written representation.

7. Identify and segment syllables in spoken words.

8. Recognize and produce rhyming words.

9. Segment sounds in initial positions.

10. Recognize parts of a story.

11. Recognize high-frequency words.

12. Apply decoding strategies to get meaning from written text.

When students learn to read and write for pleasure using literature, teachers should shift the goal of learning to read to reading to learn. Children discover reading through fiction and nonfiction texts. However, students starting with the second grade must learn to read to gather information and learn content areas. This shift represents a challenge for ELs who might comprehend short stories but may fail to understand a content passage containing academic vocabulary and concepts.

Expectations for English Learners

The expectations for ELs are similar to the expectations for native English speakers. However, teachers must consider the unique needs and assets that ELs bring to literacy.

1. The native language of the student should serve as a foundation for the development of literacy in L2.

2. In some programs, ELs must learn English and the content areas simultaneously, which requires teachers to incorporate the English Language Proficiency Standards (ELPS) as part of content area instruction. The incorporation of ELPS in the content area is required by the Texas Education Agency as well as the federal education legislation—ESSA.

3. As part of the language arts components of daily lessons, ELs will get instruction in phonemic awareness and application decoding strategies with the development of academic vocabulary as well as comprehension skills needed to master the content areas.

4. Scaffold instruction for ELs is needed to deliver comprehensible input.

5. Use the assets and knowledge children bring to the literacy process as the foundation for matching or introducing components of the second language.

6. Emphasize vocabulary development as part of instruction in the content areas. Use the multiple cognates common to English and Spanish to promote vocabulary development.

7. Use rhetorical devices and figurative language common to L1 and guide children to compare them with equivalent examples in their native language.

8. Establish the difference between explicit versus implicit language and explain how these affect meaning.

9. Review idiomatic expressions commonly used in schools.

10. Provide explicit and strategic support to students without previous schooling and students who are not literate in their first language.

The Spanish Curriculum for Elementary Grades

The Texas Spanish curriculum for elementary education follows a system similar to the English version of the program. It follows the strands of reading, writing, research, listening and writing, and oral and written conventions. Besides the reading components common to both languages, teachers must teach Spanish literacy using unique features of the language. This section presents an analysis of the unique features of the Spanish curriculum, with strategies to deliver instruction. For details about the Spanish curriculum in Texas, please go to the TEA curriculum website (TEA, 2007–2015).

1. **Role of Vowels:** Spanish has a consistent sound–symbol association, especially with the sounds of the five vowels. Because of this consistency, reading instruction begins with the five vowels. When students master the vowel system, instruction is focused on the syllable, using the most consistent consonant sounds. The most consistent consonant sounds in Spanish are—*m, n, b, p, s, d, t,* and *f.* These consonants in initial position are thus used to create open syllables; that is, the consonant-vowel (C-V) format in such syllables as *ma, me, mi, mo, mu, ba, be, bi, bo,* and *bu.* Teachers later can present the CVC format in words like *pan, sol, amo, uva, pez,* and *gas.* Teachers should next introduce words with consonant blends found in such words as *claro, grande,* and *cristal.* They can also introduce words with diphthongs and hiatus in such words as *ciudad, auto,* and *viuda* (diphthongs), and *aéreo, área,* and *caer* (hiatus). Finally, teachers should introduce those inconsistent grapheme-phonemes of the letter, *h,* the silent *u* (after the *g* or *q*), the *c,* and *g,* and less frequent letters like *k, x,* and *w* (Ford & Palacios, 2015).

2. **Basic Units for Reading Instruction:** The syllable is the key unit to decode words in Spanish. Since Spanish has a consistent grapheme–phoneme correspondence, decoding is relatively easy.

Using the syllable as the key unit for decoding is thus ideal for Spanish. However, in Spanish the real challenge is not to decode the words but to comprehend the information read. By the end of first grade, most students can decode most words. However, they might not understand and recall the information they have read. Teachers thus must be vigilant to be sure that comprehension skills develop with decoding.

3. **Sounding Words:** Since most words in Spanish can be easily decoded, there is no need to introduce an extensive list of sight words, as is done with English. Instead, teachers should use Spanish syllables to guide students in the discovery of Spanish words. Most common words in Spanish begin with an open syllable or a consonant and a vowel—CV. Based on that premise, children can create new syllables by substituting the initial consonant, i.e., **ma**, **ta**, **pa**. Table 5.5 presents a strategy to guide children to combine syllables to create words in Spanish. In this exercise, small groups of children are asked to connect two syllables from the columns and read the resulting syllable strings to see whether it is a Spanish word. When they agree it is a Spanish word, they will write in the section labeled "Word Chest." With words like *mama* (to extract milk) and *mamá* (mother), and *papa* (potato), *Papa* (the Pope) and *papá* (father), the teacher can introduce the accent marks. Depending on the age, the teacher then should explain how diacritic accents can change the meaning of words. For young learners, teachers just emphasize the pronunciation with the accent and without it and avoid extensive explanations.

Table 5.5. Discovering Spanish Words

Syllables 1	Syllables 2	Syllables 3	Syllables 4
Ma	Me	Mi	Re
Mo	Mu	Pa	Ro
Pe	Pi	Po	Ru
Pu	Sa	Se	Ta
Si	So	Su	Te
La	Le	Li	Ti
Lo	Lu	ra	To
Word Chest: mama, mamá, mami, rema, reme, mima, papa, papá. Papa, lata, Lola, puse, Lala, late, ruso, Pola, pelo, sapo . . .			

4. **Spanish homophones:** Words with identical pronunciation in Spanish (homophones) can create challenges for the writing component of Spanish literacy (Morris & Rosado, 2013). The most common problems with homophones include:

A. B and V –Barón (nobility title) and varón (male)

B. With H or without it—Hola (salutation) and ola (wave)

C. LL and Y—arrolló (hit by a car) and arroyo (a creek)

D. S and Z—Casar (get married) and cazar (to hunt)

E. S and C—Brasero (burning charcoal) and bracero (agricultural workers)

5. **Syllabication:** Understanding rules of Spanish syllabication is needed to teach decoding skills, and to identify words that require orthographic accents in Spanish. To identify syllables, students need to identify the types of vowel and how these can be clustered for syllable formation. Spanish has two types of vowels: strong/open (a, o, e) and weak/closed (I, u). A combination of these vowels creates three types of grouping: diphthongs, triphthongs, and hiatus. These groupings are important to separate words into syllables, and the application of pronunciation rules, including the rules for the use of orthographic accents.

A. **Diphthongs**—two adjacent vowels pronounced as part of the same syllable). Spanish diphthongs can happen under two conditions:

- Two weak vowels in any order: ci*u*dad (*ciu*-dad), c*ui*dado (c*ui*-da-do)

- One weak and one strong vowel: c*au*dal (c*au*-dal), c*uo*ta (c*uo*-ta), c*ue*ro (c*ue*-ro)

B. **Triphthongs**—three vowels sounds pronounced as part of the same syllable

- A combination of two weak vowels and one strong vowel pronounced as one syllable. Examples: Urug*uay* (U-ru-*guay*), m*iau* (m*iau*), limp*iau*ñas (lim-p*iau*-ñas)

C. **Hiatus**—two adjacent vowels with sounds separated, creating two syllables.

- The best example of a hiatus is the word aéreo (a-é-re-o). It has six letters with four hiatus which create four separate syllables.

6. **Orthographic accents in Spanish are used for two main purposes**—to guide pronunciation and to clarify meaning.

A. To guide readers in the pronunciation of words that violate Spanish pronunciation rules. For example, words that end in *n, s,* or a *vowel* should have the primary stress in the next-to-last syllable, like in the following examples—A-**mi**-go, **ca**-sas, y **a**man. However, Spanish has multiple words that do not follow this rule and thus the orthographic accents are used to guide their pronunciation. Some examples are: ca-**mión**, ja-**más**, and can-**té**.

B. To clarify the intended use of words spelled identically. For example, Spanish has multiple words, including monosyllabic words, with more than one meaning. For example, the word *el* with an accent represents a personal pronoun, and without it represents a definite article. See the following example: El (article) carro es de él (pronoun).

7. **Words with gue and gui:** As a rule in Spanish, the *u* is silent in the word strings **gue** and **gui**. For example, in the words *guerra* (war), and *guitarra* (guitar) the *u* is silent. To identify exceptions to this rule, Spanish uses the dieresis—two dots over the *ü*. Words that fall under this category include:

A. Words with güe—bilingüe, bilingüismo, vergüenza, pedigüeño, and paragüero.

B. Words with güi—lingüística, lingüista, pingüino, agüita, and contigüidad.

8. **Capitalization:** Spanish and English have similar capitalization rules, while a few rules differ altogether. Students developing biliteracy must identify exceptions to capitalization rules so that they can use them appropriately with the two languages. Capitalization rules that can confuse students include:

A. The days of the week, the months, the names of religions, and the adjectives of nationality are written in lower case in Spanish. For example: *lunes* (Monday), *febrero* (February), *catolicismo* (Catholic), and *americano* (American).

B. In Spanish, the day precedes the month. In English, the month precedes the day. La fecha de hoy es el 23 de Noviembre del 2016—Today's date is November 23, 2016.

For a detailed analysis of the unique features of Spanish, consult the book "*El desarrollo del español para maestros en programas de educación bilingüe* (Morris & Rosado, 2013).

Development of Biliteracy

The development of biliteracy is similar to the process native English speakers follow to develop literacy in the first language. However, when children are immersed in two languages and cultures from the start, the development of biliteracy becomes a unique process that differs from the development of literacy in L1 and L2 as separate processes. However, not all children are exposed to the two languages at the same time and under identical conditions. One child might get exposed to one language first and then get exposed to the second language at different stages of development. The process used to achieve biliteracy depends on the way children are exposed to the two languages and the route they use to achieve bilingualism.

Routes to Bilingualism

The two main types of bilingual people are those identified as simultaneous bilingual and those identified as sequential bilinguals. Simultaneous bilinguals are exposed to the two languages concurrently. Sequential bilinguals acquire the native language first and add the second language later.

Simultaneous Bilinguals: In the United States, simultaneous bilingual refers to children who were born in the country and were exposed to two languages from birth to age 5 (Baker, 2001). Most bilingual students in the nation fall into this category. Since they are exposed to both languages concurrently, bilingualism (L1+L2) is their primary mode of communication (Escamilla et al., 2014). These children use both languages to communicate as well as for schooling. With appropriate and on-grade level instruction in both languages, simultaneous emerging bilingual can become bilingual and biliterate.

Sequential Bilinguals: Sequential bilinguals are children who had some level of development in their first language when they were exposed to the second language. If these children are on grade level in L1 and have a strong foundation in L1, they can transfer multiple language features from L1 to L2. Sequential bilinguals have an advantage over simultaneous bilinguals because they have a better chance to use features of the L1 as a foundation for the development of the second language. These cross-linguistic transfers can enhance the knowledge of metalanguage strategies among learners and guide them to develop a better understanding of the features of the two languages.

Escamilla et al. (2014) suggest that for biliteracy instruction to work, an equal amount of instruction should be devoted to the development of oracy, reading, and writing as well as the explicit teaching of metalanguage strategies.

Oracy: The term *oracy* goes beyond the teaching of oral language development. It focuses on the oral language needed to accomplish literacy activities (Escamilla et al., 2014). It emphasizes the teaching of the academic and conceptual vocabulary needed to understand classroom instruction and the language used in textbooks as well as other academic written language used for learning. To develop the oracy students need to function in two languages, teachers must identify and teach students the vocabulary and concepts needed to conduct numerous activities.

Instruction for biliteracy emphasizes the teaching metalanguage, the language and concepts used to analyze and talk about language (Escamilla et al., 2014). To develop the oracy needed for biliteracy, instruction should emphasize the structures of the language required to complete the task, the academic vocabulary, and the strategies to engage students in literacy-related discourse. To succeed in these literacy tasks, learners and especially ELs must know the language structures and format to:

1. Ask for clarification

2. Propose and advocate for a course of action

3. Discuss and explain information

4. Justify an answer or a position

5. Respond to engage in a debate using polite language and convincing information

6. Express agreement and disagreement

7. Respond to hypothetical situations, using **if** and **would** constructions.

Language Structures: Learners must become familiar with the language structures used in English and Spanish to carry out multiple speech acts required in the literacy classroom, i.e., agreeing and disagreeing, providing and accepting compliments, adding and summarizing information, making requests, and using polite and professional language. Teachers can introduce key language structures to help learners succeed in these speech acts. For example, learners can be taught to use polite language to carry out multiple language functions:

1. Disagreeing—I understand your point of view, but;

2. Adding Information—That is a very interesting idea, but;

3. Building Consensus—Would you consider . . . ;

4. Asking Permission—May I have it?

5. Conflict Resolution—We can solve this by . . .

6. Asking for Help—Would you be willing to . . .

Vocabulary: Vocabulary development has been linked to reading fluency as well as speech and writing comprehension. Students who come to school with a strong vocabulary in L1 have advantages over children new to the language and those from low socioeconomic backgrounds. Students with limited vocabulary will begin school behind their peers and will continue with this gap unless teachers provide the instruction to overcome these vocabulary limitations. For Spanish-speaking emergent bilinguals, teachers must rely on the first language as a foundation for the development of vocabulary in L2.

For more advanced on-grade level bilingual students, vocabulary development and learning can happen in two languages. These students are more likely to transfer vocabulary and concepts from L1 to L2. However, identifying cognates is not automatic. Children often do not recognize cognates because these words might not be part of the lexical repertoire.

A lot of sophisticated and highly specialized English words come from Latin, and these words are common in Spanish usage. If teachers guide students to notice the connection of highly sophisticated words of Latin origin to Spanish words of regular usage, the learners will be more likely to recognize cognates. Some cognates have identical spelling and are easier to recognize, but some cognates require the child to apply metalanguage strategies to recognize the similarities between the words. For example, *amiable* and *amicable* might sound unrelated to Spanish until the student sees how these words connect with *amigo*, a common Spanish word. When the student sees how *amigo* connects to these new words, he or she might establish their connection to one another. However, students with limited vocabulary might have *amigable* in their repertoire but fail to establish the connection. To address this discrepancy, school administrators and teachers must develop literacy programs in which students get instruction in both languages until the students arrive at what Cummins calls a threshold in the language. If students reach this threshold in both languages, the recognition of cognates can become a common and accessible skill for all bilingual students.

Table 5.6 presents an analysis of sophisticated English words and their connection to Spanish words of common usage.

Table 5.6. English Words and their connections with Common Spanish Usage

Technical English Words	Spanish Equivalent	Linkage to Regular Spanish words
Amiable or amicable	Amigable	Amigo (friend)
Amorous	Amoroso	Amor (love)
Aquarium and aquatic	Acuario or acuático	Aqua or agua (water)
Aviary	Aviario	Aves (birds)
Cerebral	Cerebral	Cerebro (brain)
Clarification	Clarificación	Claro (clear)
Labio-dental	Labio-dental	Labios (lips) and dentadura (teeth)
Defunct	Difunto	Difunto (dead)
Granary	Granero	Granos (grains)
Solar and lunar	Solar and lunar	Sol (sun) and Luna (moon)
Maternal and paternal	Maternal y paternal	Madre (mother) Padre (father)
Veracious	Verdadero	Verdad (the truth)
Gratis	Gratis	Gratis (free)
Gratuitous	Gratuito	Gratis (free)

Dialogue: Teaching dialogue includes more than the social aspect of communication. It includes the dialogue needed to share and obtain information in language as well as the content areas. It requires students to learn to ask questions and to communicate information through dialogues. It requires students to present a logical, linear, and connected progression. It also requires speakers to understand the norm used to join, develop, and close conversations. Speakers also must use the appropriate register for the conversations to deliver the intended message. Teaching the language structures mentioned earlier can also improve the participation of students in dialogues.

Reading: English and Spanish are similar but with unique characteristics that merit careful consideration when implementing programs to develop biliteracy. When comparing English and Spanish, we find English characteristics that do not transfer to Spanish. For example, English literacy emphasizes the name of the letters of the alphabet with the sound they produce. Since consonants in English are more consistent than vowels, the consonants are used as a foundation for initial reading instruction. They use the connection of the letters and sound to introduce decoding strategies or word attack skills. This phonemic awareness is fundamental for the teaching of English reading.

In Spanish, teachers also introduce the letters of the alphabet with the sounds they represent. Since Spanish vowels are more consistent than the consonants, teachers use vowels and consonants to create syllables. These syllables represent the foundation for introducing initial reading instruction. Students are guided to recognize syllables and connecting them with others to create words. This does not mean that Spanish is a syllabic language, however. It just means that for reading instruction, the unit used is the syllable, not isolated sounds. Therefore, teachers must use the features of Spanish as foundation to begin literacy instruction instead of using English literacy principles.

Despite differences, multiple common strategies can still be used to achieve biliteracy. Some common components used to achieve biliteracy rely on paired literacy, authentic literature, and literature-based English language development instruction.

Paired Literacy is the preferred model to promote biliteracy among ELs. In this model literacy in L1 and L2 is introduced simultaneously in kindergarten through at least 5th grade. This model is typically used in the 50–50 dual language models. This approach differs from the traditional transitional bilingual education programs. In traditional programs, literacy instruction is presented **sequentially**, with literacy instruction first presented in L1 and followed by formal instruction presented in L2. Traditional instruction thus relies on the transfer of concepts from L1 to L2.

Authentic Literature is more appropriate to promote literacy in both languages because this literature uses the internal structure and characteristics of the target language and not the superimposed component of translated materials. This literature is also more appropriate because students may have the background knowledge needed to understand the story. If possible, teachers should avoid using translated versions of literature.

Literature-based English language development is one of the principles of whole language instruction. This approach uses literature as a foundation for the introduction of literacy skills in English and ESL content-based instruction to teach both content and language development in English. The development of biliteracy differs from the traditional monolingual process. In this process, ELs use the knowledge and skills from both to cope with linguistic and cognitive challenges to facilitate and achieve biliteracy. The Report of the National Reading Panel (August, and Shanahan 2006) says English learners who are developing biliteracy use unique strategies available only to bilingual or multilingual learners:

1. Readers use knowledge and experience in L1 as a foundation for the acquisition of L2.

2. Skills and knowledge transfer from L1 to L2 and vice versa.

3. Literacy in the first language affects the development of literacy (reading and writing).

4. English oral development facilitates the development of literacy in English.

In literacy-based ESL programs, learners use metalinguistic awareness and the oracy skills acquired while becoming bilingual as a foundation to develop both languages and achieve biliteracy.

Other strategies to engage bilingual students in the development of biliteracy are:

1. **Interactive Read Aloud.** The teacher reads aloud in L1 or L2 to the whole group and models comprehension strategies, using questioning. The teacher engages learners in reading and guides them to develop the metalinguistic awareness to notice elements that transfer from one language to the other.

2. **Shared Reading.** With the teacher's guidance, this activity lets students participate in the reading process. The teacher models the reading process, and when children feel comfortable with the reading, they are encouraged to participate and practice comprehension strategies and literacy skills. With emerging readers, the purpose is to facilitate comprehension. With advanced readers, the lesson can include the identification of such devices as simile, metaphor, and hyperbole as well as cultural components implied in idiomatic expressions.

Implementing Shared Reading: To implement shared reading, teachers must use enlarged text or multiple copies of the same book. The teacher might begin by reading the text aloud while guiding children to follow. The teacher selects specific passages to rehearse orally with students to develop the confidence to read aloud. The teacher guides students to read along to develop an awareness of rhythm and intonation. Strategies to engage students in reading aloud include:

A. Assigning parts of the text to specific students or groups of students.

B. Guiding students to read parts of the text that are repeated throughout the story.

C. Making the content cognitive accessible to ELs by dramatizing parts of the story.

D. Reading with different vocal tones to represent emotions or to stress the importance of a section. For example, if students are reading about a mean character, use a stern voice.

Writing: The development of writing skills is linked to speaking the language. People write the way they talk. The key challenge of writing is using the markings and conventions required to guide readers to decode and understand written communication. When students learn the conventions and markings, their writing communicates more effectively.

In the early stages of writing, students must understand its value for communicating. This understanding begins at home when parents leave notes for children or guide them to write for a purpose. Composing a grocery list works well with children in the early grades. Writing letters to members of the school board or local political figures requesting support or inviting them to visit the school can be used with more advanced writers.

Teachers, meanwhile, should continue to emphasize the communication properties of writing and introduce children to process writing. With this emphasis, teachers model and share writing, and they guide children to write independently and to collaborate in writing projects.

Modeled Writing: The teacher models writing by showing it as a process and a communication tool to achieve multiple purposes. Modeled writing should show how writers convey messages to meet goals. For students in the early stages of writing, teachers use traditional or electronic boards to model the process, emphasizing word separation, capitalization, and other conventions. Teachers can also model the process and describe the grammar and orthography. When in the second language, the teacher should emphasize the differences and similarities across both languages. To improve fluency, the teacher should model the use of transitions as a cohesive devise to improve the writing. In Spanish, the teacher should describe the purpose of such special markings in Spanish as the tilde to show the use of orthographic accent marks. The teacher also should describe and model the question and exclamation marks and the use of dieresis.

Modeling writing can also be used as a tool to introduce linear progression and the cohesive devices to make the story more interesting. It can also show such different types of writing as narration and rhetoric as well as responding to literature. The steps of modeling are:

1. Introduce the topic and activate the children's schemata to determine how much they know. Teachers must be sure that children new to the language and culture have the appropriate background knowledge for the selected topic. Children often have similar concepts but different vocabulary.

2. Identify the purpose of the writing as well as the intended audience. Then share the appropriate information with the students.

3. Compose the text by using the strategy of thinking aloud so that students can observe how writers compose.

4. Revise and edit the document. Teachers should guide children to read the text to be sure their ideas are clear and organized. Invite input from the students to help rewrite the text. Finally, model the use of writing conventions, using think aloud so that students understand the rationale for the format of the text, the conventions and style, and the spelling and mechanics. At the end of the writing, students should realize they were an integral part of the writing process.

Shared Writing: In shared writing, students participate more actively. This process is similar to the Language Experience Approach described earlier. For that approach, students must have a working knowledge of process writing, including the selection of the topic and assessment of the audience as well as the type of text needed to carry out the assignment. The key steps are similar to those of modeled writing and include:

1. Collectively and with the teacher's guidance, students identify the purpose of the writing. To do this, students must identify the audience and purpose of the writing. They also must agree on the message of the writing. When these components are in place, students can start composing.

2. Depending on the level, students are introduced to key vocabulary as well as the framework or format for the writing. Select students to vocalize the information and students to write the information that has been agreed upon. While the selected students write the information on the traditional or electronic board, the other students do the same on their writing pads. Provide feedback about how the students reached consensus about the ideas for the text. Guide students to see what transfers from one language to the other. This cross-linguistic connection will later be used to write in the second language.

3. When editing, read the text with the students to determine whether changes are needed and guide them to make appropriate changes. Then read the piece with the students again and guide them to check the spelling and writing conventions and make necessary revisions.

4. Use the finished writing to extend the literacy activity to reading as well as oral activities.

Dictated Texts

This strategy can be used for both groups, during the English language development (ELD) portion or the Spanish literacy segment. The teacher dictates a word for emergent writers, phrases or sentences for early writers, or a complete story to advanced writers. Students independently encode the information to comply with the writing tasks. The teacher tries to improve enunciation by using brief pauses to indicate commas and longer pauses for the end of sentences. In Spanish literacy, teachers may overemphasize some syllables to indicate the possibility of orthographic accents, dieresis, and the ñ. They might also provide information so that students understand the correct spelling of homophones, i.e., *hola* versus *ola*—this is the wave, not the greetings. They might also modify the Spanish pronunciation to establish differences between such Spanish homophones as those words with *s* or *z*, and *v* or *b*. To establish differences between the *s* and *z*, teachers might use the Castilian pronunciation of the /z/ to make students aware of the spelling. They can also guide students to notice the differences between the labiodental (v) and the bilabial (b). In this strategy, composing skills are presented in an integrated fashion inductively through the example dictated to students. As part of this dictation activity, students can practice self-correcting techniques and metalanguage skills.

Implementing dictated texts:

1. Teachers dictate the text to students. Students repeat the dictated text, phrases, or words.

2. Students are instructed to use a dedicated notebook and a new page for each dictation activity. They are also instructed to leave one line between each phrase and sentence to allow space for editing marks and corrections.

3. Students encode the information, using appropriate language conventions.

4. Teachers write and share with students the standard version of the dictated text, using it to teach grammar conventions and composing strategies. Students then use the information to correct their own writing.

5. Students read the corrected text to a peer. Both students share information and make any necessary additional corrections to the text.

6. Teachers collect the writing samples and assess them using a rubric.

For a detailed analysis of the dictated text (dictado), consult the text, *Biliteracy from the start—Literacy squared in action* (Escamilla, et al., 2014).

Metalanguage: Metalanguage is the ability to think and talk about the multiple components of language. It includes the ability to manipulate, compare, and communicate language features. It also includes the ability to compare the grapheme–phoneme connection as well as the grammar and vocabulary and language structures within and across languages (Escamilla et al., 2014). It gives children the opportunity to compare languages and identify cross-language connections to develop biliteracy. The development of metalanguage can help learners notice similarities and differences in word and sentence structures within a language and across a second language.

Translanguaging presents a similar paradigm in the sense that children develop the ability to use common elements from across language as a foundation for mastering literacy in two languages. To acquire a full biliteracy, the development of the ability to use two languages constitutes one of the most important cognitive achievements of emerging and full bilingual students.

For a detailed analysis of a program to develop biliteracy, please consult the following sources: *Biliteracy from the start* from Kathy Escamilla et al. (2014), and *Teaching for biliteracy: Strengthening bridges between languages* (Beeman & Urow, 2013).

Concurrent Translation: *Concurrent translation* describes an archaic teaching strategy used in the 1970s and '80s in bilingual classrooms in which the teacher presented the lesson in the majority language (English) and provided translations in the second language, to be sure ELs understood the lesson. This method should not be used since ELs may pay attention to the information in their native language and disregard the English version.

Literacy Assessment

Assessment describes gathering data to make instructional or programmatic decisions. It can be done formally or informally. **Formal assessment** is conducted by using standardized norm-referenced and criterion-referenced tests. **Informal or ongoing assessment** is also done to monitor instruction and to determine if changes are needed.

Standardized test scores can offer teachers clues about the potential of students in their classrooms. However, teachers should not use standardized test results alone when making instructional decisions. The two standardized scores are norm-referenced and criterion-referenced:

1. **Standardized norm-referenced testing** measures a student's performance in skills and content. These tests are administered at set intervals using a professionally developed instrument. Norm-referenced tests compare the scores of students in other geographic locations using a ranking based on the students' performance. Results are reported based on **percentiles** or the Normal Curve Equivalent (NCE). For example, a student who scored 1300 on a test with a possible maximum of 1600 gets a percentile of 70, which means that 30% of the students who took the test on that day scored higher than the student. The same student can retake the test and score lower but get a higher percentile because the second group did not do as well as the first group. Norm-referenced tests compare the performance of students, not necessarily the mastery of specific standards or objectives. The Texas bilingual education law requires students to score in at least the 40th percentile to become candidates for reclassification as fluent English speakers.

These tests are commonly used to show achievement and predict performance in the classroom. Teachers must use the results with caution because the tests often fail to measure the potential of language-minority students and ELs. Teachers should also investigate how closely the test objectives reflect the state curriculum and use the information as a foundation to plan for initial instruction. Standardized tests can produce three scores to indicate the strengths and weaknesses of students.

   A. **Percentile rank** shows the percentage of the norm group that is at, over, or under the student's raw score. It does not show the percentage of correct items.

   B. **National Curve Equivalent (NCE) score** is like the percentile rank but uses raw scores to produce the results. This measure is used in educational research because it represents a better view of the students' achievement.

   C. **Grade equivalent score** measures how a student performed on grade-level expectations. Teachers must interpret this score cautiously. For example, if a child in third grade scores 4.1 on a test, it does not necessarily mean that the child is ready to enter fourth grade. It means the child is performing well above his or her third-grade peers.

2. **Criterion-referenced tests** indicate the level of mastery attained on specific standards or instructional objectives. Results are presented based on the percentage of questions answered correctly. Traditionally, a score of 70% is required to indicate mastery of the objectives. Teacher-made tests and state-approved tests like the State of Texas Assessment of Academic Readiness (STAAR) are criterion-referenced tests because they are designed to test the mastery of standards of the state curriculum. The bilingual education law in Texas requires students to pass the STAAR and the

Texas English Language Proficiency Assessment System (TELPAS) test to become candidates for reclassification as fluent English speakers.

3. **Informal assessment** is often linked to the concepts of **authentic**, **ongoing**, and **performance-based assessment**. This assessment is part of instruction and is done to assess students' progress. Results of informal assessment can be incorporated into teaching. Following are the most common informal assessments used in the language classroom:

A. **Observation** assesses a student's use of language in instructional settings. In this assessment, teachers observe and record such specific language features as the use of irregular and regular past tense verbs or the use of the vernacular when the standard version is required.

B. **Skill checklists** track the student's development by noting which skills have become part of the child's linguistic repertoire. Traditionally, the student's characteristics at each stage of language development are used to develop a checklist.

C. **Portfolio assessment** documents the child's progress as a language user. Traditionally, teachers collect samples of student work at each stage of the process. To assess language proficiency, teachers can collect taped oral performances as well as writing, including published works, in L1 and L2.

D. **Conferencing** gives teachers and students opportunities to discuss language development. Teachers meet students to assess their performance and identify activities and instruction needed for progress.

E. **Peer review** includes students in evaluations and builds their evaluative and interactive skills. For this approach to work, teachers must discuss the guidelines for evaluation with students. Traditionally, teachers use student evaluations when assigning grades.

F. **Self-assessment** empowers students by making them responsible for and reflective of their academic performance. Teachers can guide students to self-assessment using checklists, inventories, conferences, and portfolios. Self-assessment is a major component of student-centered practices and is among the foundations of the constructivist learning theory.

Formative and Summative Evaluation

Evaluation can be divided into two main components: formative and summative. **Formative evaluation** is an informal assessment done during instruction or immediately after it. The main purpose is to monitor and improve instruction and thus learning. It provides ongoing feedback that can be incorporated in the teaching-learning cycle. It is done as part of instruction and consists of observation, checklists, questioning, and teacher feedback to students.

ELs may need to be assessed using several assessment measures because of their level of English proficiency and cultural background. Teachers should provide multiple opportunities for ELs to produce what they know using alternative ways of assessing their knowledge and skills.

Summative evaluation is formal assessment used to document performance and for accountability purposes. Summative evaluation is conducted at specific times via such formal instruments as chapter tests, final exams, term papers, and projects. The TELPAS is a summative evaluation that documents the progress of ELs until they are reclassified as fluent English speakers.

Assessment Before Instruction—Learning About Students

Teachers can get valuable information about their students before the first day of class. Although this information should not be used to prejudge students, it can give teachers an idea of their students' needs and strengths. School records contain valuable information teachers can use to develop an overview of their students' potential and needs. By examining grades from previous years as well as results of standardized tests, health records, and other documents in the permanent school records, teachers can identify and prepare for some of the instructional, emotional, and medical needs of incoming students. As with any such information, teachers must be cautious when analyzing data about ethnic and linguistic minorities to avoid inaccurate interpretations as well as stereotyping.

State Achievement Testing Program

As part of the accountability system for educators in Texas, the state has a comprehensive assessment system overseen by the Student Testing Division of the TEA. Several tests required for each grade level in Texas are described here.

Kindergarten through Grade 2: Two key assessments evaluate the reading progress of students in kindergarten to grade 2: the Texas Proficiency Reading Inventory (TPRI), and the Tejas LEE (El inventario de lectura en español de Texas). Both tests are designed to identify early reading difficulties. The TPRI is given to students in the traditional English program, and the Tejas LEE is given to students in the bilingual or special language programs. The tests cover such skills as decoding skills, phonemic and phonological awareness, and reading comprehension.

Grades 3 through 12: The STAAR tests are administered from grades 3 to 12. The tests measure English reading and language arts and the content areas of the statewide curriculum. Table 5.7 shows the testing currently required in Texas, together with the new testing requirements of the 2015 ESSA legislation (TEA, 2016).

Table 5.7. Schedule of STAAR Examinations

Subjects	Texas	Federal Requirements (ESSA)
Mathematics	Grades 3–8 Spanish Version available for grades 3, 4, 5	Grades 3–8
Reading	Grades 3–8 Spanish Version available for grades 3, 4, 5	Grades 3–8
Writing	Grades 4 and 8 Spanish Version available for grades 4	
Science	Grades 5 and 8	High School
Social Studies	Grade 8	High School
End-of-Course Examination (EOC)	English I, II & III (optional) Algebra I & II, Biology, and U.S. History	

The Spanish versions of the tests are available in grades 3 through 6 (TEA, 2004). Students in the bilingual or special language programs can take the test in Spanish or English, depending on the recommendation of the LPAC. Satisfactory performance on the tests is required for grade promotion and to obtain a high school diploma.

End-of-course (EOC) examinations measure the statewide curriculum of certain high school courses (Algebra I, Biology, English II, and U.S. History) to ensure that high academic standards are being met. Satisfactory performance on EOC tests became an additional means for students to be eligible to graduate beginning in the 1998–99 school year.

Testing Accommodations

In addition to the traditional STAAR, the TEA has two online versions of the test embedded with support for ELs (STAAR L) and students in special education (STAAR A).

1. **STAAR L for English Learners**

The STAAR L is an online linguistically accommodated English version of the regular test for grades 3–8 and some end-of-course (EOC) examinations. The Language Proficiency Assessment Committee (LPAC) will determine whether the student qualifies to take this linguistically accommodated version of the STAAR examination. A rundown of linguistically accommodated testing (LAT) is presented in the next chapter.

2. **The STAAR Alternate 2 Assessment for Special Education Student**

The STAAR L is an online instrument designed to assess the academic performance of students with cognitive disabilities receiving special education services. This version of the test was designed for grades 3–8 and high school. The test is similar to the one followed in the traditional classrooms. However, multiple accommodations are available based on the disabilities of the learners. A list of accommodations for students receiving special education services are presented in the next chapter. For a detail analysis of the standards used for these tests, please go to the TEA Test Alternative Assessment 2 at http://tea.texas.gov/student.assessment/special-ed/staaralt.

Testing in Special Language Programs

In addition to the STAAR testing, students in special language programs comply with two additional assessments.

1. **Language proficiency testing** determines and documents language proficiency in L1 and L2 (English). When the test is not available in a student's native language, the English version is administered. Results of the tests are one criterion for making entry and exit decisions in the bilingual or ESL program.

2. The **Texas English Language Proficiency Assessment System (TELPAS)** was designed to comply with the accountability system required in the federal education legislation, currently the ESSA. The legislation requires that ELs be assessed yearly in English in all language skills: listening, speaking, reading, and writing. Students begin taking the TELPAS test in kindergarten and stop when they are exited from the bilingual or ESL program. The test for the early grades is different from that for later grades.

   • **Kindergarten to grade 1** — TELPAS consists of an observation instrument assessing the areas of listening, speaking, reading, and writing. This ongoing assessment is rated holistically and is based on classroom observation and student interaction.

   • **Grades 2 through 12** — for these grades, TELPAS consists of an online multiple-choice reading exam, a writing component assessed holistically, and a holistically rated component in the area's listening and speaking component, based the interaction of students in the classroom.

TELPAS is aligned with the state curriculum (TEKS) and the English Language Proficiency Standards (ELPS). It reports results according to composite ratings equivalent to four individual linguistic levels: beginning, intermediate, advanced, and advanced high.

Key Takeaways for Competency 003

1. Identify patterns and stages of literacy in L1 and L2 (i.e., developing phonemic awareness)

2. Make the classroom environment print rich plays an important role in developing literacy skills in L1 and L2.

3. Develop reading components early through activities (e.g., phonemic awareness, phonics, vocabulary, reading fluency, and reading comprehension).

4. Use language experience charts (i.e., connection between speech and print).

5. Develop writers (e.g., emerging writers, early writers and newly fluent writers).

6. Develop activities for each stage of writing (e.g., word families, onset and rime, journal writing).

7. Use formal and informal literacy assessments (e.g., norm-referenced, criterion-referenced, and other alternative assessments).

8. Know the state assessments used in Texas (see section in this chapter to review).

9. Make instructional modifications to deliver the statewide curriculum (TEKS) to students at different stages of literacy development in L1 and L2.

10. Support students affected by such personal factors as interrupted schooling, literacy status in L1, and literacy experience.

11. Teach language features that can create confusion among ELs: antonyms (opposites, like good–bad); homonyms (similar spelling and pronunciation but different meaning, like to, two, too); homophones (same pronunciation but different meaning, like *night* and *knight*); homographs (spelled the same way, like *fine*—sum of money, good or well, or a descripton of thickness); and acronyms (words formed from the initial letters of other words, like *radar*, *sonar*, and *laser*).

References

August, D., Carlo, M., Dressler, C., & Snow, C. (2005). The critical role of vocabulary development for English language learners. Learning Disabilities Research & Practice, 20(1), 50–57.

August, D. & Shanahan, T. (2006). Developing literacy in second-language learners: Report of the National Literacy Panel on language-minority children, and youth. Mahwah, NJ: Erlbaum.

Baker, C. (2001). Foundations of bilingual education and bilingualism (3rd Ed.). Clevedon, UK: Multilingual Matters.

Beeman, K. & Urow, C. (2013). Teaching for biliteracy: Strengthening bridges between languages. Philadelphia: Carlon Publishing.

Cummins, J. 1979. Linguistic interdependence and the educational development of bilingual children. *Bilingual education paper series*, vol. 3, no. 2. ERIC Document Reproduction Service No. ED 257 312.

Lapp, D., D. Fisher, J. Flood, and A. Cabello. 2001. An integrated approach to the teaching and assessment of language arts. In *Literacy assessment of second language learners*, eds. S.

Rollins Hurley and J. Villamil Tinajero, 1–24. Boston, MA: Allyn and Bacon.

Peregoy, S., and O. Boyle. (2017). Reading, writing, and learning in ESL: A resource book for K–12 teachers (7th ed.) New York: Pearson.

Morris, L & Rosado, L (2013) Desarrollo del Español para Maestros en Programas de Educación Bilingüe. Arlington, Texas: LM Company (Modified and Enhanced).

TEA (2016). STAAR Resources. Assessment Division. Retrieved from *http://tea.texas.gov/student.assessment/staar/*.

TEA (2007–2015) 19 TAC Chapter 128. Texas Essential Knowledge and Skills. Available from *http://tea.texas.gov/curriculum/teks/*.

TEA (2007–2006) STAAR Alternate 2 Resources. Available from *http://bit.ly/1GIBhFT*.

TEA (2007–2015) 19 TAC Chapter 128. Texas Essential Knowledge and Skills for Spanish Language Arts and Reading and English as a Second Language. Retrieved from *http://bit.ly/2ig154g*.

Content-Area Teaching in Dual Language Programs

This chapter addresses Competency 004—Content-Area Instruction—of the Bilingual Education Supplemental Exam (TExES 164). It also covers selected components of Competency 006 of the ESL Supplemental Exam (TExES 154) and strategies and the integration of language and content as well as the delivery of comprehensible content-area instruction in L2, including linguistic accommodation strategies.

COMPETENCY 004

The beginning Bilingual Education teacher has comprehensive knowledge of content area instruction in L1 and L2 and uses this knowledge to promote bilingual students' academic achievement across the curriculum.

Differentiating Instruction: Second-Language Proficiency

Teachers must understand the stages of L2 development to deliver linguistically appropriate content-area instruction for ELs. The literature suggests that ELs go through five stages of second-language acquisition: preproduction, beginning, intermediate, advanced, and advanced high. Teachers must use characteristics of students during these stages as a foundation for planning and assessing content-area instruction. The following sections provide an analysis of the abilities ELs exhibit in each stage of L2 development and describe how teachers should modify instruction to provide comprehensible input.

1. **Preproduction Stage (Silent and Receptive)**

Students in the preproduction stage have minimal oral and written comprehension and might be experiencing cultural and linguistic shock. This stage is often called the silent period of L2 acquisition because students usually remain silent while trying to make sense of the language and the classroom culture. They rely on their native language for communication and usually use non-verbal communication as well as visuals like drawing to communicate.

Educational Implications—Teachers should allow students to remain silent, but they must guide them to communicate using other forms of communication, including nonverbal. The following list shows some key strategies for students at this stage (Path to Literacy, n.d.):

- Use slow speech, repetition, as well as contextualizing key content words to help students master the content.

- Supplement instruction with visuals, concrete objects and other nonverbal means to enhance comprehension.

- Avoid forcing students to speak and instead engage them in communication by using contextualized instruction.

- Write key words on the board, explain their meaning, and guide students to copy them for their records.

- Encourage the use of visual clues and manipulatives to contextualize instruction and to make concepts cognitive accessible to the learners.

- Use multimedia to present concepts and model language.

- Use interactive dialogue journals so that students can encode concepts learned in class.

- Use choral reading to expose students to the intonation and rhythm of English.

- Introduce simple yes/no and either/or questions to provide a safe environment to students to venture into the new language. Questions for this level include: Do you drink orange juice? (yes, or no). Is your shirt/blouse green or white? (either/or). If students miss the question, teachers can guide them to the right answer.

- Create a relaxed environment to help students manage cultural and linguistic shock.

- Use commands, modeling, and other techniques from the Total Physical Response method to contextualize instruction and make content accessible.

- Establish a peer support system that pairs advanced students with students at the production stage.

2. **Beginning (Early Production Stage)**

Students at the beginning stage of L2 development communicate marginally via routine responses with memorized materials. They master routine greetings and responses. They produce discrete words and phrases but might not put them together coherently. They can also respond to questions with words and phrases using familiar vocabulary. Language interference from L1 is prevalent, affecting word usage, grammar, and pronunciation. Pronunciation is understood by sympathetic listeners who try to understand them. Students might have problems producing complete sentences. They communicate with simple sentences and with verbs usually in the present tense. They have problems understanding idiomatic expressions and how humor is communicated in the new language and culture.

Educational Implications—In terms of educational implications, teachers should continue using strategies from the total physical response and natural methods to deliver comprehensible input. To contextualize instruction, teachers should provide opportunities for active listening and use visual and concrete objects to contextualize instruction (i.e., functional vocabulary). Hands-on and group activities encourage students to support each other. Teachers should introduce idioms in contextualized situations and explain the intended meaning. Teachers also can engage students via the following strategies (Path to Literacy, n.d.):

- Organize games and role-playing activities that expose students to the language and culture in a low-anxiety environment.

- Use open-ended dialogues and discussions, accepting all contributions.

- Teach students how to access information from charts, tables, graphs, and other graphic organizers.

- Ask students to read news articles at home and bring them to class. Then guide students to share information about the article in small groups and in the whole class. Then ask students to exchange articles and guide them to read for more information.

3. **Intermediate Stage**

English learners at the intermediate stage of L2 development can initiate and sustain conversations about such familiar topics as home, school, friends, and family as well as their personal background. They can ask and answer questions in contextualized situations. Their oral communication then becomes more comprehensible, despite limited grammatical accuracy and language interference. They can produce short and isolated sentences as well as strings of sentences to convey the message.

Educational Implications—Teachers should continue providing contextualized instruction while avoiding direct correction in communication activities. If students communicate unintelligibly, teachers should ask for clarification or repetition. Corrective feedback should be given indirectly by modeling and using foreign talk (exaggeration). Instruction should begin with questions (yes/no and either/or) that require one-word answers until students are ready to produce responses that require more language input. In non-communication activities, teachers can highlight errors to let students self-correct. Teachers can also:

- Guide students to use the internet to find representations of concepts discussed in class. For example, students can search traditional videos or YouTube presentations that describe mathematics, social studies, and science. If the teacher is discussing the government of the United States, students can look for developmentally appropriate videos to represent key concepts of government.

- Develop learning centers where students can interact to find information about a topic.

- Conduct jigsaw activities that require students to find information about a component of a major topic. Teachers should organize students heterogeneously by language proficiency so that they can help each other. Ideally, the same group should have at least one advanced high, one intermediate, and one beginning. Then teachers can guide students to share information and understand topic.

- Read to students aloud, stopping to check for comprehension.

- Expose students to real-life situations that require English proficiency, such as completing forms and applications for employment or doing mock job interviews.

4. **Advanced Stage**

Students at this stage progress from sentence-level utterances to paragraph-length connected discourse. Their narratives and descriptions use present, past and future tenses. They can communicate about such concrete topics as family, travel, interests and personal background as well as events they have experienced or read about. They can express facts, report incidents, and make comparisons but may have difficulties supporting or opposing an opinion by using examples. Speaking will be more standard, but the learner may still experience language interference.

Educational Implications—Teachers should guide students in developing oral and written narratives and analyzing and correcting their own work. Teachers also should introduce and clarify the meaning of technical vocabulary from the content areas before guiding students to read or introduce content area information. Teachers must identify sounds that can cause language interference and help students polish pronunciation. Teachers can also use the following activities (Path to Literacy, n.d.):

- Guide students to engage in problem-solving activities. To accomplish that, guide students to identify and explain a problem, identify a possible solution, and defend it by using the information collected.

- Expose students to the components of storytelling and guide them to share a story with peers in small groups or the whole class.

- Organize panel discussions so that students can see a topic from different views.

- Guide students to write via process writing and then ask them to share what they have written with other students.

5. **Advanced High Stage**

Students at this level participate in most formal and informal conversations on topics connected to practical, social, professional, and abstract concerns. They can present an opinion supported by evidence. They can also hypothesize about abstract topics and provide description with native-like discourse strategies. They can converse with most native speakers, although idiomatic expressions still challenge them.

Educational Implications—Teachers should continue expanding academic vocabulary development and polishing pronunciation. Because fluency can be deceptive at this level, teachers should continuously check for comprehension. For dual-language students, emphasize cross-language components, including academic vocabulary common to the two languages (cognates) and common orthographic and grammar components. Teachers can also:

- Familiarize students with the use of electronic spell-check, thesaurus, and dictionaries.

- Help students recognize key literacy terms used in most narratives, such as antonyms, synonyms, homophones, homographs, prefixes, suffixes, and so on.

- Introduce strategies for note-taking so that students can record information during instruction.

- Use strategies for direct error correction, even during communication activities. Direct error correction is acceptable at this stage because students have a functional command of the language.

- Guide students to review and edit written work, with minimal support from the teacher.

Language and Content

Teaching the content areas to ELs present unique challenges. Teachers need to consider the cultural background of the students, as well as their language proficiency in English. They also have to take into account the type of language students bring to the learning process—informal versus formal. They also need to analyze how language background and vocabulary transfer can be used to improve content area mastery. Some of these considerations are discussed here.

Dichotomy of BICS and CALP

In addition to the stages of development, Cummins (1979) established a difference between social and academic language. He called these two distinct components the Basic Interpersonal Communication Skills (BICS) and the Cognitive Academic Language Proficiency (CALP). BICS comprises the social language children acquire after two to four years of exposure to a language. Face-to-face communication in highly contextualized situations characterizes the social language. Conversely, the CALP refers to the academic language children need to succeed in the mainstream English-only classroom. This proficiency takes four to seven years to develop. Mastery of the CALP facilitates the development of content areas like mathematics, science, and social studies.

The importance of social and academic language in instruction can be described through Cummins' comparison of cognitive-demanding and -undemanding as well as through the value of context to help the understanding of content. Figure 6.1 analyzes this connection. This figure is divided into two major components—cognitive-undemanding and cognitive-demanding tasks. It is further divided into context-embedded and context-reduced activities. Anything new for learners is cognitive-demanding, although some tasks might be cognitive-undemanding for native speakers, but they can be challenging for ELs. For example, listening to a radio newscast can be cognitive-undemanding for native speakers but cognitive-demanding for ELs because it requires students to rely solely on spoken words to identify the message. When students watch a newscast on television, they have a second vehicle of communication with visual images. The television show is thus more context embedded. If the television show adds captions, it becomes even more context embedded and even easier to comprehend. The original activity of listening to the radio was cognitive-demanding and context-reduced. When the visual and captions are added, the activity remained cognitive-demanding but was easier to understand because the content was contextualized with images and captions. Since we increased the context of the communication, the activity became easier for ELs.

Teachers of ELs must teach the state curriculum with the same rigor and intensity required of native English speakers. However, teachers can modify the instructional delivery and the use of strategies to make the content cognitively and linguistically accessible to ELs. Teachers make content accessible when they add context and when they use linguistic accommodations to deliver instruction. Figure 6.1 presents an overview of the interaction of context-embedded and context-reduced instruction, with implications for the need to develop academic vocabulary to make concepts accessible to ELs.

Figure 6.1. Roles of BICS and CALP in Academic Instruction

Cognitively Undemanding	
Social Language	
BICS	
A	C
Context-Embedded Language	Context-Reduced Language
Context-Embedded Language	Context-Reduced Language
B	D
CALP	
Academic Language	
Cognitively Demanding	

Vocabulary Transfer (Cross-linguistic Transfer)

Students literate in Spanish (L1) at a level commensurate with their grade placement bring strong word-recognition skills to English (L2). Because of the historical and linguistic connection between the two languages, they share vocabulary in the content areas. Many morphological affixes (prefixes, infixes, and suffixes) from the Greek and Latin languages are common to Spanish and English. Most of these affixes are used in such academic areas as science, law, fine arts, music, and mathematics. This connection results in the development of numerous cognates—words similar in two languages. The CALP that students need to succeed in the regular classroom can be delivered through the introduction of the prefixes and suffixes common to the two languages. When students develop a working knowledge of these common affixes, it becomes easier for them to recognize the multiple cognates across languages. Tables 6.1 and 6.2 present examples of affixes and words common to English and Spanish.

Table 6.1. English-Spanish Cognates

Greek Prefixes	Meaning	English	Spanish
anti-	against	Antifreeze	Anticongelante
anfi-	on both sides of, both	Amphibious	Anfíbio
auto-	self	Autobiography	Autobiografía
bio-	life	Biography	Biografía
demo-	people	Democracy	Democracia

Table 6.1. (continued)

Greek Prefixes	Meaning	English	Spanish
dys, dis	bad, disordered	Dysentery	Disentería
endo-	within	Endoscopy	Endoscopía
Eu-	good, well	Euphemism	Eufemismo
hyper-	over, excessive	Hyperactive	Hiperactivo
Meta-	changed, different, beyond	Metaphor	Metáfora
Latin Prefixes	**Meaning**	**English**	**Spanish**
Circum/n	around, on all sides	Circumference	Circunferencia
bi-	two	Bicycle	Bicicleta
extra-	additional	Extraordinary	Extraordinario
infra-	below, under	Infrared	Infrarojo
inter-	between, among	International	Internacional
Suffixes	**Meaning**	**English**	**Spanish**
-ible	able to be, able to	Flexible	Flexible
-or	a person who	Actor	Actor
-logy	study of	Biology	Biología
-ic	pertaining to, like	Volcanic	Volcánico
-ant	a person who	Arrogant	Arrogante

Besides the influence of Greek and Latin, the Arabic culture has influenced the development of English and Spanish. Table 6.2 presents a list of cognates from the Arabic language.

Table 6.2. Cognates from Arabic Origin

English Words	Spanish Words	English Words	Spanish Words
Alcohol	Alcohol	Gauze	Gasa
Alfalfa	Alfalfa	Gazelle	Gacela
Algorism	Algorismo	Giraffe	Jirafa
Alkaline	Alcalino/na	Jar	Jarra
Apricot	Apricot	Assassin	Asesino
Admiral	Almirante	Cork	Corcho
Fanfare	Fanfaria	Almanac	Almanaque
Pants	Pantalones	Lemon	Limón
Borax	Bórax	Guitar	Guitarra
Amalgam	Amalgama	Macrame	Macramé

To take advantage of cross-linguistic transfer, teachers must guide students to identify affixes and cognates common to both languages. However, teachers must remember that knowledge of a given word in a language does not guarantee that the student will recognize similar words in the second language. Recognition of cognates must be taught explicitly. In addition to teaching the recognition of cognates and false cognates, teachers should also use methods that integrate content and language instruction.

The Integration of Language and Content

When teachers understand the linguistic background of their students, they are ready to integrate language with content instruction to make instruction accessible to ELs. Methods that accomplish this integration of language and content include the Integrated Content-based Methods, Sheltered Instruction, and the Cognitive Academic Language Learning Approach (CALLA). These methods not only introduce language in conjunction with content but also introduce students to multiple learning strategies to help ELs master the content areas and English.

Integrated Content-Based Method (ICB)

Target Population: This method can be used at any grade but requires basic proficiency in the target language.

ICB instruction combines language instruction with the teaching of content, instead of teaching language to develop English proficiency as a prerequisite for learning the content. Traditionally, this integration is done through thematic units. Thematic planning adds a new dimension for language learners because it uses the teaching of a common theme as a foundation for teaching content-based academic language. This approach requires planning because teachers must develop content and language objectives for each day of the thematic unit. In this method, an ESL-certified teacher or a teacher with specialized language preparation provides instruction. The content area and the language standards are combined to develop instruction to meet the content standards while also developing language skills. With contextualized instruction, students can follow the scope and sequence of the content standards with the same rigor as the students who speak native English. Thematic instruction allows the simultaneous integration of content areas, eliminating the artificial separation of these subjects in traditional classrooms. It also integrates the language skills of listening, speaking, reading, and writing and thus expedites the language development of ELs.

Characteristics: Learning language through grade-level instruction provides students with the academic language needed to succeed academically. Integrating content and language objectives also minimizes content-area boundaries. Because each subject uses the same themes, students get multiple opportunities to see how diverse disciplines use similar vocabulary words and concepts. Herrera and Murry (2016) suggest the following key strategies for the integration of language and content:

1. Introduction of key vocabulary:

   - Introduce the vocabulary of the unit before starting instruction. Use visuals and graphic organizers to be sure the students' cultural background does not interfere with their understanding of new concepts.

   - Teach content vocabulary as well as the high-frequency words that will be used during the unit. Post the technical vocabulary and the high-frequency words on word walls and review them periodically during the unit.

   - Use visuals to clarify the meaning of English words, expressions, and concepts that can confuse ELs.

2. Clarify and build upon background knowledge:

   - Use Know-Wants to Know-Learned (KWL) charts or ask questions to explore students' prior knowledge.

   - Make sure concepts and vocabulary in the first language do not interfere in the acquisition of new concepts. For example, the concept of a river might differ for people across the world, i.e., a small stream of water used for swimming versus a river that allows navigation of large vessels.

   - Provide a list of vocabulary words with definitions and content explanations so that students can use it as a reference to clarify meaning and learn new concepts.

3. Use collaborative strategies:

   - Use cooperative-learning strategies to guide students to share information while practicing language skills.

   - Guide students to communicate in group formats, including pairs, small groups, and whole group.

   - Organize linguistically heterogeneous grouping so that advanced students can serve as models to support the language development of students with lower proficiency.

   - Foster interdependence and accountability among group members so that everyone is responsible for meeting instructional objectives.

4. Use authentic and culturally relevant activities to integrate literacy in the content areas:

   - Use academic activities in which students use multiple language skills to achieve content area objectives, i.e., listening, speaking, reading, and writing.

- Organize problem-solving activities in which students work with real issues and real sources. For example, teachers can guide students to develop a project to identify the conditions of rivers in a city and how to improve those conditions.

5. Increase the use of graphic organizers to provide visual and organizational support to students:

   - Describe and identify the purpose of most common graphic organizers to categorize and organize information (e.g., KWL charts, T-charts, Venn diagrams, and so on)

   - Teach students how to interpret tables, graphs, and charts.

6. Develop learning centers:

   - Organize the classroom into learning centers linked to key concepts related to thematic units.

   - Provide written instruction to use the centers, including how to rotate from centers.

7. Practice assessment strategies:

   - Use informal and ongoing assessment practices as part of learning and use the assessments to modify instruction.

   - Use project-oriented activities to assess the performance of students in a group.

   - Use assessment tools, including learning logs, to evaluate content mastery and literacy development.

   - Provide rubrics to discuss expectations and use the same tool for assessment.

   - Use summative assessment (the end of the lesson or project) to determine mastery of the intended objectives.

Sheltered English Instruction

Target Population: This method can be used at any grade but requires basic proficiency in the target language to maximize benefits.

Sheltered English (SE) is an instructional approach first designed for ELs at intermediate and advanced language proficiency. This method has had many names. The most popular labels include sheltered English, content-based English language teaching (CELT), specially designed academic instruction in English (SDAIE) (Genzuk, 2009), and Sheltered Instruction Observation Protocol (SIOP) (Echevarría, Vogt, and Short, 2013).

The main purpose of SE is to make content comprehensible to ELs (Echevarría, Vogt, and Short, 2013). Like the ICB, content area instruction is integrated with language concepts, and the goal is to develop academic language. English learners get grade-level content instruction with linguistic accommodations to make it cognitively accessible to them. From the psychological standpoint, ELs are also "sheltered" from the pressure of competing with native English speakers. In Texas, grade-level content objectives come from the state curriculum—the Texas Essential Knowledge and Skills (TEKS). The language objectives come from state-approved English Language Proficiency Standards (ELPS). The integration of language and content requires teachers to know the stages of language development as well as strategies to scaffold instruction. Traditionally, an English monolingual content specialist with specialized professional development in ESL can deliver instruction in this method.

Characteristics: The key feature of this method is that it can deliver comprehensible input to ELs. To deliver the comprehensible input, content instruction is linguistically simplified through contextualized instruction, visual aids, hands-on activities, guarded or controlled vocabulary, and graphic organizers. Some of the linguistic accommodation and strategies used to make content comprehensible are as follows:

- Control the length and complexity of the sentences. Children respond better to short and simple sentences.

- Avoid the use of idiomatic expressions. If the teacher cannot avoid it, idioms should be presented with an explanation.

- Introduce technical and content vocabulary before the lesson.

- Use repetition, restatement, and paraphrasing to clarify concepts.

- Control the speed of delivery and use different intonation to emphasize the importance of concepts.

- Supplement oral presentations with diagrams, graphic organizers, and manipulatives to make content easier to understand.

- Use role-playing and more capable peers to help understanding.

- Scaffold instruction using questioning strategies to support ELs in their effort to master content and language.

- Organize content around themes and develop thematic units.

- Develop and use content objectives to determine the language skills needed to master content.

- Monitor instruction and change instruction based on results.

- Develop multicultural activities and events to validate cultural and linguistic diversity.

The SIOP Model

The Sheltered Instruction Observation Protocol (SIOP) is among the most widely used models of Sheltered English. Researchers Jana Echevarría, Mary Ellen Vogt, and Deborah Short developed the model under the auspices of the Center for Research on Education, Diversity & Excellence (CREDE) and the U.S. Department of Education (Center for Applied Linguistics, n.d.). The eight key components for lesson planning with this method are:

1. **Lesson Preparation**

Teachers develop the content and language objectives for the lesson and post them where students can see them. Teachers guide students to read the statement of content objectives for the lesson. Teachers select supplementary materials for instruction and organize activities to deliver instruction. They adapt content delivery to the students' language proficiency. Teachers use activities to make content comprehensible, i.e., graphic organizers, hands-on, manipulatives and real objects, and word walls.

2. **Building Background**

During initial instruction, teachers build the students' background knowledge. Teachers identify students' prior knowledge and link it to new information. They also introduce key vocabulary.

3. **Comprehensible Input**

During this part of the lesson, teachers modify the delivery of instruction to make it cognitively and linguistically accessible to students. Strategies for this segment include the use of short sentences and a slower rate of speech as well as avoiding idioms. Teachers also use modeling, demonstrations, visuals, and body language to make content clear. Teachers also explicitly introduce learning strategies and let students apply them.

4. **Strategies**

This component uses learning strategies to make content linguistically accessible to students. These strategies include the use of questioning strategies to promote learning as well as appropriate wait time, social interaction, and grouping.

5. **Interaction with Students**

Teachers organize the classroom to let students interact. The teacher organizes the class to allow multiple grouping to support content and language mastery. Appropriate wait time is established to allow English learners time to understand questions and process information.

6. **Practice and Application**

Students use concrete materials and manipulatives to facilitate understanding of content. They also use activities that integrate all language skills.

7. Lesson Delivery

Teachers present the statement of objectives so that students understand the purpose of the lesson. Students get linguistic accommodations and scaffolding to make content accessible to all learners. Teachers establish appropriate pacing to be sure all students can understand content and show mastery of the content.

8. Review and Assessment

Before closing instruction, teachers review the key vocabulary and concepts of the lesson. They check for understanding and reteach as needed. Teachers do a summative assessment to determine whether the content objectives were mastered.

Cognitive Method

Target Population: This method can be used at any grade but requires basic proficiency in the target language to maximize benefits.

The **Cognitive Academic Language Learning Approach (CALLA)** model for ELs was developed by Anna Chamot and Michael O'Malley (1994) and was designed to promote English language development through the content areas. The CALLA method is based on cognitive psychology in which students actively participate in learning—constructing their own knowledge. Chamot and Robbins (2005) say the main principles and objectives of this instructional method are to:

- Use prior knowledge, including language and culture, as a foundation for new learning.

- Learn the grade-level content knowledge and academic language needed to succeed in the mainstream classroom.

- Develop metalinguistic awareness and critical literacy to succeed in school and life.

- Use instructional strategies and study skills to achieve academic and learning independence.

- Develop collaborative skills and use them to improve language and content knowledge.

- Evaluate their learning methods and identify ways to become independent learners.

The model uses three main learning strategies for teaching language and content: metacognitive, cognitive, and social/affective (Chamot & O'Malley, 1994) as well as a new strategy identified as cross-linguistic (Jiménez, García, and Pearson, 1995). The explicit teaching of these strategies is a key part of the CALLA method.

Metacognitive strategies have been described as ways to conceptualize how learning takes place and how people regulate their learning. In this strategy, learners develop an understanding of their cognitive abilities and how they learn best. Learners think about the complexity of individual tasks and then select appropriate strategies to address the challenge (Hacker, Dunlosky, and Graesser, 2009). Metacognitive strategies include three key components: organization and planning for learning, self-monitoring, and self-evaluating (Reiss, 2005). An analysis of these three strategies follows:

Planning and organizing

- Identify the task and determine how much is already known.

- Make inferences based on current knowledge and determine whether predictions were correct.

- Make associations between current and new knowledge.

- Set goals and track short- and long-term assignments with a due date.

- Segment long tasks into smaller and more manageable parts.

- Select strategies to accomplish tasks.

- Identify strategies to facilitate learning different content.

- Preview a text to identify how it presents the information.

- Provide information about the topic to be discussed in class.

Monitor and Identify Problems

- Check progress of tasks completion and assess each completed learning task.

- Determine whether the information is understood. If problems surface, identify reasons.

- Check for comprehension.

- Continue conducting self-assessment and progressing toward content mastery.

- Assess weaknesses and strengths in learning the content.

- Use self-questioning to determine how well the concepts are understood.

- Complete graphic organizers to organize and categorize the information each lesson presents.

Self-Evaluation

- Assess how well the assignment or task has been carried out.

- Identify the best strategy for learning content.

- Use self-questioning techniques to be sure the new information makes sense.

- Keep a learning log to show what has been learned and what needs more development.

- Allow students time to check their comprehension of topics, using grouping, i.e., small groups and pairs.

- Provide time for students to talk with one another about the strategies they use to master concepts. For example, how did they solve a word problem in mathematics?

- Guide students to talk about the strategies they use to learn information.

Cognitive strategies use mental and physical manipulation of information to master content. These strategies can improve understanding as well as increase retention of information and process new information. These self-regulated strategies enable learners to be more flexible in how they process information, solve problems, or perform tasks. Cognitive strategies used to work with English learners include:

- Paraphrase information to make it easier to understand or to isolate the main idea or key concepts.

- Classify and organize information as a way of remembering. Guide students to do the same in groups or individually.

- Provide students with an outline of the information to be covered in class. Guide them to use the outline as a framework for note-taking and to summarize each component listed.

- Read aloud information about new concepts and guide students to discuss the information in small groups. Then recapitulate the key points with the whole class.

- Guide students to create visual images of the concepts to help remember the concepts.

- Create charts and graphs to synthesize and present content. If students can summarize and synthesize information, they most likely will remember it.

- Preview a story before reading it and identify the purpose for reading.

- Engage students in brainstorming about the concepts to be covered in class. Brainstorming can guide students to match what they know with the upcoming new information.

- Use mnemonic devices or acronyms for remembering.

- Model scanning instead of reading word for word for information.

Social/affective strategies describe activities in which students learn from each other or by interacting in groups using socially mediated learning.

Common strategies to support English learners are included in the following lists.

Students may:

- Seek support from peers to complete an assignment or study for a test.

- Use self-talk to improve confidence to complete the task.

- Use peer modeling and support as a learning strategy.

- Work in pairs or groups to complete projects and solve problems.

- Observe and interact with people from diverse backgrounds to learn about them.

Teachers may:

- Encourage the whole group to share the responsibility for the learning of individual members.

- Guide students to ask clarifying questions. For ELLs, provide key words or phrases to present the questions, i.e., Could you give an example? Could you explain that process again?

Most students benefit from explicit instruction in learning strategies. ELLs need help to cope with the dual demands of learning a new language as well as academic content. The CALLA approach is designed to help ESL students succeed in school by providing transitional instruction from ESL programs to grade-level English content instruction.

Cross-linguistic Learning Strategies

The use of cross-linguistic learning strategies is the newest researched component of the CALLA method. These strategies maintain that second-language learners bring linguistic and cognitive information that provides a foundation for learning. Bilingual and English learners use specific strategies to manage and decipher the new language and culture. These strategies previously were included under the label of metacognitive strategies. However, these strategies are so unique to bilingual people that they are now separated from this generic label.

Some cross-linguistic strategies are used to survive the beginning stages of second-language acquisition, while others such as code-switching are used continuously—even when learners become fully bilingual. A unique cross-linguistic strategy typically used to survive the initial stages of second language acquisition is simultaneous language processing. In this strategy, beginning and intermediate ESL students use knowledge of their first language as a foundation for coping with communication demands in the language they are developing. A simple question, "What are you having for lunch today?" is an example. For native English speakers, this question is simple and can be answered without much thinking. However, for beginner English learners, this question represents a challenge that might require them to use L1 as a foundation for understanding the question and responding to it. The mental process used to answer this question can be summed in the following steps:

1. The question is presented in the second language. The students use the context of the communication with visual clues to acknowledge the communication. At this point, English learners might have a clue of the meaning of the question.

2. To be sure their understanding of the question is correct, ELs then mentally translate the question into their first language. The translation in the native language is used to comprehend the question so that an oral response can be formed mentally.

3. When the learners understand the question, they then can think about the appropriate answer.

4. The learner mentally prepares a response in the native language.

5. In the last step, the learner translates the response into the second language to reply.

Figure 6.2 presents a visual sequence of the steps language learners used to answer the question.

Figure 6.2. Simultaneous Language Processing

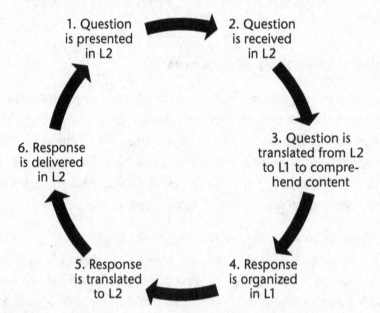

To maintain the flow of communication, these mental processes are done continuously in a few seconds. When students master the second language, they will simplify the processes and develop the automatic responses typical of native or fluent English speakers.

English learners follow strategies that are unavailable to monolingual learners. These strategies include:

- Analyze the elements that transfer from L1 and L2 as well as those that might cause language interference.

- Use code-switching (alternate use of L1 and L2) for communication as well as for performing specific speech acts, i.e., for emphasis, exclusion, ethnic identification...

- Use concurrent translations to help monolingual peers. Bilingual students are often exposed to a task beyond their cognitive development when they are required to translate for parents in adult-like situations.

- Paraphrase or translate information from L2 to L1 to remember and corroborate it.

- Recognize and use cognates (similar words in two or more languages) and false cognates (faulty association of words in two languages).

- Take notes in the first language to ensure comprehension.

- Alternate use of language to meet specific situations. For example, bilingual students might use English in school and in formal settings, use the native language at home, and both languages in the company of bilingual people.

Most ELs might use these strategies subconsciously, but the strategies can be taught explicitly to help students academically. ELs need help to cope with dual demands of learning a new language as well as academic content. The CALLA method is designed to help ESL students succeed in school by providing transitional instruction from ESL programs to grade-level English content instruction. The CALLA method follows a five-step instructional cycle described as follows:

The Instructional Cycle of the CALLA Approach

The instructional component of the CALLA approach is divided into five phases—preparation, presentation, practice, evaluation, and expansion (Chamot & O'Malley, 1994).

1. Preparation

Teachers provide students with an overview of the lesson, including a simplified description of the content and language objectives. Teachers then guide students to share prior information about the topics of the day. Through reflection, students are also guided to establish cognitive connections between the two sets of data.

2. Presentation

Teachers introduce the new information with visuals and demonstrations as well as hands-on activities. They check for comprehension and clarify key concepts. Teachers also introduce strategies to master the concepts.

3. Practice

Teachers guide students to use hand-on activities to practice and apply new concepts. This phase includes a lot of linguistic accommodation to simplify the lesson. Groups are organized to continue analyzing the content and to facilitate content and language modeling via peer or group support.

4. Evaluation

Students are guided to apply one key metacognitive strategy—assess their understanding of the concepts presented in class and determine whether they are achieving the content objectives. They can also be guided to conduct assessments of each other's work, often with a rubric.

5. Expansion

Students are guided to integrate new knowledge into what they already knew. Teachers also encourage students to link this knowledge to situations in their lives.

The ICB, SIOP and CALLA methods are the most widely used instructional methods to teach language development for English learners. These three methods use content instruction as a foundation for teaching language. The integration of language and content objectives is the most effective way to teach English learners.

Instructional Strategies

State education agencies (SEAs) identify national content and language standards, and local education agencies (LEAs) develop scope and sequence to introduce them. For English learners, SEAs must use differentiated instructional strategies for students at different stages of language and cultural development. Delivering these standards might require teachers to modify instruction using linguistic accommodations and other strategies to make language and content cognitively accessible to ELs. Moreover, SEAs and educators must understand the stages of language development to identify the accommodations needed to improve learning of the content. An analysis of the national content and language curriculum standards and a description of the stages of language development follows.

Standards for Content and Language

Content Curriculum

The United States does not have a national curriculum. SEAs develop their own curriculum standards. However, these standards vary from state to state, creating inconsistency across the nation. In response to this inconsistency, a group of state governors and commissioners of education in 2010 began an initiative to standardize the curriculum nationwide. The result of their initiative was the Common Core State Standards (CCSS).

The Common Core developed the standards for mathematics, English language arts, and literacy in the content areas. Forty-two states, the District of Columbia, four territories (the American Samoan Islands, Guam, Northern Mariana Islands, and the U.S. Virgin Islands), as well as the U.S. Department of Defense Education Activity have adopted this set of standards. The only states or territories that have chosen to follow their own standards are Texas, Virginia, South Carolina, Oklahoma, Indiana, Nebraska, Alaska, and Puerto Rico (Common Core State Standards Initiative, 2017). The Common Core Standards and selected state curricula are currently used to provide instruction in schools at the national level.

National Language Standards for ESL: The development of national standards for ESL results from the work of three national organizations—the Teaching of English to Speakers of Other Languages (TESOL) association, the World Class Instructional Design and Assessment (WIDA), and the English as a New Language Standards (ENLS) of the National Board for Professional Teaching Standards (NBPTS). TESOL is an international association dedicated to the teaching of English (2010). WIDA is a national educational consortium of state education departments whose mission is to identify appropriate standards for the teaching of English learners in K–12 settings (WIDA Consortium, 2012). NBPTS (2010) is a nonprofit national association that has developed professional standards to address the needs of English learners. These English as a New Language Standards define excellence in 12 areas of professional practice for teachers. The NBPTS also has a rigorous voluntary national teacher certification program. These associations provide the framework for the development of ESL standards in all 50 states, the District of Columbia, and the U.S. territories. Besides these national organizations, individual states have developed similar standards to teach English as a second language.

English Language Proficiency Standards (TEA, 2014): The new federal Every Student Succeeds Act (ESSA) and the Texas law (19 TAC, Chapter 74) require teachers with one or more ELs in K–12 classrooms to plan and incorporate English Language Proficiency Standards (ELPS) in the teaching of content. This mandate requires teachers to develop content objectives derived from the state curriculum and language objectives derived from the ELPS. Teachers thus must study the content objectives and identify the language skills ELs need to master the objectives. To do this, the content objectives should be communicated to the learners, sequenced to facilitate comprehension, and modified to meet the language proficiencies of the learners. These components must be developed commensurate with identified levels of linguistic proficiency of the learner to ensure that the student learns the knowledge and skills of the required curriculum. The ELPS is also aligned with the standards of the *Texas English Language Proficiency Assessment System* (TELPAS) summative assessment required of all ELs in Texas grades K–12. TELPAS documents the progress of ELs in listening, speaking, reading, and writing. The state uses linguistic data to derive a composite score to document annual growth and makes it part of a formula to reclassify ELs as fluent English proficient.

The Texas ELPS legislation requires school districts to comply with the following key provisions:

1. Provide an integrated second language instruction in the content areas.

2. Make the content cognitively and linguistically accessible to ELs.

3. As part of instruction in the content areas, build the academic language students need to succeed academically.

4. Modify instruction based on the proficiency levels of students.

5. Integrate quality on-grade level content instruction with the proficiency levels of students.

6. Modify instruction to target the language skills needed to master the content.

7. Provide explicit instruction on learning strategies to master content, which in turn makes students aware of their own learning. These strategies include:

    A. Use of prior knowledge and the schema of the learner as a foundation for new knowledge.

    B. Strategies to monitor oral and written communication.

    C. Use of strategic learning techniques to facilitate mastery of the content areas.

    D. Introduce strategies to facilitate content mastery, i.e., concept-mapping, drawing inferences, memorizing, and compare and contrast.

    E. Introduce ways and formats for requesting clarification and support from peers and the teacher as well as other strategies to help master the content.

Strategies to Integrate Language Arts with Content in L1 and L2

EL teachers use other approaches besides the ELPS to support ELs in mastering the content areas. Key approaches used for all students include the Whole Language Approach, Language across the Curriculum, and other strategies to facilitate content mastery.

Whole Language Approach: The main principle of the whole language approach (WLA) is that language should not be separated into discrete components or skills but instead experienced as a system of communication. Authentic text is preferred, especially literature and the use of language for personal communication. The concepts and strategies associated with the WLA include the following:

- Reading aloud to children

- Journal writing

- Sustained silent reading

- Higher-order thinking skills

- Student choice in reading materials

- Frequent conferences between teachers and students.

Besides the WLA, teachers can use other strategies to teach the state curriculum (the TEKS) at the grade and level of complexity required of English native speakers. Some strategies and tools to facilitate content mastery are described here.

Scaffolding originally described how adults support children in their efforts to communicate in L1. The same concept is used to facilitate language and content development for ELs. The term alludes to the provisional structure that provides support during the construction of a building and that is eliminated when the structure is complete. Following this analogy, ELLs get support to make content cognitively accessible to them until they achieve L2 mastery, and when this is done, the language support is eliminated.

Graphic organizers are used to contextualize instruction and to show relationships using visuals. The most common graphic organizers used with students are listed below:

- A semantic web or tree diagram shows relationships between main ideas and subordinated components.

- A timeline presents a visual summary of chronological events.

- A flowchart shows cause-effect relationships. It also can show steps in a process, such as the process and documentation needed to complete graduation requirements.

- The Venn diagram is a system of two circles placed in juxtaposition to show similarities and differences between two components. For example, teachers can use the diagram to show similarities and differences between two versions of Cinderella. Teachers thus can compare the traditional European version with one of the multiple versions available in the world literature, such as the Native American version (The Indian Cinderella) or the African (Mufaro's beautiful daughters: An African tale).

The SQ4R

The SQ4R is a study strategy in which the learner is engaged during the whole reading process. This strategy lets students learn and remember information read and is ideal when students begin reading to obtain content information. The acronym stands for **survey**, **question**, **read**, **reflect**, **recite**, and **review** (Tomas & Robinson, 1972). Readers engage in the following with this strategy:

(S) **Survey**—Survey material and make predictions by generating questions. Readers examine the headings as well as the captions under pictures or graphs to make predictions and generate questions.

(Q) **Questions**—Generate questions from the predictions. Readers are guided to examine how much they know about the topic to generate questions as well as determine the purpose of the reading.

(1R) **Read**—Readers read actively to answer questions. Students read the text to find answers to the generated questions.

(2R) **Reflect**—Readers reflect and monitor their comprehension as they write a summary of the information.

(3R) **Recite**—Students recite key terms and concepts.

(4R) **Review**—Readers review key concepts to determine how much they have internalized about the concepts learned through the reading.

Reciprocal teaching (Palincsar & Brown, 1984) is an instructional activity originally designed for struggling readers. However, it can be used to learn content information. Students work in small groups in which one student serves as the teacher. The teacher first models the strategy and then lets students assume the instructor's role. As part of the activity, the teacher engages students in a dialogue about parts of a text. The dialogue is structured to elicit four strategies:

1. Summarize the content of a passage.

2. Ask a question about the main idea.

3. Clarify difficult parts of the content.

4. Predict what comes next.

When students serve as the teacher, they create a peer support system to help others to master the content. This strategy also guides students to go beyond recalling information and engage the group in high-order thinking.

Planning Content and Language Instruction

Modern methods to teach English learners use the integration of content areas with language arts as the foundation for planning instruction. For ELs, this approach takes the integration a step further. The instruction is modified and integrated with learning strategies to provide ELs with the language skills needed to master the content areas.

The integration of content and language can be done by following these steps:

1. Teachers or curriculum developers study the content standards (state or national). Based on those standards, they develop the content objectives. See the content standards taken from the Texas curriculum and analyze the resulting instructional objective:

   Content Standard

   (6) (A) Geography. The student is expected to: (A) identify major land forms and bodies of water, including each of the continents and each of the oceans, on maps and globes (TEA, 2011).

   Content Objective

   After a video presentation of the continents and the oceans of the world, the learner will accurately identify the location of the continents and the oceans on a flat representation of the Earth.

2. Teachers then study the requirements of the content objectives and identify the language skills needed to master the objectives. Traditionally, content objectives require specific knowledge in one or more language skills, i.e., listening, speaking, reading and writing. Since learners will get most of the information through a narrative presented on the video, the key language skill needed to derive information is listening comprehension. Thus, the teacher must modify instruction to guide ELs to gather information from listening and through visuals.

3. When teachers identify the most important language skills needed, they analyze the state or national ESL standards and identify the most applicable language objective. See the applicable language standard and the resulting language objective from the English Language Proficiency Standards (ELPS) used in Texas.

   Language Standards—listening comprehension
   Cross Curricular: 2. (F) listen to and derive meaning from a variety of media such as video . . .

   Language Objective
   With the use of guiding questions given before a video presentation, the learner will view and study the video presentation to derive specific content information.

   In this case the language objective requires teachers to provide a set of questions so that ELs can view the video with a specific purpose and find answers to the given questions.

4. Curriculum developers and teachers must identify the specific language accommodations and strategies needed to support students at different levels of language development—beginner, intermediate, advanced and advanced high.

Here's an example of accommodations to master the language objective (El Saber Enterprises, 2009):

Beginning:

- Allow students to view the video multiple times during the learning center time.

- Provide note-taking guides.

- Use additional visuals and nonverbal communication to ensure comprehension of content.

Intermediate:

- Let students work in pairs or small groups.

- Stop the video and repeat, clarify or paraphrase key points.

- Let the students see the same part again.

Advanced:

- Let students work in pairs or small groups.

- Provide a bilingual glossary and guide students to review the vocabulary needed to understand the video.

- Let students see the whole video and then check for understanding. Identify areas that were unclear and show those parts again, stopping to check understanding.

Advanced high:

- Provide written directions so that students understand the task.

- Introduce specific techniques to enhance comprehension, i.e., note-taking, listening to the gist, questioning techniques...

- Guide students to search for videos with similar information to corroborate understanding.

Lesson Planning

Implementation Activity: Use the information about the content and language objectives and develop a lesson plan following a traditional format for one. Identify the appropriate grade level based on the complexity of the topic. Once the lesson plan is completed, compare your plan with the one that follows. Study the resulting lesson.

Table 6.3. Lesson Planning—Integration of Language and Content

1. **Grade:** Second grade

2. **Subject:** Social studies—geography

3. **Topic:** Location of the continents and oceans of the world

4. **Content Standard:** TEKS: (6) (A) Geography (TEA, 2011). The student is expected to: (A) identify major landforms and bodies of water, including each of the continents and each of the oceans, on maps and globes.

5. **Content Objective:** After a video presentation of the continents and the oceans of the world, the learner will accurately identify the location of the continents and the oceans on a flat representation of the Earth.

6. **Language Standard:** ELPS: Cross Curricular: 2. (F) listen to and derive meaning from a variety of media such as video (TEA, 2014).

7. **Language Objective:** With the use of guiding questions given before a video presentation, the learner will view and study the video to derive content information.

8. **Academic Vocabulary:** Sea, ocean, country, continent, island, cartography, and Mercator projection

9. **Materials:** Mercator projection of the world, individual maps for students, world globe, and a video.

10. **Instructional Delivery:**

    A. **Introduction/Focus:**

    1) Teacher will use a world globe to guide students to find the location of North America, the United States and Texas (focus).

    2) Teacher will use the information to identify the oceans that border the United States and introduce the concepts of continents and oceans.

    3) Teacher will indicate that today, students will watch a video to identify the names and locations of the continents and oceans of the world (statement of objectives).

(continued)

Table 6.3. Lesson Planning—Integration of Language and Content (continued)

B. **Procedure:** The teacher will:

1) introduce the video on the continents and the oceans of the world.

2) provide a set of questions and ask students to use the information from the video to answer the questions. Provide language support to ELs to be sure they understand the objective and the questions provided (accommodations).

3) pair advanced ELLs with students of lower language proficiency to create a peer-support system to answer the questions (accommodations).

4) guide students to identify the continents on a wall map.

5) guide students to identify the oceans that border each of the continents of the world.

C. **Evaluation**

Provide students with a small map of the world and individually, guide them to identify the location of the continents and the oceans of the world. Informally assess the performance of students and re-teach as needed.

D. **Re-teaching**

Using a globe of the world, guide students to spin the globe, point to a location, and identify the continent. Students should continue spinning the globe until they identify every continent and ocean.

E. **Closure**

Guide students to name and rank each of the continents by size. Guide them to name the oceans that border each of the continents and identify the largest and the smallest continent.

F. **Expansion**

Take students on an imaginary trip around the world by ship. Ask them to select a major country on one of the continents and trace the route from their city of residence to their destination, identifying the ocean(s) and the sea(s) that they must navigate to reach their destination.

The integration of language and content in lesson planning and the teaching of content with linguistic accommodations make the content accessible to English learners. This also helps ELs develop the academic language needed for further cognitive development in the mainstream classroom.

General Linguistic Accommodations to Differentiate Instruction

Some strategies to differentiate content area instruction for ELs are listed here (El Saber, 2009).

1. Create a buddy system to help beginning and intermediate students.

2. Modify instruction to let students work in pairs or small groups.

3. Segment instruction into smaller and more manageable skills.

4. For shy students or those who lack the language proficiency to communicate academic needs, develop visual symbols to communicate the need for additional guidance as well as to show understanding.

5. Allow ELs to use electronic or traditional bilingual dictionaries or glossaries to clarify the meaning of terms and concepts.

6. Allow students more time to process information and prepare appropriate responses to it.

7. Record written textbook materials from the content areas and let students listen to it while following the written version.

8. Provide students with a list of concepts and ideas to be covered during the week and guide them to study it before the lessons. As needed, use the native language to provide clarification of concepts.

9. Introduce note-taking strategies so that students learn what is important. As part of the activity, ask students to share their notes with classmates in small groups.

10. Use nonverbal communication, including facial expressions, as well as repetition and exaggerated intonation patterns to identify important information.

11. Use visuals, videos, and other technology to revisit and expand information provided in class.

12. Model standard pronunciation and emphasize the pronunciation of word endings, which is a problem Spanish-speaking ELs face.

13. Avoid the use of idiomatic expressions and figures of speech that might confuse students new to the language. If the expression cannot be replaced, describe its meaning within a context.

14. Avoid contractions initially because they can create communication problems but be sure to introduce them in class.

15. Develop word walls and document the key vocabulary of the content areas. Ask students to copy and define key vocabulary in their notebooks or on electronic devices.

16. Provide students with formats to make class presentations, defend opinions, disagree with peers, and so on.

Assessing the Content-Area Curriculum

Texas has a statewide K–12 curriculum—Texas Essential Knowledge and Skills (TEKS). The TEKS covers language arts and the content areas. Both language and content are assessed periodically through the STAAR program. Beginning in third grade, students must take examinations to insure they are mastering the state curriculum. Reading and mathematics are assessed in grades 3 to 8, writing in grades 4 and 8, science in grades 5 to 8, and social studies in grade 8. In high school, the state requires students to pass end-of-the year examinations in English, algebra, biology, and U.S. history. See chapter five for a list of required examinations for grades 3 to 12.

Technically, the STAAR assessment program affects the curriculum and the emphasis placed in the content areas. Since English language arts and mathematics are assessed in grades 3 to 8, these areas get the greatest K–8 curricular emphasis. Such areas as science, assessed in grades 5 and 8, and social studies, assessed in grade 8, are not deemed as important as the mathematics and language arts component of the state curriculum. Teachers thus must insure that the quality of instruction in these content areas is strong enough to compensate for the lack of emphasis in the K–8 curriculum. This is especially important for ELs who struggle with this lack of emphasis and face linguistic challenges with instruction in those content areas.

Considerations When Assessing ELs

When assessing ELs, teachers must account for language development of the student to be sure that language issues do not interfere in the assessment. Assessment techniques that can be used to minimize the impact of language issues include the following:

- Structured observation using a checklist to record the intended behaviors.

- Such dramatizations as role-playing or Readers' Theatre to assess students in less stressful situations.

- Drawings to represent ideas and support demonstrations or explanations.

- Fill-in-the-blanks with word banks that provide a list of words from which students choose the correct words to fill in the blanks.

Teachers should keep the following points in mind when performing assessment on ELs:

- Be aware that students from culturally diverse backgrounds might express knowledge and understanding differently.

- Recognize that ELs might understand concepts but lack the vocabulary to express their knowledge.

- Organize informal and formal activities to monitor student growth.

- Organize one-on-one interviews with ELs to explore information they bring to their learning.

- Identify the permissible linguistic accommodations to support students during tests.

Linguistic Accommodated Testing (LAT) for ELs

Linguistic accommodations are available to minimize the impact of language in content area assessment. Accommodations are based on the linguistic needs of the learners and granted with the approval of the Language Proficiency Assessment Committee (LPAC). For the examinations in mathematics, science and social studies, the state allows the following accommodations (TEA, 2016):

1. Use of a bilingual dictionary.

2. Extra time to complete the test on the same day.

3. Clarifications in English of word meanings.

4. Read aloud text (online version).

Additional linguistic accommodations and considerations that can be made in offering help to ELs are listed as follows:

1. Accommodations must not include explanations or definitions of mathematical terminology, concepts, or skills.

2. Test administrators may be allowed to translate words, phrases, or sentences as requested by students.

3. Students may request that words, phrases, and sentences be read aloud.

4. Spanish-speaking students in grades 3 through 6 may refer to both the English and Spanish test items to enhance linguistic accessibility.

5. Bilingual, monolingual, and ESL dictionaries may be used to find the meanings of appropriate words.

6. Test administrators may prepare written bilingual glossaries of appropriate words.

7. Test administrators may prepare written and pictorial ESL glossaries of appropriate words.

8. Test administrators may simplify the language used in certain test questions (in writing or orally).

9. Pictures and gestures may be used by the test administrator to illustrate the meanings of appropriate words.

Besides these linguistic accommodations, ELs with special needs might qualify for additional modifications to address specific disabilities.

Accommodations for Students in Special Education

TEA allows accommodations for students with cognitive development disabilities and students with disabilities that can affect their ability to show content mastery using the traditional STAAR examination (TEA, 2007–2016). Accommodations for students receiving special education include the use of:

1. highlighted images on text for emphasis and to improve visibility.

2. text with images or real objects of the presented concept.

3. strategies to show the relationship of images and text.

4. bolding images on text.

5. enlarged images or larger and bold text.

6. magnification devices to improve visibility.

7. Braille labels to images or whole text to help visually impaired children.

8. description of images to students with visual impairments.

9. pictures to represent key words while presenting verbal directions.

10. calculators, manipulatives, or mathematical tools to guide students to the response.

11. fraction pieces, geometric shapes, number lines, charts, money, base-ten blocks to make mathematics more concrete and solve problems.

12. personal timers set based on the needs of the learner.

13. a color-coded system, visual schedules, or handwritten reminders to guide students to complete tasks.

Key Takeaways for Competency 004

- The Texas Education Agency reports the language growth of ELs using a composite score that includes all four language skills to report language growth among ELs—beginning, intermediate, advanced and advanced high. This information is reported to the federal government to comply with the accountability system required by law.

- Interdependence of L1 and L2—cognitive and academic language proficiency in L1 has a positive effect in the acquisition of cognitive and academic proficiency in L2.

- Sheltered-Instruction uses content instruction to promote language development.

- SIOP and CALLA are two of the most popular methods to integrate content objectives and learning strategies for ELs.

- Texas as well as the new federal education legislations require teachers with English learners in their classroom to incorporate English Language Proficiency Standards (ELPS) in content area instruction.

- Texas allows linguistic accommodations for ELs taking required state assessments (STAAR).

- The Language Proficiency Admission Committee (LPAC) and the Admission Review and Dismissal (ARD) regulate and approve testing accommodations for ELs getting bilingual and special education services.

- Teachers of ELs must modify instruction to make it cognitively accessible to all students. They must develop lesson plans following the state curriculum with the integration of the ELPS to facilitate content mastery among ELs.

- The influence of the Greek, Latin, and Arabic languages have affected the development of Western languages, including English and Spanish. These languages thus have multiple common concepts and vocabulary words (cognates).

- EL teachers must differentiate instruction to address multiple needs of students in the four identified language levels.

- ELs new to the language experience cultural and linguistic shock. These students thus might go through a silent period to cope with the new language and culture.

- During the silent period, teachers should not force students to talk, but they must guide students to communicate via any other means of communication, including nonverbal.

References

Center for Applied Linguistics (CAL) (n.d.). The SIOP Model. Online *http://www.cal.org/siop/*.

Chamot, A. U., & O'Malley, J. M. (1994). The CALLA handbook: Implementing the cognitive academic language learning approach. New York: Addison-Wesley Publishing.

Chamot, A. U. & Robbins, J. (2005). The CALLA Model: Strategies for ELL Student Success Workshop for Region 10 New York City Board of Education New York, NY. Retrieved from *http://jillrobbins.com/calla/CALLAHandout.pdf*.

Common Core (2010). State Standards Initiative. Improving America's Students for Success. Online *http://www.corestandards.org/*.

Cummins, J. 1979. Linguistic interdependence and the educational development of bilingual children. *Bilingual education paper series*, vol. 3, no. 2. ERIC Document Reproduction Service No. ED 257 312.

El Saber Enterprises (2009). Flip into success: ELPS at a glance. Dallas, TX *www.elsaberenterprises.com*.

Echevarría, J., Vogt, M. & D. Short, D. (2013). Marking content comprehensible for English language learners: The SIOP model. Boston, MA: Pearson.

Genzuk, M. (2009). Specially designed academic instruction in English (SDAIE) for language minority students. University of Southern California, Center for Multicultural Research, research series. Online *http://www.usc.edu/dept/education/CMMR/SDAIE/SDAIE_Genzuk.pdf*.

Hacker, D. J., Dunlosky, J. & Graesser, A. C. (2009.). Handbook of Metacognition in Education (Eds.). New York: Routledge.

Herrera, S. & Murry, K. G. (2016). Mastering ESL/EFL methods: Differentiated instruction for culturally and linguistically diverse students (3rd ed.). Boston: Pearson.

Jiménez, R., García, G., & Pearson, P. (1995). Three children, two languages, and strategic reading: Case studies in bilingual/monolingual reading. American Educational Research Journal, 32, 67–97.

National Board for Professional Teaching Standards (NBPTS) (2010). English as a New Language Standards (2nd Ed.). Online *http://www.nbpts.org/sites/default/files/documents/certificates/nbpts-certificate-emc-enlstandards.pdf*.

Palincsar, A. S. & Brown, A. (1984). *Reciprocal Teaching of Comprehension-Fostering and Comprehension Monitoring Activities*. Cognition and Instruction, 1(2), 117–175.

Path to Literacy (n.d.). Resources for students who are blind or visually impaired. Retrieved from *http://www.pathstoliteracy.org/typical-language-development-and-second-language-acquisition*.

Reiss, J. (2005). Teaching content to English language learners: Strategies for secondary school success. White Plains, NY: Pearson.

TESOL (2010). Standard for the Recognition of Initial TESOL Program in P-12 Teacher Education. Online *http://tea.texas.gov/curriculum/teks/*.

Texas Education Agency (2014) 74.4 English language proficiency Standards. Online *http://ritter.tea.state.tx.us/rules/tac/chapter074/ch074a.html#74.4*.

Texas Essential Knowledge and Skills (TEKS) (2011). Chapter 113. Texas Essential Knowledge and Skills for Social Studies Subchapter A. Elementary. Online *http://ritter.tea.state.tx.us/rules/tac/chapter113/ch113a.html*.

TEA (2016) Linguistic accommodations allowed for students taking STAAR. Retrieved from *http://www4.esc13.net/uploads/bilingual/docs/2016_Ling_Accom_ELLs_(1).pdf*.

Tomas, E., & H. Robinson. 1972. *Improving reading in every class: A source book for teachers*. Boston: Allyn and Bacon.

World-Class Instructional Design and Assessment-WIDA (2012). English language professional development standards. Online *https://www.wida.us/*.

TExES Bilingual Education Supplemental (164) Diagnostic Test

Also available at the online REA Study Center (*www.rea.com/studycenter*).

The TExES Bilingual Education Supplemental (164) test is computer-based, so we strongly recommend that you take our online practice tests to simulate test-day conditions and to receive these added benefits:

- **Timed testing conditions**—Gauge how much time you can spend on each question.

- **Automatic scoring**—Find out how you did on the test, instantly.

- **On-screen detailed explanations of answers**—Learn not just the correct answer, but also why the other answers are incorrect.

- **Diagnostic score reports**—Pinpoint where you're strongest and where you need to focus your study.

ANSWER SHEET

1. Ⓐ Ⓑ Ⓒ Ⓓ
2. Ⓐ Ⓑ Ⓒ Ⓓ
3. Ⓐ Ⓑ Ⓒ Ⓓ
4. Ⓐ Ⓑ Ⓒ Ⓓ
5. Ⓐ Ⓑ Ⓒ Ⓓ
6. Ⓐ Ⓑ Ⓒ Ⓓ
7. Ⓐ Ⓑ Ⓒ Ⓓ
8. Ⓐ Ⓑ Ⓒ Ⓓ
9. Ⓐ Ⓑ Ⓒ Ⓓ
10. Ⓐ Ⓑ Ⓒ Ⓓ
11. Ⓐ Ⓑ Ⓒ Ⓓ
12. Ⓐ Ⓑ Ⓒ Ⓓ
13. Ⓐ Ⓑ Ⓒ Ⓓ
14. Ⓐ Ⓑ Ⓒ Ⓓ
15. Ⓐ Ⓑ Ⓒ Ⓓ
16. Ⓐ Ⓑ Ⓒ Ⓓ

17. Ⓐ Ⓑ Ⓒ Ⓓ
18. Ⓐ Ⓑ Ⓒ Ⓓ
19. Ⓐ Ⓑ Ⓒ Ⓓ
20. Ⓐ Ⓑ Ⓒ Ⓓ
21. Ⓐ Ⓑ Ⓒ Ⓓ
22. Ⓐ Ⓑ Ⓒ Ⓓ
23. Ⓐ Ⓑ Ⓒ Ⓓ
24. Ⓐ Ⓑ Ⓒ Ⓓ
25. Ⓐ Ⓑ Ⓒ Ⓓ
26. Ⓐ Ⓑ Ⓒ Ⓓ
27. Ⓐ Ⓑ Ⓒ Ⓓ
28. Ⓐ Ⓑ Ⓒ Ⓓ
29. Ⓐ Ⓑ Ⓒ Ⓓ
30. Ⓐ Ⓑ Ⓒ Ⓓ
31. Ⓐ Ⓑ Ⓒ Ⓓ
32. Ⓐ Ⓑ Ⓒ Ⓓ

33. Ⓐ Ⓑ Ⓒ Ⓓ
34. Ⓐ Ⓑ Ⓒ Ⓓ
35. Ⓐ Ⓑ Ⓒ Ⓓ
36. Ⓐ Ⓑ Ⓒ Ⓓ
37. Ⓐ Ⓑ Ⓒ Ⓓ
38. Ⓐ Ⓑ Ⓒ Ⓓ
39. Ⓐ Ⓑ Ⓒ Ⓓ
40. Ⓐ Ⓑ Ⓒ Ⓓ
41. Ⓐ Ⓑ Ⓒ Ⓓ
42. Ⓐ Ⓑ Ⓒ Ⓓ
43. Ⓐ Ⓑ Ⓒ Ⓓ
44. Ⓐ Ⓑ Ⓒ Ⓓ
45. Ⓐ Ⓑ Ⓒ Ⓓ
46. Ⓐ Ⓑ Ⓒ Ⓓ
47. Ⓐ Ⓑ Ⓒ Ⓓ
48. Ⓐ Ⓑ Ⓒ Ⓓ

DIAGNOSTIC TEST

TIME: 2.5 hours

48 multiple-choice questions

In this diagnostic test, you will find examples of test questions similar to those you are likely to encounter on the TExES Bilingual Education Supplemental test. Read each question carefully and choose the best answer from the four possible choices. Mark your responses on the answer sheet provided on page 150.

1. Martín is a middle school advanced second language learner. He produced this non-standard statement that got his teacher concerned: "Teacher, this center is worser than the other." Based on this speech sample, this student is

    A. overgeneralizing grammatical rules.

    B. experiencing language interference.

    C. applying the concepts from L1 to L2.

    D. imitating the speech sample of native English speakers.

2. Transitional bilingual education (TBE) is the program of choice for most school districts. This program is identified as a subtractive and early-exit program. Identify the rationale for the popularity of this program.

    A. Extensive research supports the program's effectiveness.

    B. The program promotes the development of biliteracy.

    C. The program allows the early reclassification and exiting of students.

    D. The program promotes the maintenance of both languages.

3. One of the key features of the Coral Way Elementary program in Dade County, Florida, was which of the following?

   A. The program was the first non-compensatory modern dual language program in the United States.

   B. The program was designed to teach English to Cuban refugees.

   C. The program was developed as a political propaganda machine against communism.

   D. The program represents an example of subtractive bilingualism.

4. In 1975 Congress passed the Individuals with Disabilities Education Act (IDEA). One key provision of this legislation is the use of strategies to address individual needs of students in school. To address these needs, school districts began requiring the use of Individualized Education Plans (IEP) and the implementation of _____ to deliver instruction.

   A. differentiated instruction

   B. a policy to require schools to use formal instruments to access student progress

   C. a policy to gather input from parents and guardians

   D. English Language Proficiency Standards (ELPS)

5. The developmental bilingual education (DBE) program was established as an alternative to the transitional bilingual education (TBE) model. These two programs may look similar, but they have one key difference. The DBE program is

   A. a remedial program that promotes the maintenance of L1 and L2.

   B. a late-exit program designed to maintain L1 and L2.

   C. an early-exit program designed to promote English and Spanish development among ELs.

   D. a program designed to reclassify students as fluent English speakers early in the process.

6. Jana is a new EL going through the silent stage of second language acquisition. After two weeks in school, she still refuses to communicate orally. What strategies can the teacher use to address the needs of students at this stage?

    A. Avoid forcing students to speak but engage them in communication by using contextualized instruction.

    B. Supplement instruction with visuals, concrete objects and other nonverbal means to enhance comprehension.

    C. Encourage the use of visual clues and manipulatives to contextualize instruction and to make concepts cognitive accessible to the learners.

    D. Options A, B, and C

7. In the last decade, two-way dual language programs have received support from mainstream groups. The goal of the programs is to promote biliteracy. However, the programs are most popular because they

    A. allow the maintenance of L1 and L2.

    B. allow the inclusion of native English-speaking children.

    C. are supported by the U.S. Department of Education.

    D. are grounded in solid scientific research.

8. Knowledge about phonemic awareness and syllabication is a prerequisite for the development of English

    A. reading.

    B. writing.

    C. speaking ability.

    D. listening comprehension.

9. What is the key disadvantage of the pullout approach to teach ELs?

   A. Children do not want the program because they feel embarrassed about placement in the ESL program.

   B. Children may feel uncomfortable spending most of the time in mainstream classrooms.

   C. Children can fall behind academically when they are pulled out for ESL instruction.

   D. Children might be unable to learn English with this approach.

10. The cases that promoted the signing of the Equal Education Opportunity Act (EEOA) of 1974 were which of the following?

   A. *Brown v. Board of Education of Topeka, Kansas,* and *Castañeda v. Pickard*

   B. *Keyes v. School District 1(Denver),* and *Lau v. Nichols*

   C. *ASPIRA v. New York City Board of Education,* and *Rios v. Reed*

   D. *Plyler v. Dow,* and *U.S. v. Texas*

11. The theory that best describes how the bilingual child organizes information in the brain is

   A. the common underlying proficiency.

   B. the separate underlying proficiency.

   C. the separate balloons theory.

   D. basic interpersonal communication skills.

12. Which strategy can be used to assess reading comprehension for students who are not proficient readers?

   A. Drawing inferences

   B. Graphic organizers

   C. Written reflections

   D. Oral retelling of the story

13. At least three main variables affect language acquisition: sociocultural factors, language development, and academic development. Which of the following identifies the most important sociocultural factors that can affect the acquisition of a second language in the United States?

    A. Self-esteem and the socioeconomic status of the native English-speaking groups

    B. The perceived social and psychological distance between the groups

    C. Prejudice against the new group and the economic impact of social programs for ELLs

    D. Past injustices committed against the new group as well as the district's dropout rate

14. English words of Latin origin are easier to comprehend for Spanish-speaking ELs because

    A. Latin is a language of prestige in the world.

    B. English comes from the Latin.

    C. Spanish is a Romance language.

    D. Spanish has a strong connection to Greek.

15. To ensure cognitive growth and academic success in the second language, students should

    A. be exposed to a culture-free curriculum.

    B. be exposed to the importance of racial and linguistic harmony.

    C. be allowed to reach the threshold level in L1.

    D. become fully assimilated to American life and the English language.

16. Identify one of the key characteristics of the native language acquisition process.

    A. It is a process that begins and ends with formal schooling.

    B. It is acquired subconsciously in contextualized and meaningful situations.

    C. It is learned in meaningful situations with the use of direct corrective feedback from adults and caregivers.

    D. It is taught deductively in a supportive environment.

17. Ms. Blanchard uses a strategy with her fifth grade students to guide them to monitor their comprehension as they read independently. She instructs students to stop and check whether they understand the main ideas before moving to the next section. This comprehension practice fosters which of the following?

A. Metacognition

B. Fluency

C. Decoding

D. Vocabulary

18. Ms. Villegas has a class of beginner and intermediate English learners. Identify the strategies that can be used to support students at these stages of development.

A. Provide direct corrective feedback to improve oral communication.

B. Provide contextualized instruction and avoid direct error correction in communication activities.

C. Engage students in activities that require extensive written and communication responses.

D. Options A, B, and C

19. According to concurrent research, ELs generally go through specific stages of second-language acquisition. These stages are preproduction, early production, speech emergence, and intermediate and advanced fluency. Identify the stage in which students begin understanding basic written information accompanied by concrete objects and based on prior experiences.

A. Preproduction

B. Early production

C. Speech emergence

D. Intermediate and advanced fluency

20. Effective approaches for teaching English as a second language are

    A. student-centered and communication-driven.

    B. sequenced based on the complexity of the grammatical structures and are teacher-controlled.

    C. geared toward grammaticality with little emphasis on communication.

    D. teacher-centered and multicultural in nature.

21. Identify the statement that best represents the rationale for implementing initial reading instruction in the student's native language.

    A. Reading skills are transferable from L1 to L2.

    B. Reading skills are identical in L1 and L2.

    C. Reading skills are confusing for ELs.

    D. Reading skills affect the cognitive process in bilingual students.

22. Marcos is a 5-year-old student in the process of first language acquisition. He often produces such statements as "This lollipop is the bestest, Mom." Based on this speech sample, this child is

    A. applying language rules.

    B. experiencing language interference.

    C. applying the concepts from L1 to L2.

    D. imitating the speech sample of cartoons on television.

23. Mr. Bollinger conducted a jigsaw activity with his fifth grade bilingual students. As part of this activity, he divided the class in groups of six students and asked them to research subcomponents of a common topic. Once the information was gathered, he asked students to come back to the group to share the information and write a summary of the main topic. What might be the main linguistic benefit of this type of activity?

    A. Students are required to use language to achieve a common goal.

    B. Students are required to write to complete an assignment.

    C. Students have the chance to work independently.

    D. Less capable students can rely on others to do their work.

24. Identify the most appropriate evaluation techniques that promote self-directed learning for ESL students.

   A. In the writing samples of beginner ELs, discuss the source of the problem and allow students time to determine the necessary correction(s).

   B. In activities designed to polish the English pronunciation of advanced students, record their speech electronically and allow enough time for them to evaluate their own performance.

   C. In communication activities, provide immediate and specific feedback, emphasizing the areas in which improvement is needed.

   D. In communication activities, provide direct feedback and guide students to produce Standard English.

25. Soledad is a middle school Latino student who was born and raised in South Texas. She grew up in the barrios (Latino enclaves), where Spanish and English are used consistently. She functions and communicates well in bilingual and bicultural environments. However, this year she is experiencing problems in science and social studies. She often complains that the language in books differs from the language she knows. Which component of the language is she lacking?

   A. Basic interpersonal communication skills (BICS)

   B. Cognitive academy linguistic proficiency (CALP)

   C. Phonology and syntax

   D. English for special purposes (ESP)

26. English and Spanish have multiple cross-linguistic connections. Identify the components that transfer from one language to the other.

   A. The derivational and inflectional morphemes

   B. The pronunciation of the vowel system

   C. The derivational morphemes and root word from the Greek and the Latin

   D. Options A, B, and C

27. Identify the statement that best describes the similarities between the pronunciation of English and Spanish consonant blends.

    A. Spanish lacks consonant blends, while English has a large number of them.

    B. Unlike Spanish, English has multiple and unique consonant blends (clusters) with *s* in the initial position.

    C. Spanish has five consonant digraphs.

    D. Options A, B, and C

28. English learners at the advanced and advanced-high stages of English development

    A. might still experience L1 interference.

    B. use their first language as a foundation for mastering English.

    C. need continuous guidance to polish English features.

    D. Options A, B, and C

29. The key English feature(s) that can affect English pronunciation for Spanish-speaking ELs is/are which of the following?

    A. Spanish does not have the concept of long and short vowel sounds.

    B. The grapheme-phoneme correspondence of English can be deceptive.

    C. Spanish does not have the concept of vowel digraphs.

    D. Options A, B, and C

30. Which of the following creates an additional syllable when it occurs in a word?

    A. A diphthong

    B. A hiatus

    C. A triphthong

    D. A dieresis

31. Which of the following is the main advantage of using content-based programs to teach language and content to ELs?

    A.   Instruction in these programs can be adjusted to suit ELs from diverse linguistic backgrounds.

    B.   ELs obtain grade-level content instruction through the use of linguistic accommodations.

    C.   ELs can use their native language as a foundation for mastering the second language.

    D.   Explicit language instruction can be eliminated from their instructional program.

32. What is the purpose of using the orthographic accents and the dieresis in Spanish?

    A.   To identify important words in the language

    B.   To identify words of foreign origin

    C.   To identify words that deviate from Spanish pronunciation rules

    D.   To help students learn the rules of pronunciation in Spanish

33. From the phonological perspective, what is the common feature of the following set of words?

could	tomb	ache	school	calm

    A.   The words are borrowed from a foreign language.

    B.   The words contain medical terms.

    C.   The words present spelling challenges for children new to the language.

    D.   The words contain silent letters.

34. Under Texas law, school districts must offer bilingual education services if

    A.   a school has an enrollment of 20 or more ELs in need of services.

    B.   the school district has an enrollment of 20 or more ELs.

    C.   the district has an enrollment of one or more ELs with legal U.S. residency.

    D.   the district has an enrollment of 20 or more ELs at the same grade level with a common native language.

35. What are the similarities between the Language Proficiency Assessment Committee (LPAC) and the Admission Review and Dismissal (ARD)?

    A.   Both are mandated by the Federal Bilingual Law.

    B.   Both are mandated by the Individuals with Disabilities Education Act (IDEA).

    C.   The committees regulate admission and dismissal to the bilingual and special education programs, respectively.

    D.   Both committees should have at least one parent, two teachers, and an administrator.

36. In the last few years, the two-way dual language programs have received public support in the United States. The main reason for this popularity is because the program

    A.   allows the maintenance of L1 and L2.

    B.   allows the inclusion of children from mainstream groups in the program.

    C.   has been endorsed by the U.S. Department of Education.

    D.   is grounded on solid scientific research.

37. What was the key contribution of the Lau Remedies to the education of ELs in the United States?

    A.   It started English as a second language (ESL) programs to address the needs of ELs.

    B.   It forced the U.S. Congress to enact dual language legislation.

    C.   It established the criteria for the implementation of special language programs for ELs.

    D.   It guided state legislators to enact English-only legislation.

38. The key distinction between the one-way and the two-way dual language program is the

    A.   language goal of the programs.

    B.   academic goal of the programs.

    C.   student population served.

    D.   percentage of language distribution in the programs.

39. One of the most effective strategies or methods for students in the preproduction stage of language development is the total physical response (TPR). Besides this command-based approach, teachers can promote language development by

    A. using direct teaching instruction on the structure of the language.

    B. modeling the language and contextualizing instruction through the use of concrete objects.

    C. using questions that call for one short answer, including yes/no and either/or questions.

    D. using questions that call for open-ended answers.

40. Identify the statement that best describes differences between English and Spanish vowel digraphs.

    A. English has multiple vowel digraphs, while Spanish has three.

    B. English has three main vowel digraphs, while Spanish has none.

    C. Spanish and English have multiple vowel digraphs.

    D. Spanish does not have vowel digraphs, while English has a large number of them.

41. Identify the statement that best represents the connection between reading and writing.

    A. Reading and writing skills develop concurrently rather than sequentially.

    B. Formal reading instruction should precede writing.

    C. Reading and writing develop sequentially and in a structured manner.

    D. Reading and writing should be postponed until children are completely fluent in the second language.

42. The identification of syllables in Spanish literacy is vital because

    A. Spanish is a syllabic language.

    B. Spanish has good grapheme-phoneme correspondence.

    C. syllabication is one of the principles of phonemic awareness.

    D. syllables are the foundation for teaching Spanish reading.

43. Identify the key single event that added the largest number of non-English speaking minorities to the United States.

    A. The Human Rights Act 1974

    B. The annexation of the American Southwest

    C. The Spanish-American War of 1898

    D. Options A and C

44. When assessing the academic achievement of ELs, teachers have to take into account the

    A. stages of language development of the learners.

    B. elements that transfer from L1 to L2.

    C. native cultures of the learners.

    D. Options A, B, and C

45. The current Texas bilingual education and special language programs legislation mandates and/or allows which of the following programs?

    A. Bilingual education from kindergarten to upper elementary

    B. Transitional bilingual education in middle school and high school

    C. Dual language instruction in K–12

    D. Options A and C

46. When planning instruction for ELs in Texas, teachers are required to:

    A. Use the curriculum standards developed by individual school districts.

    B. Use the curriculum standards of the state.

    C. Use the content area standards legislated for the nation.

    D. Use the content area standards developed by textbook developers.

47. The primary goal of a home language survey is to determine

    A. whether children qualify for the one-way and two-way dual language programs.

    B. whether parents have the linguistic background needed to support their children in school.

    C. whether further screening is needed to determine placement in a special language program.

    D. Options B and C

48. Bilingual students have access to instructional strategies not commonly available to monolingual learners. These strategies include codeswitching and which of the following?

    A. Paraphrase or translate information from L2 to L1 to remember and corroborate it.

    B. Identify and use cognates to improve vocabulary development in both languages.

    C. Analyze the elements that transfer from L1 to L2 as well as those that might cause language interference.

    D. Options A, B, and C

DIAGNOSTIC TEST
ANSWER KEY

1.	A.	17.	A.	33.	D.
2.	C.	18.	B.	34.	D.
3.	A.	19.	C.	35.	C.
4.	A.	20.	A.	36.	B.
5.	B.	21.	A.	37.	C.
6.	D.	22.	A.	38.	C.
7.	B.	23.	A.	39.	B.
8.	A.	24.	B.	40.	D.
9.	C.	25.	B.	41.	A.
10.	B.	26.	C.	42.	D.
11.	A.	27.	B.	43.	B.
12.	D.	28.	D.	44.	A.
13.	B.	29.	D.	45.	D.
14.	C.	30.	B.	46.	B.
15.	C.	31.	B.	47.	C.
16.	B.	32.	C.	48.	D.

DIAGNOSTIC TEST
ANSWER EXPLANATIONS

1. **A.** The correct answer is (A). When a student overgeneralizes language structures, including the use of the comparative in the example ("worser" for "worse"), the student is applying the regular use of the comparative (*er*) to an exception to the rule. This overgeneralization is typical to all students, including ELs. The provided information does not support possible language interference (B and C). Most English native speakers in middle school have eliminated this overgeneralization, and option (D) can thus be ruled out.

    Competency 002: First- and Second-Language Acquisition and Development

2. **C.** The correct answer is (C). Students in the TBE program are exited from the program after two to three years. Current research suggests that dual language programs, not the TBE (A), provide the best opportunity for ELs to achieve academic parity with native English speakers. Because of the TBE program's goal and short duration of three to four years, it does try to maintain both languages, and thus no biliteracy is developed (B).

    Competency 001: Foundations of Bilingual Education

3. **A.** The correct answer is (A). The Coral Way Elementary program in Florida was a dual language program for Cuban refugees in the 1960s. It was designed to maintain English and Spanish, not to teach English only (B). The new program was design to help Cuban children in their adjustment to U.S. schools, not necessarily as political propaganda against communism (C). The program was additive (not subtractive) in nature because it aimed at maintaining the two languages (D). Most of the refugees were middle class in Cuba, but it was the first model of non-compensatory dual language program.

    Competency 001: Foundations of Bilingual Education

4. **A.** The correct answer is (A). The key principle of differentiated instruction is the adjustment of instruction to address the linguistic and cognitive needs of the children, as well as their levels of readiness for the required instructional objectives. Option (B) is incorrect because using only data from formal assessment to deliver appropriate instruction is too limited in scope. Using input from parents and guardians (C) can generate valuable information, but not necessarily to deliver instruction. Using ELPS as part of content area instruction is a required practice for English learners; however, its use is only one of the components needed to develop differentiated instruction.

    Competency 004: Content Area Instruction

5. **B.** The correct answer is (B). The developmental bilingual education program is an enriching, additive, late-exit program of five to six years and is designed to promote bilingualism. The

program is neither remedial (A) nor early exit (C). It is not designed to reclassify students early (D). On the contrary, the program is identified as late-exit.

Competency 001: Foundations of Bilingual Education

6. **D.** The answer is (D). Options (A), (B), and (C) all describe portions of the process teachers should use to allow children to remain silent while also engaging in communication.

Competency 004: Content Area Instruction

7. **B.** The correct answer is (B). Two-way dual language programs allow the participation of native English speakers. Since the programs are not only for language minorities, the public has a better perception of them. They allow the maintenance of both languages (A) and are grounded in some form of research (D), but these are not the main reasons for the popularity of the programs. The U.S. Department of Education does not have an official policy about the use of specific programs (D) to meet the needs of ELs.

Competency 001: Foundations of Bilingual Education

8. **A.** The correct answer is (A). The ability to connect letters with sounds (phonemic awareness) and syllabication (phonological awareness) constitute the two key principles for successful initial reading instruction. These two components may have a degree of influence in the development of writing (B), but not as strong as compared with reading. In most cases, children master these skills through reading and transfer them to writing. Phonemic awareness and syllabication have minor influence in the development of speaking (C), and listening comprehension (D) compared with reading skills.

Competency 003: Development and Assessment of Literacy and Biliteracy

9. **C.** The correct answer is (C). In the pullout system, children are removed from the classroom to get English language development for a determined period of the day. While getting ESL instruction, the students will miss instruction in the content areas and can fall behind academically. Options (A) and (B) describe elements that may be true but fail to explain the key disadvantage of the pullout program. Option (D) is incorrect because students in the pullout program can develop some levels of English proficiency, but they do so at the expense of learning content.

Competency 001: Foundations of Bilingual Education

10. **B.** The correct answer is (B). Both the *Keyes* and *Lau* rulings dealt with discriminatory education practices in public schools. In response to these rulings, the U.S. Congress enacted the Equal Education Opportunity Act of 1974. The legislation prohibited discrimination based on race, color or national origin in institutions receiving federal funding. Choice (A) is incorrect because the *Brown* (1954) ruling may have had an impact on the legislation, since it also deals with discriminatory practices, but *Castañeda v. Pickard* came after the EEOA became law. The *ASPIRA v.*

New York City Board of Education and *Rios v. Read* (C) ruling also came after the enactment of the EEOA legislation. Choice (D) is incorrect because the *Plyler v. Doe* ruling dealt with the rights of undocumented children to public education, and the *U.S. v. Texas* ruling came seven years (1981) after the enactment of the legislation.

Competency 001: Foundations of Bilingual Education

11.   **A.**   The correct answer is (A). The dominant theory of second-language acquisition suggests that people store information in a language-free environment common to L1 and L2, the common underlying proficiency. Because language information is stored in a common environment, learning a second language does not diminish students' mental capabilities. Proponents of the separate underlying proficiency (SUP) say that L1 and L2 split the mental space, which can result in semilingualism or the inability to develop proficiency in either language. Research suggests that the SUP model (B) accurately describes what happens in the brain of a child learning a second language. Option (C) is incorrect because it refers to the SUP model mentioned in option (B). Option (D) describes the social language, which does not connect with how the brain is organized.

Competency 002: First- and Second-Language Acquisition and Development

12.   **D.**   Oral retelling is a good strategy to use when having emergent and beginning readers recall the main elements of the story. It lets students recall key events and details of the story even before they become fluent readers. Options (A), (B), and (C) describe informal assessment techniques used with students who are already reading and writing at the intermediate and advanced levels.

Competency 003: Development and Assessment of Literacy and Biliteracy

13.   **B.**   The correct answer is (B). The perceived social and psychological distance describes how ELs see their relationship with members of mainstream groups. If they perceive themselves as socially equal, second language acquisition becomes easy. However, if both groups perceive themselves as different, it can lead to social isolation, which hinders second language acquisition. Self-esteem, socioeconomic status (A), prejudices (C) and past injustices against the group (D) can affect interaction with the group, but these features are encompassed in the "perceived and social psychological distance" concept suggested in option (B).

Competency 002: First- and Second-Language Acquisition and Development

14.   **C.**   The answer is (C). Spanish comes from the Latin, the language of the Romans. From this connection, the term Romance language emerged. English is a Germanic language but has influence from the Latin and the Greek languages. Thus, most English words of Latin origin might be English/Spanish cognates, and consequently easier to understand for Spanish-speaking ELs. Option (A) is incorrect because Latin was a prestigious language as part of the Roman Empire. However, today the language is practically dead since it does not have native speakers. Choice (B)

is incorrect because as stated earlier, English is not of Latin origin. Spanish has a strong connection with the Greek, but this does not address the reason why Spanish-speaking children have facility to recognize Latin-based words.

Competency 004: Content Area Instruction

15. **C.** The correct answer is (C). The Canadian researcher Jim Cummins suggested that ELs must arrive at a threshold level in their native language to transfer language and cognitive strategies from L1 to L2. Students reach the threshold level when they develop a strong literacy foundation in their native language. A culture-free curriculum (A), racial and linguistic harmony (B), and assimilation (D) may affect the language and cognitive growth of ELs, but none of these choices individually account for the cognitive and academic growth of ELs.

Competency 002: First- and Second-Language Acquisition and Development

16. **B.** The correct answer is (B). The term *language acquisition* is used to describe the process that children follow in their attempt to decipher and use language. Generally this process begins at birth and continues through life; however, when used in the school setting, some features of the process are replaced by direct instructions (learning). First-language acquisition happens subconsciously when children try to understand the language spoken around them. Parents and caregivers teach language concepts indirectly through meaningful interactions in contextualized situations. Parents provide corrective feedback to children indirectly through modeling. Choice (A) is incorrect because the acquisition of a first language is a process that begins prior to formal schooling. A first language is acquired subconsciously in meaningful situations, but direct corrective feedback is rarely used to support the process (C). Choice (D) is incorrect because first language acquisition is not taught deductively—i.e., through direct instruction.

Competency 002: First- and Second-Language Acquisition and Development

17. **A.** The correct answer is (A). Metacognition encompasses awareness and self-regulation of one's own thinking as comprehension occurs. Self-monitoring, or stopping to self-assess and check one's own understanding, is most related to metacognition. Options (B), (C), and (D) focus on reading skills that are important to comprehension, but they do not relate directly to self-monitoring.

Competency 003: Development and Assessment of Literacy and Biliteracy

18. **B.** The correct answer is (B). Students at the beginning and intermediate levels of second language acquisition can benefit from contextualized instruction to get meaning from instruction. They are beginning to experience success with the language, but they are not ready to accept direct error corrections in communication activities. Direct corrections can inhibit communication and affect further development in the language. Based on this explanation, the rest of the options can be ruled out.

Competency 004: Content Area Instruction

19. **C.** The correct answer is (C). Students at the speech-emergence stage communicate in phrases using words with high semantic value. They are also beginning to understand the print concept. They can understand speech and written communication presented in contextualized situations and accompanied with visuals. In the preproduction stage (A), students lack basic language skills and may rely on nonverbal communication to make their point. Thus, it is unlikely that they can understand written communication. In the early production stage (B), students communicate using language at the social level in everyday situations. Print awareness is taking place, but the main emphasis at this stage is the development of basic oral communication. The intermediate and advanced fluency stage (D) represents a higher level of proficiency in which students communicate using simple sentences. However, the language is not fully developed, and their speech may experience language interference as well as overgeneralizations. Their literacy development is beyond the basic recognition skills to which the question alludes.

Competency 002: First- and Second-Language Acquisition and Development

20. **A.** The correct answer is (A). Effective methods to teach a second language should revolve around the student and his or her communication needs. "Student-centered and communication-driven" describes an effective approach to teaching a second language. Choice (D) calls for the opposite, teacher-centered, and does not represent best teaching practices. Choices (B) and (C) call for the teaching of a second language following a grammatical syllabus. Research does not support a grammar-based approach to teaching languages.

Competency 002: First- and Second-Language Acquisition and Development

21. **A.** The correct answer is (A). Research on second language acquisition suggests that a strong literacy development in L1 can facilitate the acquisition of similar levels of proficiency in L2. Language-specific variables, with literacy and metacognitive strategies, can transfer from L1 to L2. Reading skills are not identical in L1 and L2 (B), but the strategies to develop the skills might be similar. Reading skills might be confusing for ELs (C) and can affect the cognitive process in bilingual students (D), but these options do not represent the rationale for implementing initial reading instruction in L1.

Competency 003: Development and Assessment of Literacy and Biliteracy

22. **A.** The correct answer is (A). When children overgeneralize as with "bestest," they are applying grammar rules. The overgeneralizing indicates they have passed the stage of mere repetition and are decoding the grammar of the language. Such overgeneralization is typical of native English speakers acquiring a language and does not show any interference from a language. This statement eliminates choices (B) and (C). Choice (D) is incorrect, but it can be confusing for students taking the test because cartoons like "Rugrats" often use such overgeneralization to mimic

the speech of children. However, the continuous overgeneralization typical of children cannot be attributed to cartoons on television.

Competency 002: First- and Second-Language Acquisition and Development

23. **A.** The correct answer is (A). Language development is enhanced when students use the language for a meaningful purpose. In this case, students were guided to research a project that required reading, sharing, and summarizing information to accomplish the task. Writing (B) and working independently (C) are only two components of the total project. Option (C) is incorrect because all students should be responsible for their own work.

Competency 004: Content Area Instruction

24. **B.** The correct answer is (B). The question calls for activities that promote self-directed learning. Advanced students have enough knowledge about the language to analyze the source of the errors and make their own corrections. Students at the beginning stage of second language acquisition might not have enough knowledge to do that. Thus, option (A) is incorrect. In communication activities (C), ESL teachers do not provide direct corrective feedback but instead are encouraged to provide indirect feedback by modeling the structures in question. The same principle applies to option (D) because direct corrections are not the best tool during communication activities. However, teachers can note the grammatical problems and design a grammar lesson to teach the concepts.

Competency 003: Development and Assessment of Literacy and Biliteracy

25. **B.** The correct answer is (B). Soledad has the basic interpersonal skills (BICS) in Spanish and English, but she lacks the language needed to do well academically—the Cognitive academic linguistic proficiency (CALP). Based on this explanation, options (A), (C), and (D) can be ruled out.

Competency 004: Content Area Instruction

26. **C.** The correct answer is (C). English and Spanish have a large number of common derivation morphemes and root words. The languages thus also share a large number of cognates—words similar in two or more languages. Option (A) is incorrect because it contains inflectional morphemes, a unique feature of English— especially oral language, past and past participle, comparative and superlative, the present progressive, and the plurals. Both languages have five letters to represent the vowels, but in English these represent multiple phonemes—12 to 15 phonemes. Based on these explanations, option (D) is ruled out.

Competency 003: Development and Assessment of Literacy and Biliteracy

27. **B.** The correct answer is (B). Both Spanish and English have multiple consonant blends, or clusters. English has a number of such blends/clusters that occur in the first position—as we see, for example, in *splash*, *spring*, and *scream*. In Spanish, these clusters can happen in the medial position, and they are always preceded by the vowel *e*. Spanish indeed has five consonant digraphs (C), but the question asks about consonant blends, not digraphs. Option (A) is incorrect because, as we've established, both languages have multiple consonant blends. Based on these explanations, option (D) can be ruled out.

Competency 003: Development and Assessment of Literacy and Biliteracy

28. **D.** The correct answer is (D). ELs at the advanced stage of English development might still experience language interference (A), and they still might rely on L1 to master the second language (B). Both advanced and advanced-high students still need instructional guidance to improve English pronunciation.

Competency 004: Content Area Instruction

29. **D.** The correct answer is (D). The five Spanish vowels are pronounced with the same duration (A). The Spanish grapheme-phoneme correspondence is more consistent than in English (B). English has multiple vowel and consonant digraphs that create problems for all ELs. Spanish has five consonant digraphs and no vowel digraphs (C).

Competency 003: Development and Assessment of Literacy and Biliteracy

30. **B.** The correct answer is (B). The presence of a hiatus—two strong vowels—automatically signals a separation into two syllables. For example, in the word—*creo*—the *e* and the *o* are strong vowels, creating two different syllables. In words with diphthongs (A) and triphthongs (D), the vowels are pronounced as part of the same syllable. Words like *veo,* which have a hiatus, have two syllables, while a word like *muy* (diphthong) or miau (triphthong) are monosyllabic because the triphthongs and diphthong are pronounced as part of the same syllable. The dieresis (D), the tilde over the ñ, does not affect the number of syllables in a word.

Competency 003: Development and Assessment of Literacy and Biliteracy

31. **B.** The correct answer is (B). Through the use of content-based instruction ELs get exposed to language and content concurrently. With linguistic accommodations, they can comprehend the content and at the same time learn the academic language needed for further development. Content-based instruction does not take into account the native language of the learners; therefore, option (A) is not relevant. Option (C) is incorrect because content-based methods do not allow for the use of the students' native language for instruction. Option (D) is a faulty statement, since content-based instruction is not designed to replace explicit language instruction.

Competency 004: Content Area Instruction

32. **C.** The correct answer is (C). The purpose of the orthographic accents and dieresis is to make readers aware that the words do not follow the traditional pronunciation rules. Special markings thus are required to guide pronunciation. Based on this explanation, the other options can be ruled out.

Competency 003: Development and Assessment of Literacy and Biliteracy

33. **D.** The correct answer is (D). All the words contain at least one letter that is not pronounced. Because the question emphasizes the phonological perspective, the other options can be ruled out.

Competency 003: Development and Assessment of Literacy and Biliteracy

34. **D.** The correct answer is (D). Texas bilingual education legislation requires districts to offer bilingual or special language programs if the district identifies 20 or more ELs with a common native language. This includes students district-wide, not school-wide (A and B). Legal residence is not taken into account to determine the need for bilingual or special language services (C).

Competency 001: Foundations of Bilingual Education

35. **C.** The correct answer is (C). The ARD regulates and manages students in special education. The LPAC does the same for students in the bilingual or special language programs. Choice (A) is incorrect because no federal law mandates bilingual education. A federal IDEA legislation regulates special education (B). The composition of the committees is different (D). In special education, the parent of the child is part of the committee, wheras the LPAC uses a parent representative.

Competency 001: Foundations of Bilingual Education

36. **B.** The correct answer is (B). The two-way dual language program was designed to serve language minority and language majority students. Children from mainstream groups thus can participate in the program and become bilingual. Despite this public support, the U.S. Department of Education has not officially endorsed the program (C). The program allows the maintenance of L1 and L2 (A) and is based on research (D), but these features alone do not account for its popularity.

Competency 001: Foundations of Bilingual Education

37. **C.** The correct answer is (C). Because of the *Lau* ruling (1972), the U.S. Department of Health Education and Welfare created the Lau Remedies in 1975 to force compliance of the ruling. A key component of the Lau Remedies was the diffusion of the criteria used to develop effective language programs to support ELs. ESL became a component of bilingual education, not a program in isolation (A). Although the Lau Remedies did not affect federal legislation (B), they did affect state legislation, as states began removing English-only legislation (D) and enacting laws to implement special language programs for ELLs.

Competency 001: Foundations of Bilingual Education

38. **C.** The correct answer is (C). The one-way, also known as developmental bilingual education, serves language minority students (e.g., Spanish-speaking students), while the two-way serves both language minority and language majority students (e.g., Spanish-speaking and native English speakers). The language (A) and academic (B) goals of both programs are the same: to perform well academically and to maintain both languages. Both programs also follow a similar format for the distribution of L1 and L2 (D).

Competency 001: Foundations of Bilingual Education

39. **B.** The correct answer is (B). Children in the preproduction stage of second language acquisition usually cannot communicate verbally. They are analyzing and "cracking" the language code. Thus, the use of commands as well as contextualizing instruction and using concrete objects as teaching tools can promote language development. Option (A) calls for the use of direct instruction on the structure of the language. This option might not be developmentally appropriate because students at the preproduction stage lack the language skills necessary to benefit from direct instruction. Short answers like yes/no and either/or are usually used with students who are at the early production stage of second-language acquisition (C). Children in the preproduction stage (D) do not have the language skills to understand and address open-ended questions.

Competency 002: First- and Second-Language Acquisition and Development

40. **D.** The correct answer is (D). A vowel digraph is created when two vowels in a word represent one sound—*cool*, *book*, or *feet*. Vowel digraphs are common in English but do not exist in Spanish. In Spanish every vowel is pronounced. Based on this explanation, we can rule out the remaining options.

Competency 003: Development and Assessment of Literacy and Biliteracy

41. **A.** The correct answer is (A). Research studies suggest that literacy emerges naturally and concurrently—emergent literacy. Contrary to that position, proponents of **reading readiness** suggest that the child must master specific subskills (B and C) to fully engage in reading and writing. This group also suggests that formal reading instruction (D) should be postponed until children are fluent. The emergent literacy movement has replaced these positions.

Competency 003: Development and Assessment of Literacy and Biliteracy

42. **D.** The correct answer is (D). Since the vowel system and most consonants in Spanish are very consistent, syllables are used for initial reading instruction. Spanish and English are alphabetic language, not syllabic (A). Spanish has a good grapheme-phoneme correspondence (B), but the key element is the almost perfect correspondence of the vowel system. Option (C) is incorrect. Syllabication is part of phonological awareness.

Competency 003: Development and Assessment of Literacy and Biliteracy

43. **B.** The correct answer is (B). The annexation of Texas, California and the rest of the American Southwest added large numbers of Spanish speakers as well as large numbers of Native-American tribes with their own languages living in the region. Human rights legislation did not directly affect the number of non-English speaking minorities in the country. Ruling out option (A) also rules out option (D) because it includes option (A) as well as (C). Option (C) by itself is a strong distractor since as a result of the Spanish-American War (1898), the Spanish government ceded the territories of Puerto Rico and Guam to the United States.

Competency 001: Foundations of Bilingual Education

44. **A.** The correct answer is (A). Teachers and administrators need to identify the levels of language development of the learners to be sure their language proficiency does not interfere in the assessment of the content areas. The elements that transfer from L1 to L2 (B) and the native culture of the learners (C) are generally taken into account when planning instruction, but not necessarily when assessing content. Based on the data provided, option (D) can be ruled out.

Competency 004: Content Area Instruction

45. **D.** The correct answer is (D). The state legislation requires bilingual education from kindergarten to upper elementary, and dual language instruction is allowed in K–12. It also required bilingual or ESL in middle school and ESL in high school. The legislation did not mandate TBE in high school (B).

Competency 001: Foundations of Bilingual Education

46. **B.** The correct answer is (B). School districts in Texas are required to implement instruction using the state approved curriculum. Option (A) is incorrect because individual school districts are not allowed to develop their own curriculum standards. Option (C) is incorrect because the United States does not have a national curriculum. Under the new federal education law—ESSA—this option of developing a national curriculum is officially prohibited. Option (D) is incorrect because textbook developers are required to use the state curriculum to develop textbooks.

Competency 004: Content Area Instruction

47. **C.** The correct answer is (C). The home language survey has two key questions designed to identify the primary language of the child and the language spoken at home. If a language other than English is indicated in the survey, the district must further screen to determine whether the child qualifies for a special language program. Based on this explanation, the options (A), (B), and (D) can be ruled out.

Competency 001: Foundations of Bilingual Education

48. **D.**   The answer is (D). Bilingual students use their linguistic and cultural knowledge as a foundation for development in both languages. Comparing L1 and L2 is a general strategy that bilingual people use consistently. When comparing the two languages, students are able to identify those elements that transfer and those that do not. All these strategies are commonly used among bilingual learners.

Competency 004: Content Area Instruction

TExES Bilingual Education Supplemental (164)

Practice Test

Also available at the online REA Study Center *(www.rea.com/studycenter).*

The TExES Bilingual Education Supplemental (164) test is computer-based, so we strongly recommend that you take our online practice tests to simulate test-day conditions and to receive these added benefits:

- **Timed testing conditions**—Gauge how much time you can spend on each question.

- **Automatic scoring**—Find out how you did on the test, instantly.

- **On-screen detailed explanations of answers**—Learn not just the correct answer, but also why the other answers are incorrect.

- **Diagnostic score reports**—Pinpoint where you're strongest and where you need to focus your study.

ANSWER SHEET

1. Ⓐ Ⓑ Ⓒ Ⓓ
2. Ⓐ Ⓑ Ⓒ Ⓓ
3. Ⓐ Ⓑ Ⓒ Ⓓ
4. Ⓐ Ⓑ Ⓒ Ⓓ
5. Ⓐ Ⓑ Ⓒ Ⓓ
6. Ⓐ Ⓑ Ⓒ Ⓓ
7. Ⓐ Ⓑ Ⓒ Ⓓ
8. Ⓐ Ⓑ Ⓒ Ⓓ
9. Ⓐ Ⓑ Ⓒ Ⓓ
10. Ⓐ Ⓑ Ⓒ Ⓓ
11. Ⓐ Ⓑ Ⓒ Ⓓ
12. Ⓐ Ⓑ Ⓒ Ⓓ
13. Ⓐ Ⓑ Ⓒ Ⓓ
14. Ⓐ Ⓑ Ⓒ Ⓓ
15. Ⓐ Ⓑ Ⓒ Ⓓ
16. Ⓐ Ⓑ Ⓒ Ⓓ
17. Ⓐ Ⓑ Ⓒ Ⓓ
18. Ⓐ Ⓑ Ⓒ Ⓓ
19. Ⓐ Ⓑ Ⓒ Ⓓ
20. Ⓐ Ⓑ Ⓒ Ⓓ
21. Ⓐ Ⓑ Ⓒ Ⓓ
22. Ⓐ Ⓑ Ⓒ Ⓓ
23. Ⓐ Ⓑ Ⓒ Ⓓ
24. Ⓐ Ⓑ Ⓒ Ⓓ
25. Ⓐ Ⓑ Ⓒ Ⓓ
26. Ⓐ Ⓑ Ⓒ Ⓓ
27. Ⓐ Ⓑ Ⓒ Ⓓ

28. Ⓐ Ⓑ Ⓒ Ⓓ
29. Ⓐ Ⓑ Ⓒ Ⓓ
30. Ⓐ Ⓑ Ⓒ Ⓓ
31. Ⓐ Ⓑ Ⓒ Ⓓ
32. Ⓐ Ⓑ Ⓒ Ⓓ
33. Ⓐ Ⓑ Ⓒ Ⓓ
34. Ⓐ Ⓑ Ⓒ Ⓓ
35. Ⓐ Ⓑ Ⓒ Ⓓ
36. Ⓐ Ⓑ Ⓒ Ⓓ
37. Ⓐ Ⓑ Ⓒ Ⓓ
38. Ⓐ Ⓑ Ⓒ Ⓓ
39. Ⓐ Ⓑ Ⓒ Ⓓ
40. Ⓐ Ⓑ Ⓒ Ⓓ
41. Ⓐ Ⓑ Ⓒ Ⓓ
42. Ⓐ Ⓑ Ⓒ Ⓓ
43. Ⓐ Ⓑ Ⓒ Ⓓ
44. Ⓐ Ⓑ Ⓒ Ⓓ
45. Ⓐ Ⓑ Ⓒ Ⓓ
46. Ⓐ Ⓑ Ⓒ Ⓓ
47. Ⓐ Ⓑ Ⓒ Ⓓ
48. Ⓐ Ⓑ Ⓒ Ⓓ
49. Ⓐ Ⓑ Ⓒ Ⓓ
50. Ⓐ Ⓑ Ⓒ Ⓓ
51. Ⓐ Ⓑ Ⓒ Ⓓ
52. Ⓐ Ⓑ Ⓒ Ⓓ
53. Ⓐ Ⓑ Ⓒ Ⓓ
54. Ⓐ Ⓑ Ⓒ Ⓓ

55. Ⓐ Ⓑ Ⓒ Ⓓ
56. Ⓐ Ⓑ Ⓒ Ⓓ
57. Ⓐ Ⓑ Ⓒ Ⓓ
58. Ⓐ Ⓑ Ⓒ Ⓓ
59. Ⓐ Ⓑ Ⓒ Ⓓ
60. Ⓐ Ⓑ Ⓒ Ⓓ
61. Ⓐ Ⓑ Ⓒ Ⓓ
62. Ⓐ Ⓑ Ⓒ Ⓓ
63. Ⓐ Ⓑ Ⓒ Ⓓ
64. Ⓐ Ⓑ Ⓒ Ⓓ
65. Ⓐ Ⓑ Ⓒ Ⓓ
66. Ⓐ Ⓑ Ⓒ Ⓓ
67. Ⓐ Ⓑ Ⓒ Ⓓ
68. Ⓐ Ⓑ Ⓒ Ⓓ
69. Ⓐ Ⓑ Ⓒ Ⓓ
70. Ⓐ Ⓑ Ⓒ Ⓓ
71. Ⓐ Ⓑ Ⓒ Ⓓ
72. Ⓐ Ⓑ Ⓒ Ⓓ
73. Ⓐ Ⓑ Ⓒ Ⓓ
74. Ⓐ Ⓑ Ⓒ Ⓓ
75. Ⓐ Ⓑ Ⓒ Ⓓ
76. Ⓐ Ⓑ Ⓒ Ⓓ
77. Ⓐ Ⓑ Ⓒ Ⓓ
78. Ⓐ Ⓑ Ⓒ Ⓓ
79. Ⓐ Ⓑ Ⓒ Ⓓ
80. Ⓐ Ⓑ Ⓒ Ⓓ

PRACTICE TEST

TESTING TIME: 4 hours and 45 minutes

80 multiple-choice questions

In this practice test, you will find examples of test questions similar to those you are likely to encounter on the TExES Bilingual Education Supplemental Exam. Read each question carefully and chose the best answer from the four possible choices. Mark your responses on the answer sheet provided on page 178.

1. Mike is enrolled in a class of all-Latino students in a program that provides instruction one day in Spanish and the other in English. The goal of the program is to promote proficiency in L1 and L2. In which program is Mike enrolled?

    A. Bilingual program

    B. Transitional bilingual education

    C. Two-way dual language program

    D. One-way dual language program

2. Identify the program(s) whose main goal is to promote biliteracy among students.

    A. The one-way dual language program of the United States

    B. The two-way dual language programs of the United States

    C. The dual language immersion programs in Canada

    D. All of the above

3. English learners (ELs) might have problems understanding the following statement:
    The politician met his Waterloo once he faced public opinion.
    What must ELs know to understand the statement?

    A. The concepts of metaphor and allusion

    B. The concept of a simile

    C. The concept of allusion

    D. The concept of a hyperbole

4. Identify the statement that best describes the concept of Sheltered English.

    A. It is a program designed to teach ESL and bilingual education to ELs.

    B. It is the Canadian version of the bilingual education program.

    C. It is a program designed to teach ESL through instruction in the content areas.

    D. It is an example of a submersion program designed to promote bilingualism among students.

5. Identify the technique(s) that best represent the implementation of Sheltered English.

    A. Speaking slowly in English and providing support in L1 to promote listening comprehension

    B. Using nonverbal communication to promote comprehension

    C. Evaluating the mastery of the content taught at least once per week

    D. Using visuals and hands-on activities as well as contextualizing instruction to ensure comprehension

6. Some of the acceptable forms of linguistic accommodation for mathematics and science testing in Texas are:

    A. oral translation, linguistic simplification and one-to-one instruction.

    B. reading assistance as well as the use of a bilingual dictionary and a glossary.

    C. L1 and L2 side-by-side questions and tutoring in English only.

    D. simplification of the content tested and techniques from sheltered instruction.

7. Traditionally, newcomer programs are designed to address the language and cultural needs of students

    A. from low socioeconomic backgrounds.

    B. from non-traditional backgrounds without prior schooling.

    C. from non-Spanish speaking backgrounds.

    D. at the intermediate and advanced level of English proficiency.

8. Students who arrive at the threshold level of L1 have which of the following advantages?

    A. They develop the positive self-esteem needed to acquire a second language.

    B. They develop a deep understanding of culture and its implications for the acquisition of L2.

    C. They possess the foundation in L1 needed to transfer to L2.

    D. They can compare and contrast the two languages.

9. Which of the following was the main contribution of the landmark case of *Lau v. Nichols*?

    A. It mandated the creation of a bilingual education program in San Francisco.

    B. It empowered the Office for Civil Rights (OCR) to force school districts to provide better education to linguistic minority students.

    C. It forced other states to develop bilingual education programs.

    D. It resulted in the signing of federal legislation mandating bilingual education in the United States.

10. Before the European colonization of North America, large numbers of Native Americans communicated and conducted business using sign language. This example of communication represents which of the following facts about pre-Columbian America?

    A. Native American groups were living peacefully in America before the European invasion.

    B. Native American groups invented American Sign Language and used it for communication before the European colonization.

    C. Linguistic diversity was a prevalent feature in North America.

    D. In pre-Columbian America, the incidence of mute and deaf people was higher than in Europe.

11. Under the direction of the Bureau of Indian Affairs, large numbers of Native American children were removed from their homes and sent to boarding schools. Because of this program, Native American children

    A. became bilingual and bicultural.

    B. experienced language loss.

    C. became highly educated and returned to their reservations.

    D. left the reservations for American urban centers.

12. Because of language loss, large numbers of Native American languages have disappeared. However, the resurgence of bilingual education programs has revitalized some of these languages, with one group increasing the number of speakers to more than 150,000. The group that best represents this language revitalization is the

    A. Cherokee.

    B. Navajo.

    C. Choctaw.

    D. Apache.

13. Language diversity is often perceived as a threat to national unity. Proponents of this view say that language and cultural diversity can lead to Balkanism or division. However, World War II showed the value of language diversity. Identify the historical term or concept that best represents the value of bilingualism in supporting the war effort.

    A. The Navajo Code Talkers Program

    B. The Tuskegee Pilot Program

    C. The admission of Hawaii as the 50th state

    D. The launching of the *Sputnik* satellite

14. Linguistic diversity characterized the life of the 13 American colonies. However, linguistic diversity was later perceived as a threat to national security. Identify the primary event or document that guided Americans to embrace English-only legislation.

    A. The Revolutionary War

    B. The 10th Amendment of the U.S. Constitution

    C. The Vietnam War

    D. World War I

15. Identify the event or events that promoted the modern revival of bilingual education in American public schools.

    A. The United Nations (UNESCO) proclamation of 1953

    B. The Cuban Revolution of 1959

    C. Court challenges led by linguistic minority groups

    D. All of the above

16. The reauthorization of the ESEA of 1984 moved away from the compensatory nature of bilingual education and helped in the implementation of dual language programs. However, the actual legislation that allowed the implementation of dual language programs was

    A. the No Child Left Behind legislation of 2001.

    B. the Elementary and Education Act of 1994.

    C. the Every Student Succeeds Act (ESSA).

    D. Options A and C

17. The federal ESSA and corresponding Texas legislation require school districts to integrate English Language Proficiency Standards (ELPS) when providing instruction in English to ELs. To comply with ELPS implementation, teachers are required to

   A.   provide content area instruction based on the English proficiency levels of the students.

   B.   decrease the rigor and intensity of content instruction to make content comprehensible to ELs.

   C.   provide linguistic accommodations to make the content comprehensible to ELs.

   D.   Options A and C

18. Besides the legislation(s) that required the inclusion of English Language Proficiency Standards (ELPS) in school districts nationwide, the ESSA changed multiple mandates from the NCLB. Identify the new mandates of this legislation.

   A.   Moved the accountability for ELs from Title III to Title I (Education of Disadvantaged Students).

   B.   Prohibited the interference of the federal government with states' ability to set their own academic standards.

   C.   Required school districts to follow-up former ELs for four years after reclassification.

   D.   All of the above

19. Identify the court case that made racial segregation illegal in the United States.

   A.   *Plessy v. Ferguson*

   B.   *Brown v. Board of Education*

   C.   *Meyer v. Nebraska*

   D.   None of the above

20. The implementation of quality bilingual education was challenged in which of the following court cases?

    A. *ASPIRA v. New York* (1974) and *Lau v. Nichols* (1974)

    B. *Keys v. Denver, Colorado* (1973) and *Serna v. Portales* (1974)

    C. *Rios v. Read* (1978) and *Castañeda v. Pickart* (1981)

    D. All of the above

Use the information below to answer questions 21–23 that follow.

Mike and Brenda are second graders attending a special language program in a local elementary school. Mike is an American-born native English speaker while Brenda is an immigrant native speaker of Spanish. They are participating in a program that follows the 90/10 model and whose goal is to promote biliteracy and bilingualism.

21. Based on the information provided, Mike and Brenda are part of which of the following programs?

    A. One-way dual language

    B. English immersion

    C. Two-way dual language

    D. English enrichment

22. Based on the instructional model selected (90/10), which of the two students will be directly involved in a language immersion process 90% of the time?

    A. Mike

    B. Brenda

    C. Both of them

    D. Neither of them

23. One of the key benefits of this type of program is that Mike and Brenda

    A. can interact freely and share cultural information.

    B. can help each other to become bilingual and bicultural.

    C. can become friends.

    D. Options A and B

Use the information below to answer questions 24–26 that follow.

Rodolfo, Enrique, and Alicia are five-year-old children going through the admission process to public schools in Texas. As part of Texas state law, each of the parents completed a Home Language Survey. As part of the screening process, a certified bilingual teacher interviewed the children in Spanish. Below are the results of the survey, with comments from the bilingual teachers involved in the interview process.

Home Language Survey (HLS)

Questions	Rodolfo	Enrique	Alicia	Teachers' Note
What language is spoken in your home most of the time?	Spanish	Español	Inglés	Language Proficiency Testing required for Rodolfo and Enrique.
What language does your child (do you) speak most of the time?	Spanish	English	Inglés	Alicia and Rodolfo are monolingual Spanish speakers. Enrique has some basic command of English.
What language do you speak most of the time?	Spanish	Spanish	Inglés	All three children are fluent in Spanish. Rodolfo seems to have some form of lisping when communicating in Spanish.

24. Based on the data gathered, what is the next step in the process?

    A. All three children have to be officially tested for oral language proficiency.

    B. Alicia does not have to be tested since she is an English speaker.

    C. All three children can be admitted to a special language program.

    D. Only Rodolfo clearly qualifies for admission to a special language program.

25. What action should the Language Proficiency Assessment Committee (LPAC) take to address the lisping found in Rodolfo's speech?

    A. Rodolfo should be assigned to the special education classroom to receive speech support.

    B. Since Rodolfo qualifies for special education, no further language testing should be done at this time.

    C. Ignore the speech issue and continue with the screening process for possible admission to the special language program.

    D. The LPAC should stop language testing since the group does not have jurisdiction over students with special needs.

26. In the case of Alicia, the data gathered from the HLS showed that she might be fluent in English. However, informal data gathered by the bilingual teacher suggest that the information might not be reliable. What should the LPAC do in the case of Alicia?

    A. Alicia should be placed in the traditional English-only program.

    B. No further testing should be done since the parents might not want the child in the special language program.

    C. Oral testing should proceed as scheduled.

    D. All of the above

Use the representation of the Dual Iceberg Analogy to answer questions 27 and 28 that follow.

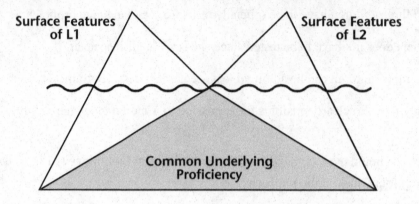

(adapted from Cummins, 1984)

27. Based on the L2 acquisition model represented with the iceberg analogy, where do bilingual people store information about the meaning system of the language (semantic) and the content area knowledge?

    A.   In the surface features of L1 and L2

    B.   In the Common Underlying features of the languages

    C.   In the surface features of L2

    D.   In the surface features of L1

28. The Separate (L1 and L2) and Common Underlying proficiencies represented in the Iceberg analogy has been used to represent the value of

    A.   late-exit programs.

    B.   learning two languages.

    C.   early-exit programs.

    D.   using visual representations to represent abstract concepts.

Use the information below to answer questions 29 and 30 that follow.

Comparison between Spanish and English

Key Components	English	Spanish
Consonant Digraphs	Multiple examples: *know*, *school*, *church*, *shirt*	It has five consonant digraphs: **CH**: choza, **LL**: calle, **RR**: carro, **QU**: quiero, **GU**: guerra
Initial consonant clusters/blend	Multiple examples: *speak*, *spring*, *street*, *splash* *slate*, *plate*, *smoke*, *snow*, *scream*	None, these clusters happen only in medial position, preceded by the vowel E—e*spero*, e*spri*mir, e*scu*ela
The Alphabet/ phonemes	26 letters/44 sounds	27 letters/27 sounds
Grapheme-phonemes	5 letters/12–15 sounds	5 letters/5 sounds

29. Based on the characteristics of Spanish presented in the table above, which of the following are the resulting implications for initial reading instruction in Spanish?

    A.   The vowel system and the resulting syllables can be used for initial reading instruction.

    B.   The use of onset and rhymes is a valuable strategy to teach Spanish reading.

    C.   Spanish is a syllabic language, thus syllables are the logical units of Spanish reading.

    D.   All of the above

30. According to the information in the table, Spanish-speaking English learners (ELs) might have problems with the pronunciation of which of the following?

    A.   Final consonant clusters

    B.   The *th* and *sh* sounds

    C.   Initial consonant clusters

    D.   Spanish vowels

31. The development of second language proficiency is best achieved when

    A. the language of instruction leads to the development of functional communication skills in L2.

    B. the language is taught deductively by involving students with activities in which they use language and derive language principles subconsciously.

    C. instruction is contextualized and presented with meaningful memorization drills.

    D. students are exposed to idiomatic expressions and tongue twisters to facilitate communication.

32. Identify the statement that best sums the research associated with the development of proficiency in L2 and age of first exposure to the language.

    A. Children exposed to L2 before puberty develop a near native pronunciation in the second language.

    B. Given the appropriate instruction, children exposed to L2 after puberty will develop similar language proficiency as children who came into contact at an earlier age.

    C. Children exposed to L2 after puberty master pronunciation, grammar and reading better than younger children.

    D. All of the above

33. Second-language learners often experience problems with the semantic and cultural components of the English language. Which language component will most likely be impacted by this situation?

    A. The use and understanding of figurative language and idioms

    B. The application of phonological analysis

    C. The use of syntactic and phonological components

    D. The application of the lexical and structural components

34. Standard American English is the language variety

    A. commonly accepted and spoken by the general U.S. population.

    B. imposed by the government.

    C. used in official government documents, schools and the media.

    D. used as a lingua franca in a large number of former African colonies.

35. One of the best predictors of success in the acquisition of literacy in L2 is the

    A. ESL program selected by the district.

    B. level of literacy achieved in L1.

    C. level of acculturation achieved in the native culture.

    D. method used for the teaching of listening, speaking, reading, and writing.

36. Graphophonemic differences between L1 and L2 can result in

    A. syntactic interference between L1 & L2.

    B. language interference at the phonological and spelling levels.

    C. positive language transfer between the language structures in L1 and L2.

    D. semantic differences between L1 and L2.

37. Identify the statement that best describes differences between English and Spanish consonant digraphs.

    A. English has multiple consonant diagraphs, while Spanish has three.

    B. English has multiple consonant diagraphs, while Spanish has multiple diphthongs.

    C. Spanish and English have multiple consonant diagraphs and diphthongs.

    D. Spanish and English have multiple consonant blends.

38. Identify the statement(s) that best describe(s) the international status of the English language.

    A. English is the world's third most spoken language.

    B. English is used as a lingua franca in former colonies of Great Britain in Asia and Africa.

    C. English is spoken as a first or second language in more than 100 countries.

    D. All of the above

39. Identify the option that presents accurate information about the Spanish language.

    A. Spanish is the third most spoken language in the world.

    B. Spain is the country with the largest number of Spanish speakers.

    C. The United States is the country with the second-largest number of Spanish speakers.

    D. All of the above

40. Which of the following statements best represent(s) the structure of the word "homelessness"?

    A. It contains three free morphemes.

    B. It contains two derivational morphemes and one inflectional morpheme.

    C. It contains one free morpheme and three derivational morphemes.

    D. It contains a root word and two derivational morphemes.

41. Which literacy component must an EL analyze to get meaning from the idiomatic expression in the next sentence? Life is full of lemons, and your only option is to make lemonade.

    A. Connotation versus denotation

    B. Simile

    C. Alliteration

    D. All of the above

42. Which of the following are characteristics of the L1 acquisition process that can be adapted to teach ELs?

    A. Communication is highly contextualized.

    B. There is no direct error correction during communication.

    C. The purpose of the communication is to get information.

    D. All of the above

43. Story retelling in both Spanish and English is an assessment strategy designed for non-readers. This strategy is designed to assess

    A. comprehension, sentence formation, and vocabulary development.

    B. oral language development as well as writing skills.

    C. listening, speaking, reading and writing skills.

    D. knowledge of literary pieces and literary writing styles.

44. TELPAS, the instrument used to document the linguistic progress of ELs in Texas, uses checklists to document progress of students in Pre-kindergarten to grade 1. This assessment represents an example of

    A. effective teaching strategies.

    B. informal teaching strategies.

    C. formal assessment strategies.

    D. informal assessment strategies.

45. The alphabetic principle describes children's ability to understand that

    A. English and most European languages are alphabetic languages.

    B. letters and letter combinations represent specific sounds.

    C. children must memorize the alphabet before the introduction of formal reading.

    D. learning the alphabet is a prerequisite for the introduction of dictionary skills.

46. Which of the following best defines the term "cognates."

    A. Words with similar or identical spelling and meaning in two or more languages

    B. Homophones in two languages

    C. Homographs in two languages

    D. Words with similar spelling and pronunciation but different meanings

47. Identify the number of syllables and the number of phonemes in the word "thought."

    A. Two syllables and three phonemes

    B. One syllable and three phonemes

    C. Three syllables and six phonemes

    D. Two syllables and three phonemes

48. Identify the statement that best describes the word "brought."

    A. It contains two syllables and three phonemes.

    B. It contains a consonant blend, one consonant trigraphs, and a vowel digraph.

    C. It contains two consonant blends and one vowel digraph.

    D. It contains seven graphemes, two syllables, and one consonant blend.

49. Identify the number of morphemes in the word "mistrustful."

    A. Two morphemes

    B. Three morphemes

    C. Four morphemes

    D. Five morphemes

50. Identify the pair of words that best represents consonant digraphs:

    A. clue—brew

    B. church—shirt

    C. scream—first

    D. cat—bag

51. Niurka is a 5-year-old native Spanish speaker in the process of second language acquisition. She often produces such statements as "I don't know nothing." Based on this speech sample, Niurka is

    A. overgeneralizing colloquial English.

    B. experiencing language interference.

    C. applying the concepts from L2 to L1.

    D. imitating the colloquial speech pattern of children in school.

52. The third person singular, possessive and the short and long plurals are examples of

    A. derivational morphemes.

    B. function words.

    C. inflectional morphemes.

    D. free morphemes.

53. Identify the two key features of inflectional morphemes.

    A. They come from the Latin and the Greek, and they do not change the syntactic classification of the word.

    B. They are native of English, and they can change the syntactic classification of the words.

    C. They are suffixes native of English.

    D. They can precede or follow derivational morphemes, and they come from the Greek and the Latin languages.

54. First language acquisition and especially oral language development appear to be the result of

    A. imitation and stimulus from the environment and practice.

    B. innate abilities, imitation and memorization.

    C. environmental influences, practice and memorization.

    D. innate mechanism, imitation and environmental influences.

55. McKinley is a 3-year-old child who produces such statements as "more Dada," "open door," and "no baby." Based on this speech sample, McKinley is going through which of the following stages of first language acquisition?

    A. Holophrastic

    B. Babbling

    C. Telegraphic

    D. Egocentric

56. The key feature of a balanced reading program is that it uses

    A. a balance between the receptive and productive skills of the language.

    B. a balance between theory and application of reading concepts.

    C. phonics instruction as the primary method to teach English reading.

    D. best practices from skill-based and meaning-based approaches.

57. Identify the statement that best describes the advantages of using the Language Experience Approach to teach reading to language minority students.

    A. It provides the schema or experiential background to facilitate the comprehension of the story.

    B. It uses the vocabulary and the experience common to both language minority and mainstream students.

    C. It minimizes the possibility of errors because of idiomatic expressions from both L1 and L2.

    D. It facilitates reading by ensuring a positive match between L1 and L2.

58. Identify the activity that parents can use to promote emergent literacy indirectly or subconsciously.

   A.   Guide children to follow and read the subtitles used in movies and television programs.

   B.   Play board games that require students to read rules and information to succeed.

   C.   Guide children to translate English stories in their native language.

   D.   Share stories (storytelling) and write them down. Let the child see how the story looks in print.

59. Elizabeth is an advanced ESL learner from Puerto Rico experiencing adjustment problems in school. Since she learned academic English in Puerto Rico, her vocabulary is always very formal. Students say that she uses "book English." Her peers often make jokes about her word choice during social gatherings. They called her "the professor." What type of communicative competence is Elizabeth lacking?

   A.   Grammatical

   B.   Sociolinguistic

   C.   Discourse

   D.   Strategic

60. In upper elementary, reading becomes more challenging and meaningful for students because at this stage

   A.   interest in reading fades as students find other preferred activities.

   B.   students are still developing skills in fluency and decoding.

   C.   students use reading to get information to succeed in the content areas.

   D.   students have a harder time choosing books to read on their own.

61. A key challenge that children in upper elementary experience when moving from the stage of "learning to read" to "reading to learn" is to

A. use graphic organizers to learn and present information.

B. understand the organizational patterns of the text to read better.

C. develop an understanding of academic English.

D. predict the content of the writing.

62. Which of the following strategies are commonly used to implement the instructional activity of reciprocal teaching?

A. Asking a question about the main idea

B. Clarifying difficult parts of the content

C. Predicting what comes next

D. All of the above

63. Convergent research suggests that when bilingual children acquire languages sequentially, they

A. transfer language features from L1 to L2 and vice versa.

B. transfer the phonology of L1 to L2 and vice versa.

C. experience confusion and frustration with the linguistic codes of both languages.

D. may experience language loss.

64. Bilingual students use the cumulative knowledge and skills acquired in and through both languages as a mechanism to solve problems and to cope with linguistic and academic challenges. When they encounter new concepts, they use this cumulative knowledge as a framework to understand new information. Which of the following terms best describes this capability unique to bilingual people?

A. Language transfer

B. Bilingualism

C. Translanguaging

D. Code switching

65. The CALLA and the SIOP are programs to

    A. teach English as a second language.

    B. integrate language and content.

    C. integrate ELs and gifted and talented students.

    D. promote dual language and biliteracy.

66. Convergent research shows that sheltered English instruction is more appropriate for students who are

    A. field independent and have a strong foundation in L1.

    B. at the intermediate or advanced proficiency level in English.

    C. native speakers of a language other than Spanish.

    D. already literate in their native language.

67. When analyzing and interpreting assessment data from culturally and linguistically diverse (CLD) students, assessors must consider that

    A. the main objective of assessment is to make students feel valued and wanted in school.

    B. students go through different stages of development, and these stages should not affect the way that children are assessed.

    C. the students might show potential differently because of linguistic and cultural influences.

    D. students may have culture and language deficits that can preclude them from effective participation in the testing.

68. In indirect instruction, the role of questioning is to guide students into discovery. Questions in this approach are used to

    A. refocus and probe for deeper analysis of the content.

    B. keep students engaged.

    C. promote equity and equality among linguistic minority students.

    D. promote deductive teaching.

69. Preview–review is a traditional strategy to ensure comprehension in the content areas. Which of the following statements best describes this strategy?

    A. English and L1 is used at the start of instruction.

    B. Translation is used as a teaching tool.

    C. L1 is used to introduce the content and to sum instruction delivered in L2.

    D. L1 and L2 are separated throughout instruction.

70. When teachers explore the knowledge that children bring to the lesson and then provide additional details to prepare them for the content of the day, they are

    A. strengthening the language background of the child.

    B. expanding the schemata needed to comprehend new content.

    C. facilitating second language acquisition.

    D. providing students with the vocabulary needed to understand the lesson.

71. The main purpose of semantic mapping is to

    A. teach geography concepts to ELLs.

    B. identify critical features of a concept.

    C. connect concepts in L1 and L2.

    D. present a graphic representation of a process.

72. Marisela develops a study guide to be sure that she synthesizes the content of a class and check what she knows about that content. Which strategy is she using?

    A. Cognitive

    B. Social

    C. Metacognitive

    D. Memory

73. Joe is literate in his native language and has a strong background in math, social studies, and science. When he came to the United States, he used the knowledge that he acquired in his native language as a foundation for learning new concepts in English. Which strategy is he using?

    A. Metacognitive

    B. Cognitive

    C. Social

    D. Mnemonic

74. A key strategy to help students gather information from textbooks is to

    A. teach the technical vocabulary needed to understand the content.

    B. teach the format used in textbooks and discuss how each part can increase comprehension.

    C. teach cognates in L1 and L2 and explain how this knowledge can facilitate the understanding of new concepts.

    D. provide a glossary of terms related to the content areas.

75. Sheltered Instruction is among the most popular alternatives to serve the cognitive and linguistic needs of ELs because

    A. the program introduces students to learning strategies.

    B. the instructor does not have to be bilingual.

    C. the program provides content area instruction with language development.

    D. All of the above

76. To develop academic language used in the content areas, English and Spanish use

    A. French-based words.

    B. German-based words.

    C. Latin- and Greek-based words.

    D. Hindu-European languages.

77. When teachers ask students to perform a real-world task to show mastery of a concept or a standard, the teacher is implementing

    A. a meaningful and active assessment.

    B. an authentic assessment.

    C. an ongoing assessment.

    D. a hands-on project.

78. What is the main advantage of using hands-on activities and visuals when teaching the content areas to English learners?

    A. It makes the content cognitive accessible to the students.

    B. It makes the class more interesting for the learners.

    C. It favors visual learners.

    D. It favors kinesthetic learners.

79. Ms. Torres developed a science test in English for ELs fourth grade students. The test had illustrations to improve students' comprehension. For beginner ESL children, she also read the questions to be sure the language did not interfere with assessment. These testing modifications are examples of

    A. formative evaluation.

    B. strategies to improve the performance of English learners.

    C. strategies to support English learners.

    D. linguistic accommodation.

80. Second-language learners often experience problems with schema and the cultural framework required to understand English. Which language component will more likely be affected by this lack of background knowledge?

    A. The use and understanding of figurative language or idioms

    B. The application of phonological analysis

    C. The use of syntactic and phonological components

    D. The application of the lexical and structural components

PRACTICE TEST
ANSWER KEY

1. D.	21. C.	41. A.	61. B.
2. D.	22. A.	42. D.	62. D.
3. C.	23. D.	43. A.	63. A.
4. C.	24. A.	44. D.	64. C.
5. D.	25. C.	45. B.	65. B.
6. B.	26. C.	46. A.	66. B.
7. B.	27. B.	47. B.	67. C.
8. C.	28. A.	48. B.	68. A.
9. B.	29. A.	49. B.	69. C.
10. C.	30. C.	50. B.	70. B.
11. B.	31. A.	51. B.	71. B.
12. B.	32. D.	52. C.	72. C.
13. A.	33. A.	53. C.	73. B.
14. D.	34. C.	54. D.	74. B.
15. D.	35. B.	55. C.	75. D.
16. B.	36. B.	56. D.	76. C.
17. D.	37. A.	57. A.	77. B.
18. D.	38. D.	58. D.	78. A.
19. B.	39. C.	59. B.	79. D.
20. C.	40. D.	60. C.	80. A.

1.   **D.**   The correct answer is (D). Since the class is composed of Latino students, it is considered a one-way program. If the class had combined language minority and language majority students, it would have been a two-way program (C). Since the goal of the program is to promote biliteracy, the Transitional Bilingual (B) and the generic descriptor bilingual program (A) can be ruled out.

> *Competency 002: First- and Second-Language Acquisition and Development*

2.   **D.**   The correct answer is (D), all of the above. The one- and two-way programs in the United States and the immersion programs in Canada were designed to promote bilingualism and biliteracy.

> *Competency 002: First- and Second-Language Acquisition and Development*

3.   **C.**   The correct answer is (C). The expression alludes or refers to the Battle of Waterloo, in which English soldiers defeated the supposedly unbeatable French forces under Napoleon. Option (A) contains part of the answer—allusion—but includes the concept of metaphor, which is not in the statement. A metaphor is a figure of speech that compares two ideas. Example: His cotton candy words did not convince her. In this case the speaker compares the stickiness and overly sweet taste of cotton candy to imply that the speaker's sticky-sweet words failed to persuade his audience. The statement does not contain a simile (B). A simile differs from a metaphor in its use of "like" or "as" to make its implicit comparison. Example: She sings like an angel. A hyperbole (D) is an exaggeration. Example: I am so hungry that I could eat a horse.

> *Competency 002: First- and Second-Language Acquisition and Development*

4.   **C.**   The correct answer is (C). Sheltered English focuses on the delivery of content in contextualized situations together with English language development. Students with different primary languages get content instruction in English. However, teachers use strategies whose goal is to facilitate comprehension and acquisition of English as well as the content areas. The primary goal of the program is not to promote bilingual education (A), but to teach English and content concurrently. No direct connection exists between sheltered instruction and the bilingual education programs in Canada (B). Option D contains incorrect information because submersion does not lead to bilingualism. Contrary to Sheltered Instruction, students in submersion are placed in the all-English classroom without any linguistic support.

> *Competency 004: Content Area Instruction*

5. **D.** The correct answer is (D). One of the key features of Sheltered English is the delivery of comprehensible input through hands-on discovery learning and contextualized instruction. Speaking slowly (A), using nonverbal communication (B) to promote comprehension, and checking for understanding (C) are among the features of Sheltered English, but individually they do not represent the best answer.

    Competency 004: Content Area Instruction

6. **B.** The correct answer is (B). Since the goal is testing the content, upon approval from the LPAC, teachers can provide reading assistance and event translating as well as the use of bilingual dictionaries and a glossary of terms. Teachers cannot provide one-to-one instruction during testing (A), nor tutoring (C) during testing. Teachers cannot simplify the content, especially during testing (D).

    Competency 004: Content Area Instruction

7. **B.** The correct answer is (B). Newcomer centers were designed as transitional programs to help students in their linguistic and cultural adjustment to the country. Students without prior schooling and refugees from war are assigned to these centers for six months to two years. When they arrive to the U.S., most refugees are poor, but the SES (A) is not a prerequisite for admission to these programs. The language background (C) and the level of proficiency (D) are taken into account when grouping students, but these are not the primary reason for admission to the program.

    Competency 001: Foundations of Bilingual Education

8. **C.** The correct answer is (C). When students achieve an advanced level of development in L1 (threshold), they can use this information as a foundation for learning a second language. Developing positive self-esteem (A) can improve learning, but it is not the primary implication of the Threshold Hypothesis. Achieving the threshold in L1 (B) does not necessarily impart the cultural knowledge needed to affect L2 acquisition. Expecting students at this level to compare and contrast two languages (D) is unrealistic. Some level of comparison can be done later.

    Competency 002: First- and Second-Language Acquisition and Development

9. **B.** The correct answer is (B). The Lau ruling did not mandate bilingual education (A) in San Francisco or create a federal law (D) mandating bilingual education. The court indicated that the San Francisco School District must take affirmative steps to improve the education of ELs. The OCR used the ruling as a foundation for the development and implementation of programs to address the needs of ELs. The ruling made districts aware of the need to develop better programs for ELs, but it did not force (C) states to develop a specific program.

    Competency 001: Foundations of Bilingual Education

10.   **C.**   The correct answer is (C). Because of linguistic diversity typical of North Americans, Native American groups were forced to use signs to communicate among themselves. Option (A) is incorrect because the scenario does not provide data to suggest that Native American groups were living peacefully in America. Option (D) is incorrect because American Sign Language was developed during the onset of the 19th century, when deaf education was introduced in the United States.

Competency 001: Foundations of Bilingual Education

11.   **B.**   The correct answer is (B). A key result of the boarding schools for Native Americans was language loss. In these schools, children were forced to assimilate and learn English. Option (A) is incorrect because the goal of the program was not to promote bilingualism. Children instead were often punished for speaking the home language. Option (C) is incorrect because these programs were designed to provide basic education and assimilate children to the American language and culture. Option (D) is incorrect because Native Americans often faced discrimination in the United States, and children thus were unlikely to be moved to American urban centers.

Competency 001: Foundations of Bilingual Education

12.   **B.**   The correct answer is (B). The Navajos have the largest number of speakers in the country at about 150,000. More than 155 Native American languages are estimated to still be spoken in the U.S., though a large number are endangered or have fewer than 10,000 speakers. The Cherokee and the Apache have under 23,000, and the Choctaw have under 10,000. Thus, options (A), (C), and (D) are incorrect.

Competency 001: Foundations of Bilingual Education

13.   **A.**   The correct answer is (A). During War II, the United States' enemies, especially the Japanese, intercepted and decoded American messages using English. To make decoding more difficult, U.S. forces created a program using Navajo speakers as radio operators—the Code Talkers. Since Navajo was a relatively unknown language, the Japanese were never able to decode the system. Because of the Navajo Code Talkers Program, the lives of a large number of American soldiers were saved. Option (B) is incorrect because the Tuskegee Pilot Program was a program to train and involve African American pilots in the war effort. The admission of Hawaii as a state (C) happened in 1959, and World War II ended in 1945. Option (D) is incorrect because it refers to the Soviet launching of the first artificial satellite in 1957.

Competency 001: Foundations of Bilingual Education

14.   **D.**   The correct answer is (D). Before World War I, German was commonly used in public schools in the United States. Because of Germany's participation in the war and the resulting xenophobia, multiple state legislatures, including that of Texas, adopted English-only legislation. This legislation prohibited the use of languages other than English in school. Option (A) is incorrect

because linguistic diversity was common among the American colonists. However, the colonists were unified against England. Option (C) is incorrect because the 10th Amendment states that the powers not directly allocated to the central government are automatically given to the states. Since the U.S. Constitution did not mention education or an official language for the country, these two components became the responsibilities of state government. The Vietnam War (C) did not have a direct impact on the enactment of English-only legislation. During the war, states like Texas eliminated English-only legislation and experimented with bilingual education.

Competency 001: Foundations of Bilingual Education

15. **D.** The correct answer is (D). All the events listed in options (A), (B), and (C) led to the rebirth of bilingual education in the 1960s. In 1953, the United Nations Educational, Scientific and Cultural Organization (UNESCO) planted the seeds for this by issuing a proclamation (A) supporting the use of native language instruction to teach children. The Cuban Revolution (B) forced large number of Cubans to immigrate to the United States. With the use of funds to support refugees, Dade County school district established a dual language program in the Miami area. This program became a national model. Multiple court cases, including *Lau v. Nichols* and *Serna v. Portales*, forced school districts nationwide to offer programs to meet the educational needs of linguistic minorities (C).

Competency 001: Foundations of Bilingual Education

16. **B.** The correct answer is (B). The ESEA of 1994 under President Bill Clinton allowed the development of dual language programs. The legislation allowed the participation of native English speakers, which resulted in the development of the two-way dual language programs. Option (A) is incorrect because the emphasis of the No Child Left Behind Act was English language development, not dual language. The ESSA began implementation in 2016, and it is too early to determine its impact. Based on the explanation provided, option (D) is incorrect.

Competency 001: Foundations of Bilingual Education

17. **D.** The correct answer is (D). The ELPS legislation requires school districts to deliver content-area instruction to the level and rigor required of native English speakers (A). However, districts must adjust the delivery to make it comprehensible to ELs. To make content accessible to ELs, teachers can segment (chunking) instruction and implement multiple linguistic accommodation to improve comprehension (C). Option (B) is incorrect under any circumstances because the curriculum cannot be modified to remove the rigor required of all students.

Competency 001: Foundations of Bilingual Education

18. **D.** The correct answer is (D)—all of the above. The new legislation reemphasized the rights of the states to establish their own accountability process (B). It also moved the accountability requirements from bilingual education of Title III to Title I (A). The ESSA legislation also

mandated state education agencies (SEA) to follow up students exited from the special language programs for four years. This mandate requires Texas to increase the follow-up services from two to four years.

Competency 001: Foundations of Bilingual Education

19. **B.** The correct answer is (B). In *Brown v. Board of Education of Topeka, Kansas*, the court eliminated the separate but equal doctrine established under *Plessy v. Ferguson* (1896). Based on this explanation, option (A) can be ruled out. The *Meyer v. Nebraska* case challenged a Nebraska law that prohibited teaching foreign languages in school. The case went to the U.S. Supreme Court where the law was declared unconstitutional, based on the provision of the 14th Amendment. The equal protection clause of the 14th Amendment was used throughout the country in cases seeking bilingual education.

Competency 001: Foundations of Bilingual Education

20. **C.** The correct answer is (C). *Rios v. Read* challenged the quality of bilingual education offered to ELs in the Patchogue-Medford school district in New York. In *Castañeda v. Pickard* the quality of bilingual education was also challenged. The court mandated a series of guidelines for the implementation of quality bilingual programs. *ASPIRA v. New York*, *Lau v. Nichols* (A), and *Serna v. Portales* (B) were the first successful court cases, which in turn built momentum for bilingual education throughout the country. Those cases sought to improve the quality of education of ELs in general. In *Keyes v. Denver*, a group of African American and Hispanic parents argued that their segregated schools were inferior to white schools. The U.S. Supreme Court ruled that the segregation was unintentional but mandated that the school district remedy it.

Competency 001: Foundations of Bilingual Education

21. **C.** The correct answer is (C). The two-way dual language program serves language majority (Mike) and language minority (Brenda) students. The goal of this program is to promote biliteracy and bilingualism. The one-way dual language program serves language minority students only learning two languages (A). Choice (B) is incorrect because the goal of the English Immersion program is to teach English only, not bilingualism. Choice (D) is incorrect because the term English enrichment is linked to the one-way dual language program, not the two-way program.

Competency 001: Foundations of Bilingual Education

22. **A.** The correct answer is (A). In the 90/10 model, students received 90% of instruction in the non-dominant language (Spanish); consequently, Mike will be immersed in the second language, Spanish. Brenda, on the other hand, will be taking 90% of instruction in her native language, Spanish. Based on this explanation, options (C) and (D) can be ruled out.

Competency 001: Foundations of Bilingual Education

23. **D.** The correct answer is (D). When students from different cultural backgrounds come in contact within a supportive learning environment, they indirectly and directly exchange cultural and linguistic information. Moreover, they can rely on each other for support when the instruction is delivered in their second language for instruction. That is, Mike will help Brenda with English and Brenda will do the same with Spanish. Becoming friends (C) is a possibility but not the main goal of this type of program.

Competency 001: Foundations of Bilingual Education

24. **A.** The correct answer is (A). All three children have to be tested in Spanish and English to determine proficiency in both languages. In the case of Alicia (B) the parents indicated that English is the native language of the child but the notes from the teacher suggest otherwise. In cases like this, the students have to be tested. The data does not support admission to the special language program, i.e., bilingual, dual language (C and D).

Competency 003: Development and Assessment of Literacy and Biliteracy

25. **C.** The correct answer is (C). Lisping describes the misplacement of articulators to pronounce the sounds of the /s/ and /z/. Three conditions have been recorded: placing the tongue between the upper and lower teeth (lingual), touching the upper teeth (dental), and raising the tongue that results in the emission of a lateral sound (lateral). These pronunciation problems can be a developmental feature that can disappear as the child matures. Thus, there is no need to refer the child to special education, nor to stop the screening process for possible admission to the special language program (D). However, if the situation persists and it interferes in communication, a referral to the Admission Review and Dismissal (ARD) Committee might be initiated. The bilingual teacher is not qualified to determine if the child needs special education support (B). Thus, the child cannot be assigned to the special education classroom (A).

Competency 001: Foundations of Bilingual Education

26. **C.** The correct answer is (C). Testing should proceed as scheduled to corroborate information. However, no placement should be done prior to receiving results from the oral proficiency testing (A) and the decision of the LPAC. Parents who do not want their children in the special language program often provide inaccurate information in the HLS (B). If the student qualifies for the program, and if the parents do not agree with the placement, they can sign a "parental denial form" to move the child to the traditional English program. Based on the explanation, we can rule out option (D)—all of the above.

Competency 001: Foundations of Bilingual Education

27. **B.** The correct answer is (B). Once information is acquired and internalized through L1 or L2, it goes into a language-free environment called the Common Underlying Proficiency (CUP). For bilingual people, the information and abstractions stored in this section can be easily retrieved

and communicated through either language. Memorized information, culturally-bound communication strategies, and the phonology of the individual languages will remain with the respective language, and information not fully internalized can be housed in L1 or L2 (A, B, and D). However, when these concepts are fully internalized they are transferred to the CUP and become readily available to the speakers.

Competency 002: First- and Second-Language Acquisition and Development

28. **A.** The correct answer is (A). In the late-exit programs, students received information using two languages. Once this information is learned, it is transferred to the CUP. Thus, with longer exposure to the two languages, the learner will become more proficient in both languages. With the ability to add information using two languages the information stored in the CUP will increase, impacting the knowledge base of the learner. Based on this explanation, option (C)—early exit programs—can be ruled out. Options (B)—learning in two languages—reinforces the value of learning in two languages but it does not address the full implications of the theory. (D) is incorrect because it just indicates a superficial fact that visuals are good to represents abstract concepts.

Competency 002: First- and Second-Language Acquisition and Development

29. **A.** The correct answer is (A). The consistent grapheme-phoneme correspondence of Spanish, and especially the almost perfect connection of the vowel system, makes the syllable the ideal structure for initial reading instruction. However, Spanish is an alphabetic language, not a syllabic language, as incorrectly stated in option (C). The use of onset and rhymes (B) is a valuable tool to compensate for the grapheme-phoneme inconsistency of English, but it has little value for the teaching of Spanish literacy. Based on the information presented, option (D) ("all of the above") can be ruled out.

Competency 003: Development and Assessment of Literacy and Biliteracy

30. **C.** The correct answer is (C). Based on the information presented, Spanish-speaking students might have problems with initial consonant clusters because in Spanish these consonants do not happen in initial position. They occur in medial position and these are preceded by the vowel *e*, as in the words **es**pero, **es**toy, **es**primir, and ex**pl**icar. Options (A) and (B) present true information—Spanish-speaking ELs generally have problems with the pronunciation of the *th* and *sh* (B), and they also have problems with final consonant cluster (A) but none of these features are presented in the table used for the question. Option (D) is incorrect because these students should not have problems pronouncing sounds of the vowel system of their native language.

Competency 003: Development and Assessment of Literacy and Biliteracy

31. **A.** The correct answer is (A). Second-language development is best achieved when instruction is geared toward meaningful and functional tasks in the language. This approach can facilitate

and increase the motivation for L2 learning. Option (B) presents a convoluted and contradictory explanation involving inductive and deductive teaching. Deductive and inductive instruction can be used to teach a second language. However, inductive or indirect teaching works better than direct instruction with young learners. Option (C) looks fine until "meaningful memorization" is introduced. Memorization is not the best tool to promote proficiency in L2. Option (D) is incorrect because idiomatic expressions and tongue twisters are useful activities to promote basic communication skills but fail to go beyond that.

Competency 002: First- and Second-Language Acquisition and Development

32. **D.** The correct answer is (D)—all of the above. Children exposed to the second language before puberty develop native-like pronunciation (A). However, adults rely on their native language as a foundation for the development of L2. This reliance often leads to language interference at the phonological level. Adults are better at handling the grammar and the abstract components of the language (C). Learners who contact the language after puberty can still develop the same level of proficiency as those who did earlier (B). Therefore, children have advantages over adults at the phonological level, but adults might have advantages in all other areas.

Competency 002: First- and Second-Language Acquisition and Development

33. **A.** The correct answer is (A). English uses multiple figures of speech and idioms to communicate meaning (semantics). Understanding the connotative nature of this figurative language requires students to know and have experience with the target culture. Students new to the culture will take this communication literally, and it can create problems. Neither the application of phonological analysis (B) nor syntax (C) will be directly affected by lack of cultural knowledge.

Competency 003: Development and Assessment of Literacy and Biliteracy

34. **C.** The correct answer is (C). The standard version of the language is the variety used by the most powerful social groups of the nation. It is used in government, the media and in the education system. Generally, it differs from the popular version used by the population from low socio economic background (A). The government promotes the use and development of Standard English, but it does not impose it (B). The English variety used in most former African colonies is British English, not necessarily American Standard English (D).

Competency 002: First- and Second-Language Acquisition and Development

35. **B.** The correct answer is (B). Language and reading skills are transferable from L1 to L2. When children develop a strong foundation in L1 and master reading, they can develop similar skills in the second language. The ESL program used in the district (A) and the methods used (D) to teach language can have an impact, but it will be minimal compared with the levels of literacy in

L1. Choice (C) can be ruled out because it uses faulty information. Students get acculturated to a second language, not their native language.

Competency 003: Development and Assessment of Literacy and Biliteracy

36. **B.** The correct answer is (B). Differences between the grapheme (letters) and phonemes (sounds) can create confusion among ELs. Such grapheme-phoneme inconsistency as in the following English words—sugar (sh), emotion (sh), and **ch**evron (sh)—can confuse students new to the language. With this explanation, (C)—positive language transfer—can be ruled out. These differences most likely are not going to interfere with syntax (A) or with the meaning system (D) of L1 and L2.

Competency 003: Development and Assessment of Literacy and Biliteracy

37. **A.** The correct answer is (A). A consonant digraph is created when two letters are used to represent one sound. English has multiple consonant digraphs. This characteristic affects Spanish-speaking ELs because Spanish has only five consonant digraphs—*ch, ll, rr, qu,* and *gu.* Options (C) and (D) thus can be ruled out. Option (B) is incorrect because the question addressed consonant digraphs, not diphthongs.

Competency 003: Development and Assessment of Literacy and Biliteracy

38. **D.** The correct answer is (D). English is the language of business, and it is spoken as a first or second language in 106 countries. Former English colonies like India, Pakistan, Nigeria, Uganda, and Zimbabwe use English as a common language.

Competency 002: First- and Second-Language Acquisition and Development

39. **C.** The correct answer is (C). The United States has about 41 million native Spanish speakers and 11.6 million bilingual Spanish/English speakers. This population is second only to Mexico (B). Spanish is the second most spoken language in the world, surpassed only by Chinese (A). Based on the explanation, option (D) can be ruled out.

Competency 002: First- and Second-Language Acquisition and Development

40. **D.** The correct answer is (D). The word has three units of meaning (morphemes): the root word, *home,* and two derivational morphemes, *less* and *ness.* In this case the root word, *home,* is also a free morpheme. The morpheme *ness* is not a free morpheme (A). The word does not contain inflectional (B) morphemes (plurals, third person singular, past tense, possessive, past participle, present progressive, comparative, and superlative). Option (C) is incorrect because it mentions four morphemes instead of three.

Competency 003: Development and Assessment of Literacy and Biliteracy

41. **A.**   The correct answer is (A). A large number of English expressions use implied meaning (connotation) to communicate information. ELs might get confused when trying to decipher the information relying on the literal meaning (denotation). The sentence uses a metaphor, not simile, to imply life is a bowl of lemons (B). Alliteration is not needed to understand the statement. Alliterations describe the use of successive words with the same first consonant sound—Peter Piper, Coca-Cola, Best Buy, and PayPal.

Competency 002: First- and Second-Language Acquisition and Development

42. **D.**   The correct answer is (D). Children are eager to learn the language so that they can communicate and meet their needs. They are concerned with delivering and obtaining information, not grammar. Parents should not correct children. They should model and contextualize information so that it becomes easier to understand. All these features can be incorporated to teach ELs.

Competency 002: First- and Second-Language Acquisition and Development

43. **A.**   The correct answer is (A). In story retelling, teachers read a story aloud and ask students to retell the story to assess comprehension, vocabulary development and communication skills. Option (B) is partially correct. Story retelling assesses oral language development, but it does not address writing skills. Option (D) is also incorrect because in story retelling the student is not required to use reading and writing skills.

Competency 003: Development and Assessment of Literacy and Biliteracy

44. **D.**   The correct answer is (D). Checklists and teacher observations are common examples of ongoing or informal assessment. Based on the description, option (C) can be ruled out. Options (A) and (B) are incorrect because they refer to teaching strategies, not assessment strategies.

Competency 003: Development and Assessment of Literacy and Biliteracy

45. **B.**   The correct answer is (B). The alphabetic principles suggest that letters of the alphabet represent the sounds of the language. It also implies that speech can be represented in print, which can be reversed back to speech. Option (A) presents a fact but does not describe the alphabetic principle. Option (C) presents an opinion not supported by research. Memorizing the alphabet will not hurt, but it does not guarantee that children will understand the alphabetic principle. Option (D) presents a plausible statement but is unrelated to the question. The introduction of dictionary skills is unrelated to the development of the alphabetic principle.

Competency 003: Development and Assessment of Literacy and Biliteracy

46. **A.**   The correct answer is (A). Cognates are words with similar meaning in two or more languages. Most cognates come from the Greek and the Latin, and they constitute the key vocabulary of the content areas (social studies, mathematics, science, music and the arts). Homophones (B) are words pronounced and spelled similarly, but they have different meanings (hare and hair). Homo-

graphs are words spelled alike but that can have more than one meaning (*bear* the animal and *bear* the action of carrying a baby or a weapon). Option (D) describes false cognates, which are words that only appear to be cognates. Example: the English/Spanish words lecture (oral presentation) and lectura (reading).

Competency 002: First- and Second-Language Acquisition and Development

47. **B.** The correct answer is (B). The word "thought" has seven letters but is monosyllabic. It has three phonemes – one consonant digraph (the "th"), a consonant trigraph (the "ght"), and a vowel digraph (the "ou") representing one sound each – for a total of three sounds. Choices (A), (C), and (D) are incorrect based on the previous explanation.

Competency 002: First- and Second-Language Acquisition and Development

48. **B.** The correct answer is (B). *Brought* contains seven letters representing one syllable. It contains one consonant blend (*br*), a vowel digraph (*ou*), and a consonant trigraph (*ght*). Choice (A) is incorrect because the word is monosyllabic, with one consonant blend (C). It contains seven letters but only one syllable (D).

Competency 003: Development and Assessment of Literacy and Biliteracy

49. **B.** The correct answer is (B). The word contains a prefix (*mis*), the root word (*trust*), the morpheme that calls for an adjective (*ful*) for a total of three units of meaning. Options (A), (C), and (D) are incorrect based on the previous explanation.

Competency 003: Development and Assessment of Literacy and Biliteracy

50. **B.** The correct answer is (B). The first and final sounds of *church* and the first sound of *shirt* represent diagraphs because the first two graphemes represent one sound. Option (A) is incorrect because the words *clue* and *brew* contain initial consonant blends, not digraphs. Option (C) is also incorrect because both letters contain consonant clusters or blends. The individual sounds are blended to create a unique sound combination. Option (D) is incorrect because all letters in the words are pronounced.

Competency 002: First- and Second-Language Acquisition and Development

51. **B.** The correct answer is (B). The sentence uses double negatives, which is unacceptable in standard English. The child is experiencing language interference because in Spanish double negatives are permitted and often required. (A) is incorrect because the child is not overgeneralizing. She is using a principle from her native language to construct a sentence in the new language. Option (C) is incorrect because the child is transferring elements from the first to the second language, not the other way around. There might be a remote possibility that the child is imitating speech patterns from the playground (D).

Competency 002: First- and Second-Language Acquisition and Development

52. **C.** The correct answer is (C). The question identifies three of the eight inflectional morphemes of the English language. The remaining morphemes are the present progressive (*ing*), the comparative (*er* or *better*) superlative (*est* or *best*), past tense (*ed*), and the participle (*en*). Based on the explanation, options (A), (B), and (D) are incorrect.

Competency 002: First- and Second-Language Acquisition and Development

53. **C.** The correct answer is (C). Inflectional morphemes are also called inflectional endings because they occur at the end of the word. Options (A) and (B) are incorrect because inflectional morphemes are native to English, and they do not change the syntactic classification to the word attached. Option (D) is incorrect because inflectional morphemes always follow derivational morphemes.

Competency 003: Development and Assessment of Literacy and Biliteracy

54. **D.** The correct answer is (D). Current research suggests that language development results from innate abilities, imitation of parents and caregivers, and stimulus from the linguistic community. Option (A) is incorrect because it fails to mention the most important component: the role of nature. Option (B) is incorrect because memorization alone does not describe the intricate process of first language acquisition. Option (C) is incorrect because practice and memorization do not play an important role.

Competency 002: First- and Second-Language Acquisition and Development

55. **C.** The correct answer is (C). In the telegraphic stage of first language acquisition, children produce two- and three-word statements. Choice (A) is incorrect because the child is going beyond the one-word stage—holophrastic. Choice (B) is incorrect because children at the babbling stage do not produce intelligible or standard words. Choice (D) is incorrect because egocentric does not describe a specific stage of language development. It describes a stage of social development.

Competency 002: First- and Second-Language Acquisition and Development

56. **D.** The correct answer is (D). A balanced reading program combines phonics instruction, a skill-based approach, to teach decoding skills, with features from the whole language, a meaning-based approach, to teach reading. Option (A) is incorrect because the main thrust of a balanced reading program is not directly related to the formal teaching of the four skills of the language. As we consider option (B), it makes sense to establish a balance between theory and application, but there is no direct connection with the balanced reading program. Option (C) is incorrect because a balanced approach uses not only phonics skills but also whole language strategies.

Competency 003: Development and Assessment of Literacy and Biliteracy

57. **A.** The correct answer is (A). The main reason for the creation of the Language Experience Approach was to eliminate the discrepancy between the background knowledge that the child brings to the reading process and the experiential background required to understand the story—i.e., the schema of the author. Option (B) is incorrect because it eliminates the need to discuss the schema of the story by exposing children to a common experience and guiding them to dictate a story using the experience. Option (C) is incorrect because students will use their own vocabulary in the story. If they use idioms, these are probably known to children in the group. Option (D) is incorrect because the main purpose of the LEA is not to contrast language but to make content easier to decode and understand.

Competency 003: Development and Assessment of Literacy and Biliteracy

58. **D.** The correct answer is (D). Storytelling and reading to children can guide them to notice the correlation between the letters and the sounds they produce. This phonemic awareness is a foundation for learning to read—emergent reading. (A) is incorrect because children at the emergent reading stage are unable to read or comprehend the subtitles of movies and television shows. (B) is also incorrect because children at the emergent stage cannot read instructions for board games. (C) is incorrect because translating stories alone does not guarantee that children will develop the readiness to begin reading.

Competency 003: Development and Assessment of Literacy and Biliteracy

59. **B.** The correct answer is (B). The learner is unable to switch registers (communication styles) based on the context of communication. This language feature is identified as sociolinguistic competence. The concept of communicative competence has been defined based upon another three components: grammatical, discourse, and strategic. The grammatical component (A) describes the ability of the learner to apply grammar of the language. Discourse competence (C) refers to the ability of the learners to present an argument in a cohesive fashion. And the strategic competence describes the ability of the child to maintain the flow of communication to achieve the communicative purpose.

Competency 002: First- and Second-Language Acquisition and Development

60. **C.** The correct answer is (C). Students in fourth grade and up typically have more difficulty reading to learn because it requires an understanding of the format for expository writing. This is especially important because students must learn the content areas to succeed academically. Losing interest in reading (A), lacking fluency and decoding (B) are challenges that upper-elementary students face, but these options individually do not represent their most important challenge. Problems with choosing books to read on their own (D) is not a real challenge for upper-elementary students.

Competency 004: Content Area Instruction

61. **B.**   The correct answer is (B). When reading informational text, students must analyze the text structure and organizational pattern of the writing. The faster they learn to decipher the structure of text, the faster they will retrieve information and the better they will read. Using graphic organizers (A) and developing academic English (C) are important but secondary strategies that students must master to move to the stage of "reading to learn." Predicting the content (D) is an effective strategy for narrative text, but it loses its effectiveness with expository writing.

   Competency 004: Content Area Instruction

62. **D.**   The correct answer is (D). Reciprocal teaching requires students to participate in cooperative learning groups in which each student has a role in discussing the text by posing questions, clarifying confusing sections, and making predictions.

   Competency 004: Content Area Instruction

63. **A.**   The correct answer is (A). When students learn a first language and then are exposed to the second, they can transfer multiple components of the experience to the second language. Children may experience language interference when they transfer the phonology of L1 to L2 (B), but the impact should be minor when compared with the benefits of transferring other language features. There is no evidence to show sequential bilingual experience confusion or frustration (C), or language loss (D).

   Competency 002: First- and Second-Language Acquisition and Development

64. **C.**   The correct answer is (C). The term translanguaging has been coined to describe the cumulative experience and skills that bilingual students use to address new linguistic and cognitive challenges. This cumulative knowledge acquired through two different languages goes beyond language transfer (A) and codeswitching (D). Translanguaging goes beyond being bilingual (B) and encompasses the knowledge, experiences and skills developed when facing challenges in two languages and two cultural milieus.

   Competency 004: Content Area Instruction

65. **B.**   The correct answer is (B). The Cognitive Academic Language Learning Approach (CALLA) model and the Sheltered Instruction Observation Protocol (SIOP) are programs designed to teach the content areas using language strategies to facilitate comprehension. This added linguistic modifications indirectly promotes language development. The main purpose of these programs is to teach content, not necessarily to teach ESL (A) or to promote dual language (D). English development comes as a by-product of the methods. The methods were designed for all ELs, not necessarily for gifted and talented students (C).

   Competency 004: Content Area Instruction

66. **B.** Sheltered English provides content and language instruction in contextualized situations to make sure students can understand the content. Because English is the only language of instruction, a minimum command of the language is necessary to get the program's full benefit. Having a strong foundation in L1 (A) and being literate in the language (D) are good predictors of second language acquisition, but there is no direct connection with specific ESL methods like sheltered English. Option (C) is incorrect because the native language of the students plays a minimal role in the choice of ESL methods.

Competency 004: Content Area Instruction

67. **C.** The correct answer is (C). Culture shapes how children behave and perform in school. Linguistic limitations can also affect the ability of children to show capabilities and potential. The option of making students feel valued and wanted (A) is a noble cause but should not be the main concern when assessing CLD learners. Option (B) presents a true statement when it indicates that students go through different stages of development, but that choice is invalidated when it says that these should not affect how students are assessed. The term cultural deficit used in (D) invalidates the answer because CLD learners cannot be considered culturally deficient. They bring with them their language and culture.

Competency 004: Content Area Instruction

68. **A.** The correct answer is (A). In indirect instruction, students are guided to discover and build their knowledge. However, teachers should guide students to identify important concepts. Questioning techniques are used to analyze and develop an in-depth knowledge of important components in the lesson. Questions can also be used to keep students engaged (B), but their main purpose goes beyond keeping students engaged. Promoting equity and equality among linguistic minorities (C) is commendable, but questioning in indirect teaching is designed for more specific purposes. Because indirect teaching by definition promotes inductive learning, option (D) is incorrect.

Competency 004: Content Area Instruction

69. **C.** Preview–review is a traditional bilingual education strategy designed to teach content using two languages. The content is introduced in L1, and the technical vocabulary and the lesson are presented in L2, and L1 is then used again to review the content. The use of both languages at the start of instruction (A) is incorrect because it fails to specify the order and indicate that L1 is used again at the end. Choice (B) is incorrect because translation is not used in this strategy. The concept of language separation (D) is probably maintained in the preview-review strategy, but it is not the strategy's key characteristic.

Competency 004: Content Area Instruction

70. **B.**   The correct answer is (B). English language learners often have trouble understanding content because they may lack the necessary background to internalize new concepts. By examining the knowledge that children bring to the lesson and providing the missing content, teachers expand the schema needed to acquire new content. The question deals with getting students to understand new content, not necessarily with language development (A). Second language acquisition (C) and vocabulary development (D) will help the student, but the question does not address language development by itself.

Competency 004: Content Area Instruction

71. **B.**   The correct answer is (B). Semantic mapping visually represents interconnected features of a concept. This interrelatedness can be represented with words or visuals. For example, the concept of landscape can be linked to pictures of lakes, rivers, mountains, grass, trees, and other features that represent possible attributes of the concept. *Mapping* relates to geography (A), but the intended meaning of the word goes beyond geography. People can use semantic mapping to contrast concepts in L1 and L2 (C), but the process was not designed to accomplish that. (D) describes a possible mapping but does not represent semantic mapping.

Competency 004: Content Area Instruction

72. **C.**   The correct answer is (C). Metacognitive strategies describe ways to conceptualize how learning occurs. These strategies divide into two classifications: organization and planning for learning, and self-monitoring and self-evaluating. Cognitive strategies (A) describe techniques to improve understanding, increase retention of information, and apply new information. Social strategies (B) describe techniques for learning from each other in social situations—peer or group format. Option (D) describes strategies for promoting rote memorization of facts. Examples of this strategy include the use of songs, acronyms, and mnemonics to remember facts or rules.

Competency 004: Content Area Instruction

73. **B.**   The correct answer is (B). Cognitive strategies use techniques to improve retention of content and such prior knowledge as information acquired in L1 as a foundation for acquiring new concepts. Metacognitive strategies (A) describe the ability to conceptualize how learning occurs, not the transfer of information from L1 to L2. Social strategies (C) describe ways to acquire new knowledge in social settings. The use of mnemonic devices is part of a rote memory strategy, which has no correlation with transferring content from L1 to L2.

Competency 004: Content Area Instruction

74. **B.**   The correct answer is (B). The format for organizing information in a textbook differs from the traditional narrative format used in children's literature. Students need to use such

resources as glossaries, indexes, text boxes, highlighted areas, graphics, and visuals to increase comprehension. Teaching technical vocabulary (A) as well as using cognates (C) and glossaries (D) are good strategies for helping students gather information from textbooks, but neither represents the best answer.

Competency 004: Content Area Instruction

75. **D.**   The correct answer is (D). Sheltered Instruction introduces students to multiple strategies to contextualize instruction and enhance comprehension. It also incorporates content and language objectives (C) to ensure students can benefit from instruction delivered in their second language. Monolingual teachers with specialized preparation in second language acquisition (B) deliver instruction.

Competency 004: Content Area Instruction

76. **C.**   The correct answer is (C). English and Spanish use a large number of Latin- and Greek-based words in most content areas, including social studies, math, science, arts and music. English is a Germanic language, while Spanish is Latin-based. Both use some words from the French and perhaps from other European languages, but not to the extent that they rely on Latin and Greek words.

Competency 004: Content Area Instruction

77. **B.**   The correct answer is (B). When students use content information to solve real problems or perform a real-world task, they are engaging in authentic assessment. Choice (A) uses such generic terms as meaningful and active to describe a technical term—authentic assessment. Ongoing assessment (C) is done as part of instruction, and it might not be authentic. Hands-on project (D) is not precise enough to describe the assessment described in the question.

Competency 004: Content Area Instruction

78. **A.**   The correct answer is (A). The use of concrete objects and visuals can facilitate comprehension of content area instruction. The use of these activities contextualizes instruction and makes it easier to understand. It might make the class more interesting (B) and more appealing to visual learners (C) and kinesthetic learners (D), but those are not the main reasons for using these activities.

Competency 004: Content Area Instruction

79. **D.**   The correct answer is (D). When the purpose is to test content area information, teachers must be sure that language does not interfere with assessment. Using visuals and reading the questions for ELs can minimize the impact of language in assessing content mastery. The information presented does not provide information to determine whether the test was formative (A) or summa-

tive. The linguistic accommodations were not designed to improve or support the performance of ELs (B and C), but to promote equity and fairness in the assessment.

Competency 003: Development and Assessment of Literacy and Biliteracy

80. **A.** The correct answer is (A). Understanding figurative language in English requires learners to understand American culture and how language is used in daily speech. Traditionally, ELs fail to capture the implied meaning in these idioms, creating communication problems. Choices (B), (C), and (D) are incorrect because phonology and syntax do not rely heavily on culture to convey meaning.

Competency 003: Development and Assessment of Literacy and Biliteracy

SELF-ASSESSMENT GUIDES

Texes Bilingual Education Supplemental Diagnostic Test

Competency 001: Foundations of Bilingual and ESL Education

2	3	5	7	9	10	34
35	36	37	38	43	45	47

___/14

Competency 002: First- and Second-Language Acquisition and Development

1	11	13	15	16	19	20
22	39					

___/9

Competency 003: Development and Assessment of Literacy and Bilingual Literacy

8	12	17	21	24	26	27
29	30	32	33	40	41	42

___/14

Competency 004: Content Area Instruction

4	6	14	18	23	25	28
31	44	46	48			

___/11

223

Texes Bilingual Education Supplemental Practice Test

Competency 001: Foundations of Bilingual and ESL Education

7	9	10	11	12	13	14
15	16	17	18	19	20	21
22	23	25	26

___/19

Competency 002: First- and Second-Language Acquisition and Development

1	2	3	8	27	28	31
32	34	38	39	41	42	46
47	50	51	52	54	55	59
63

___/22

Competency 003: Development and Assessment of Literacy and Bilingual Literacy

24	29	30	33	35	36	37
40	43	44	45	48	49	53
56	57	58	79	80

___/18

Competency 4: Content Area Instruction

4	5	6	60	61	62	64
65	66	67	68	69	70	71
72	73	74	75	76	77	78

___/21

NOTES

NOTES

NOTES

NOTES

NOTES